THE CAMBRIDGE BIBLE COMMENTARY

NEW ENGLISH BIBLE

GENERAL EDITORS

P. R. ACKROYD, A. R. C. LEANEY
J. W. PACKER

JEREMIAH 26–52

THE BOOK OF THE PROPHET
JEREMIAH
CHAPTERS 26–52

COMMENTARY BY

ERNEST W. NICHOLSON
Lecturer in Divinity in the University of Cambridge
Fellow and Dean of Pembroke College

CAMBRIDGE UNIVERSITY PRESS

Published by the Syndics of the Cambridge University Press
Bentley House, 200 Euston Road, London NW1 2DB
American Branch: 32 East 57th Street, New York, N.Y.10022

© Cambridge University Press 1975

Library of Congress Catalogue Card Number: 74–80357

ISBNS
0 521 20497 6 hard covers
0 521 09867 X paperback

First published 1975

Printed in Great Britain
at the University Printing House, Cambridge
(Euan Phillips, University Printer)

GENERAL EDITORS' PREFACE

The aim of this series is to provide the text of the New English Bible closely linked to a commentary in which the results of modern scholarship are made available to the general reader. Teachers and young people have been especially kept in mind. The commentators have been asked to assume no specialized theological knowledge, and no knowledge of Greek and Hebrew. Bare references to other literature and multiple references to other parts of the Bible have been avoided. Actual quotations have been given as often as possible.

The completion of the New Testament part of the series in 1967 provides a basis upon which the production of the much larger Old Testament and Apocrypha series can be undertaken. The welcome accorded to the series has been an encouragement to the editors to follow the same general pattern, and an attempt has been made to take account of criticisms which have been offered. One necessary change is the inclusion of the translators' footnotes since in the Old Testament these are more extensive, and essential for the understanding of the text.

Within the severe limits imposed by the size and scope of the series, each commentator will attempt to set out the main findings of recent biblical scholarship and to describe the historical background to the text. The main theological issues will also be critically discussed.

Much attention has been given to the form of the volumes. The aim is to produce books each of which will be read consecutively from first to last page. The introductory material leads naturally into the text, which itself leads into the alternating sections of the commentary.

The series is accompanied by three volumes of a more general character. *Understanding the Old Testament* sets out to provide the larger historical and archaeological background, to say something about the life and thought of the people of the Old Testament, and to answer the question 'Why should we study the Old Testament?'. *The Making of the Old Testament* is concerned with the formation of the books of the Old Testament and Apocrypha in the context of the ancient near eastern world, and with the ways in which these books have come down to us in the life of the Jewish and Christian communities. *Old Testament Illustrations* contains maps, diagrams and photographs with an explanatory text. These three volumes are designed to provide material helpful to the understanding of the individual books and their commentaries, but they are also prepared so as to be of use quite independently.

P. R. A.
A. R. C. L.
J. W. P.

EDITOR'S PREFACE

The commentary on the first twenty-five chapters of Jeremiah has already been published (Cambridge, 1974). For the convenience of readers the introductory sections in vol. I ('Jeremiah's ministry in its historical setting', 'The book of Jeremiah', and 'The religious ideas of the book of Jeremiah') have been reprinted in this concluding volume.

I take this opportunity of expressing my thanks to Professor P. R. Ackroyd, Professor A. R. C. Leaney and Mr J. W. Packer, the General Editors of the Series, for their generous help and advice in preparing the commentary. I am also much indebted to the staff of the Cambridge University Press for their invaluable work on my typescript. As ever, my wife's patience and encouragement have been inexhaustible.   E. W. N.

CONTENTS

THE FOOTNOTES TO THE
N.E.B. TEXT

The footnotes to the N.E.B. text are designed to help the reader either to understand particular points of detail – the meaning of a name, the presence of a play upon words – or to give information about the actual text. Where the Hebrew text appears to be erroneous, or there is doubt about its precise meaning, it may be necessary to turn to manuscripts which offer a different wording, or to ancient translations of the text which may suggest a better reading, or to offer a new explanation based upon conjecture. In such cases, the footnotes supply very briefly an indication of the evidence, and whether the solution proposed is one that is regarded as possible or as probable. Various abbreviations are used in the footnotes.

(1) Some abbreviations are simply of terms used in explaining a point: *ch(s).*, chapter(s); *cp.*, compare; *lit.*, literally; *mng.*, meaning; *MS(S).*, manuscript(s), i.e. Hebrew manuscript(s), unless otherwise stated; *om.*, omit(s); *or*, indicating an alternative interpretation; *poss.*, possible; *prob.*, probable; *rdg.*, reading; *Vs(s).*, version(s).

(2) Other abbreviations indicate sources of information from which better interpretations or readings may be obtained.

Aq.　Aquila, a Greek translator of the Old Testament (perhaps about A.D. 130) characterized by great literalness.

Aram.　Aramaic – may refer to the text in this language (used in parts of Ezra and Daniel), or to the meaning of an Aramaic word. Aramaic belongs to the same language family as Hebrew, and is known from about 1000 B.C. over a wide area of the Middle East, including Palestine.

Heb.　Hebrew – may refer to the Hebrew text or may indicate the literal meaning of the Hebrew word.

Josephus　Flavius Josephus (A.D. 37/8–about 100), author of the *Jewish Antiquities*, a survey of the whole history of his people, directed partly at least to a non-Jewish audience, and of various other works, notably one on the *Jewish War* (that of A.D. 66–73) and a defence of Judaism (*Against Apion*).

Luc. Sept.　Lucian's recension of the Septuagint, an important edition made in Antioch in Syria about the end of the third century A.D.

Pesh.　Peshitta or Peshitto, the Syriac version of the Old Testament. Syriac is the name given chiefly to a form of Eastern Aramaic used by the Christian community. The translation varies in quality, and is at many points influenced by the Septuagint or the Targums.

Sam. Samaritan Pentateuch – the form of the first five books of the Old Testament as used by the Samaritan community. It is written in Hebrew in a special form of the Old Hebrew script, and preserves an important form of the text, somewhat influenced by Samaritan ideas.

Scroll(s) Scroll(s), commonly called the Dead Sea Scrolls, found at or near Qumran from 1947 onwards. These important manuscripts shed light on the state of the Hebrew text as it was developing in the last centuries B.C. and the first century A.D.

Sept. Septuagint (meaning 'seventy'); often abbreviated as the Roman numeral (LXX), the name given to the main Greek version of the Old Testament. According to tradition, the Pentateuch was translated in Egypt in the third century B.C. by 70 (or 72) translators, six from each tribe, but the precise nature of its origin and development is not fully known. It was intended to provide Greek-speaking Jews with a convenient translation. Subsequently it came to be much revered by the Christian community.

Symm. Symmachus, another Greek translator of the Old Testament (beginning of the third century A.D.), who tried to combine literalness with good style. Both Lucian and Jerome viewed his version with favour.

Targ. Targum, a name given to various Aramaic versions of the Old Testament, produced over a long period and eventually standardized, for the use of Aramaic-speaking Jews.

Theod. Theodotion, the author of a revision of the Septuagint (probably second century A.D.), very dependent on the Hebrew text.

Vulg. Vulgate, the most important Latin version of the Old Testament, produced by Jerome about A.D. 400, and the text most used throughout the Middle Ages in western Christianity.

[...] In the text itself square brackets are used to indicate probably late additions to the Hebrew text.

(Fuller discussion of a number of these points may be found in *The Making of the Old Testament* in this series.)

TABLE OF EVENTS IN THE SEVENTH AND SIXTH CENTURIES B.C. BEARING ON
THE BOOK OF JEREMIAH

Judah		Egypt	Babylon
Manasseh 687–642 Amon 642–640 Josiah 640–609		Psammetichus I 664–610	Nabopolassar 626–605
	Death of Assurbanipal of Assyria about 630 Call of Jeremiah to be a prophet 627 Josiah's reformation based upon the book of Deuteronomy 621 Fall of Nineveh 612 Battle of Megiddo and Josiah's death 609	Necho II 610–594	
Jehoahaz (Shallum) 609 Jehoiakim 609–598	Egypt defeated by Nebuchadrezzar at Carchemish 605		Nebuchadrezzar 605–562
Jehoiachin 598–597	Capture of Jerusalem by Nebuchadrezzar and the deportation of Jehoiachin and other leading citizens into exile in Babylon 597		
Zedekiah 597–587	Fall of Jerusalem to Nebuchadrezzar and a second and more extensive deportation of Judaeans to Babylon 587. Judah henceforth organized as a province of Babylonian empire	Psammetichus II 594–589 Hophra 589–570	
Gedaliah (governor) 587–?	Jeremiah taken into exile in Egypt soon after assassination of Gedaliah Jehoiachin released by Amel-Marduk (Evil-merodach) from prison in Babylon 562	Amasis 570–526	Amel-Marduk (Evil-merodach) 562–560 Neriglissar 560–556 Labashi-Marduk 556 Nabonidus 556–539 Babylon conquered by Cyrus (550–530), King of Persia. End of exile 539

THE BOOK OF THE PROPHET

JEREMIAH

✳   ✳   ✳   ✳   ✳   ✳   ✳   ✳   ✳   ✳   ✳   ✳   ✳

JEREMIAH'S MINISTRY IN ITS HISTORICAL
SETTING

Jeremiah received his call to be a prophet in the thirteenth
year of the reign of Josiah king of Judah (640–609 B.C.; see
1: 2), that is, in 627 B.C. His ministry took place during the
period from this year until not long after 587 B.C. when a group
of Judaeans, fearing reprisals by the Babylonians because of the
assassination of Gedaliah whom Nebuchadrezzar had appointed
governor of Judah after the destruction of Jerusalem, forced
Jeremiah to accompany them into exile in Egypt (cp. 43:
1–7). The last recorded episode of his career took place there
and it was there, we must presume, that he eventually died. He
came from Anathoth, about 3 miles (about 4·8 km) north of
Jerusalem, and was the son of a priest, Hilkiah, though there is
nothing to suggest that Jeremiah himself was a priest. Jeremiah's prophetic ministry spanned a period of over forty
years and covered the reigns of the last five kings of Judah.
These years, though they began with renewed hopes under
Josiah, saw the decline and fall of Judah and the destruction
of Jerusalem at the hands of the Babylonians under Nebuchadrezzar, the ablest monarch of the neo-Babylonian empire
which emerged and rose to power towards the end of the
seventh century B.C.

Josiah was the grandson of Manasseh whose long reign
(687–642 B.C.), according to the author of 2 Kings 21, saw a
resurgence of Canaanite and other pagan cults which his
father Hezekiah had suppressed by a reformation carried out
towards the end of the eighth century B.C. (2 Kings 18: 3 ff.).

I

Manasseh is portrayed in 2 Kings 21 as a patron and innovator of pagan cults and practices on a scale hitherto unsurpassed in Judah. His son and immediate successor Amon (642–640 B.C.), about whom we know very little, was assassinated by a group of his courtiers. His assassins were themselves executed by a popular rising among the people, who placed his son Josiah on the throne.

Josiah proved himself to be a courageous leader of the nation. He gained independence for his kingdom from the Assyrians who had held Palestine and neighbouring lands in subjection for more than a century. We cannot be certain when Josiah made his first move to shake off the Assyrian yoke. The last years of the reign of the Assyrian king Assurbanipal, who died shortly before or shortly after 630 B.C., were troubled ones for the Assyrians, largely because of internal struggles, and it is possible that Josiah took advantage of this to make his move for national independence. But though independence was achieved, the struggle to maintain it went on and we know that Josiah was killed in battle at Megiddo against the Egyptians in 609 B.C. when he was attempting to prevent them from getting across to help the Assyrians against the Babylonians whose rise to a position of power and control of the Near East was beginning at that time.

What Josiah is most remembered for in the Old Testament, however, is the reformation he carried out on the basis of 'the book of the law' found in the temple in the eighteenth year of his reign (622 B.C.; 2 Kings 22: 1 – 23: 25; cp. 2 Chron. 34 which presents a different account, strikingly divergent in a number of ways from that in 2 Kings, but which, if used with caution, provides some supplementary information to that given in 2 Kings). Scholars are almost unanimously agreed that 'the book of the law' was the book of Deuteronomy with the exception of a few chapters, for the reforms carried out by Josiah, especially his centralization of worship in Jerusalem, reflect closely the main demands of Deuteronomy. The information supplied by the narrative in 2 Kings 22: 1 – 23: 25

together with a study of Deuteronomy itself has revealed that this book was composed probably during the second half of the seventh century B.C., though a few chapters (most of chs. 1–4 and 29–34) are generally agreed to have been added some time later, very probably during the period of the exile.

Deuteronomy was the product of a group of reformers who sought to renew the nation's loyalty to its God, Yahweh, and to extirpate the Canaanite religion and cults which had gained widespread popularity among the people and threatened to submerge Yahwism altogether. In a preaching style striking for its intensity and sense of urgency they emphasized God's love for his people, his redemption of them from bondage in Egypt and his gracious gift to them of the good land of Canaan, all of which was intended to evoke a response of love and fidelity from Israel, God's chosen people. The book is imbued with warnings against the danger of apostasy, of worshipping other gods, and laws are set forth to deal with any attempt to encourage such worship. The abolition of all sanctuaries apart from 'the place' appointed by God for the nation's cult is demanded. (Various considerations make it clear that 'the place' is to be identified with Jerusalem.) The nation is described as under an oath of obedience to the divine will, the law as set forth in the central section of the book (chs. 12–26). Promises of blessing as reward for faithfulness are set forth but also threats of the dire consequences of apostasy and disobedience (ch. 28). (For fuller detail, see *Deuteronomy* in this series.)

We know almost nothing of Jeremiah's life during the reign of Josiah and can only infer what the content of his message was during those years. For although there are many narratives in the book describing incidents and events in his life during the reigns of Jehoiakim and Zedekiah, there is none dealing with the period of Josiah's reign. Furthermore only one short passage in the book is explicitly dated in the reign of Josiah (3 : 6–11) and it is almost certainly not from Jeremiah but was composed by the Deuteronomic authors to whom the book owes its present form (see the discussion of the composition of

3

the book on pp. 10–16). The evidence suggests that the most intense period of Jeremiah's ministry took place during the reigns of Jehoiakim and Zedekiah. This is not surprising, for the period during which these two kings reigned contrasted sharply with the years of revival, reformation and hope under Josiah. We note also that in 605/4 B.C. Jeremiah made a collection of the oracles which he had hitherto spoken and now applied them anew to the situation at this time under Jehoiakim (see ch. 36). This also points to the new and intensified activity of the prophet which began with the advent of Jehoiakim to the throne.

Although we cannot be certain, it is possible that some of the sayings in, for example, chs. 2 and 3 of the book derive from the earliest years of Jeremiah's ministry. The bitter attack here on the nation's 'harlotry', its worship of the Canaanite god Baal, would certainly fit the period immediately after his call in 627 B.C. when as yet Josiah's reformation was not inaugurated (or was only in its initial stages) and the apostasy which had flourished under Manasseh would very probably still have been widespread. In addition, some of the sayings in these chapters, especially those which portray Israel as the unfaithful 'bride' of Yahweh, may be evidence of the influence on the young Jeremiah of the preaching of the great eighth-century prophet Hosea. Likewise, the impassioned appeal to the nation to turn again to God in passages such as 3: 12f., 19–22; 4: 1–9 would also fit the early years of the prophet's ministry. The evidence suggests that as time went on, and especially during the reigns of Jehoiakim and Zedekiah, Jeremiah became increasingly convinced that the nation's rebellion against God was so deep-seated that judgement was inevitable and that only through judgement could a new beginning be made. A number of commentators believe that the sayings in the early chapters of the book announcing the coming of the 'foe from the north' derive from the earliest years of Jeremiah's ministry and some have suggested that the foe in question at this stage in his preaching was the Scythians, a name used rather loosely

4

for marauding bands known from this period. But the book as it now stands clearly identifies the 'foe from the north' with the Babylonians; accordingly, it seems more likely that the oracles announcing the terrifying approach of the 'foe from the north' belong to the later stages of the prophet's ministry. They fit the early years of Jehoiakim's reign well.

What Jeremiah's attitude was towards Josiah's reformation can only be inferred. The one passage in the book (11: 1–17) which would indicate that he enthusiastically supported the reformation is very probably not from Jeremiah but from the Deuteronomic editors of the book (see the commentary on this passage in the previous volume on pp. 107 ff.). What we can say, however, is that Jeremiah held Josiah in the highest esteem (see 22: 15f.) and this, coupled with the aims and intentions of the reformation, which the prophet could only have welcomed, points to the strong probability that he shared the hopes to which Josiah's reforming zeal gave rise. Indeed it is possible that as a result of the reformation he withdrew from his ministry for some years. This would account for the absence of any information about his activity during Josiah's reign and for the difficulty in assigning more than a few oracles and sayings to that period. It is true that in time Jeremiah seems to have become disenchanted with the reformation. But this was not because he believed it to have been in any way wrong or even deficient in the first instance but evidently because in some circles the law which had been the foundation of the reformation became the basis for a new orthodoxy which resulted in an easy complacency and blinded the nation to the ever new and challenging word of God. In this way the law was being reduced to nothing more than a fetish (see the commentary on 8: 8–9).

As we have seen, Josiah was tragically killed at Megiddo in 609 B.C. He was succeeded by his son Jehoahaz (Shallum) who was acclaimed king by the people. But he reigned for only three months before being deposed by Pharaoh Necho, the victor at Megiddo, who placed another son of Josiah, Eliakim (whose name as king was Jehoiakim), on the throne (cp. 22: 10–12). Under Jehoiakim (609–598 B.C.) Judah remained subject to Egypt until 605 B.C. The Egyptians exacted a heavy tribute from Judah and as if this was not a heavy enough economic burden on the nation, Jehoiakim himself, probably early in his reign, set about building a new and grandiose palace for himself for which he incurred a scathing condemnation from Jeremiah (see 22: 13–17). Jehoiakim turned out to be the very opposite of all his father Josiah had been. Not only was he a tyrant, but under him the reforms enacted by his father lapsed. He was Jeremiah's bitterest enemy. We know that he executed a prophet, one Uriah, whose message is said to have been similar to Jeremiah's, and that but for the protection afforded Jeremiah by certain state officials he too would have been removed from the scene by Jehoiakim (26: 20–4; cp. 36: 19, 26).

It is recorded in 26: 1 that at the beginning of Jehoiakim's reign Jeremiah preached his famous temple sermon in which he condemned as false the popular belief that the mere presence of the temple in Jerusalem was a guarantee against divine judgement upon the nation for its rebellion against God. (This sermon was subsequently edited and developed by the Deuteronomic editors of the book and is now found in 7: 1–15.) This in itself is evidence that Josiah's reformation had now ceased to be effective. In addition, pagan practices of the most heinous nature, the Molech cult, the chief characteristic of which was human sacrifice, again became popular (cp. 7: 31f.) as also did the cult of 'the queen of heaven' (cp. 7: 18).

As a result of all this and the disastrous policies which Jehoiakim pursued, Jeremiah's ministry now entered its most vigorous period. He became the unrelenting opponent of the king and proclaimed the inevitable judgement of God upon the nation. Very probably it was during these early years of Jehoiakim's reign that the oracles announcing the devastation to be wrought upon the country by the 'foe from the north' were proclaimed by the prophet.

6

For a few years the Babylonians were not an immediate threat to Judah. But this state of affairs was soon to be drastically altered. In 605 B.C. Nebuchadrezzar defeated the Egyptians at Carchemish on the Euphrates and was poised to invade Palestine itself. It was probably these events which prompted Jeremiah to compile a scroll of the oracles which he had hitherto uttered and have them re-proclaimed as a unit in the temple by his scribe Baruch (cp. ch. 36). If up to that point his oracles of judgement had been ignored or dismissed as false, in the new situation which had now come about, they took on a frightening significance for the people whose confidence was now severely shaken: the 'foe from the north' had terrifyingly materialized!

The danger which loomed for the nation at this time was overcome when, in 604 B.C., Jehoiakim submitted to the Babylonians. But his loyalty to Nebuchadrezzar was short-lived and as a result of further war between the Babylonians and the Egyptians in 601 B.C. he rebelled against his overlord. It was not for some time that Nebuchadrezzar was able to march in power to quash Judah's rebellion, though he engaged some Aramaean, Moabite and Ammonite contingents to harass Jehoiakim in the meantime (cp. 2 Kings 24: 2). Late in 598 B.C., however, the Babylonian army invaded Judah and besieged Jerusalem, Jehoiakim died (he may have been assassinated), and his eighteen-year-old son, Jehoiachin, succeeded him. When, however, only three months later, that is, in 597 B.C., Jerusalem fell to the Babylonians, the young king and his mother as well as various officials and other top-ranking citizens were carried into exile in Babylon (cp. Jer. 13: 18; 22: 24–7). Jehoiachin's uncle Mattaniah, whose throne-name was Zedekiah, became king and was to be the last reigning monarch of Judah.

Under Zedekiah the nation's decline continued. He appears to have been a weak ruler easily manipulated by his nobles. His position was not helped by the fact that Jehoiachin, though in exile, appears to have been regarded officially by the Baby-

7

lonians as still being king of Judah. The exiles themselves regarded him as king, whilst in Judah itself it was popularly believed that Jehoiachin and the exiles would soon be brought back to Jerusalem (28: 1–4). Such a state of affairs would have placed limitations on Zedekiah's authority.

Jeremiah inveighed against the optimistic beliefs which sprang up after 597 B.C. that God was about to destroy the power of Babylon and return the exiles to the homeland. He announced that the yoke of Babylon would remain upon the neck of not only Judah but the other kingdoms of Syria-Palestine (ch. 28). At the same time he declared that God's blessing was already upon those in exile and that the future restoration of the nation would be brought about by God through these exiles (ch. 24), whilst those who had remained in the homeland were under divine judgement soon to befall them. He wrote to the exiles in Babylon encouraging them to settle down and assuring them of God's care for them and their ultimate redemption from bondage (ch. 29).

Because of this he became increasingly the object of abuse at the hands of his fellow countrymen and more than once during the reign of Zedekiah, and especially during the final years of it, he suffered greatly and at times came near to losing his life (cp. 20: 1f; 37; 38). He was regarded as a traitor and was condemned and isolated. Though we cannot date precisely those passionate and intensely personal outbursts of Jeremiah commonly referred to as his 'confessions' (cp. 11: 18 – 12: 6; 15: 10–18; 17: 14–18; 18: 19–23; 20: 7–13, 14–18), it is in every way probable that they belong at least for the most part to this period of his ministry.

Notwithstanding the assault on Judah and Jerusalem by the Babylonians in 598–597 B.C. and its dire consequences, the spirit of rebellion continued and given the opportunity would flare up into activity. Probably as a result of disturbances in Babylon in 594 B.C. (cp. 29: 21–3), Zedekiah became party to an attempted coalition between Edom, Moab and Tyre with a view to rebellion against the Babylonians and consultations

Jeremiah's ministry

between ambassadors of these states took place in Jerusalem
(cp. ch. 27). But for reasons unknown to us nothing came of
this attempt. Jer. 51: 59 may be an allusion to Zedekiah's
desire to reassure Nebuchadrezzar of his continued loyalty.

But if the plans on this occasion came to nothing, outright
rebellion was to come but a few years later. By 589 B.C.
Zedekiah had committed himself irrevocably against the
Babylonians. His reasons are not known to us. Undoubtedly
the same nationalistic spirit which exhibited itself earlier and
which was sustained by promises by popular prophets of an
imminent reversal of the set-backs and exile of 597 B.C.
asserted itself again. In addition, the Egyptians now as in times
past entered the scene with encouragement to Zedekiah and
assurances of military backing. Nebuchadrezzar did not delay
to attack. Early in 588 B.C., the ninth year of Zedekiah's reign,
the Babylonian army reached Jerusalem and besieged it whilst
at the same time setting about reducing and gaining control of
such strongholds as they had not already taken. Jerusalem had
a brief respite later in the year when the promised, but in the
end ineffectual, Egyptian help materialized and forced the
Babylonians to lift the siege on Jerusalem (cp. 37: 3–5). But
the Egyptians were quickly routed by the Babylonians who
promptly surrounded Jerusalem again. Resistance continued
for months. During this time and probably also before it
Zedekiah considered surrendering and suing for peace. He
consulted Jeremiah who had all along called for submission to
Nebuchadrezzar (cp. 21: 1–7; 37: 1–10, 17f.; 38: 14–23). But
in spite of the prophet's message and counsel, the resistance
was carried on until 587 B.C. when the city had exhausted its
food supplies (cp. 2 Kings 25: 2f.; Jer. 52: 5f.). Zedekiah got
out of the capital by night in an attempt to escape but was
captured near Jericho and brought to Nebuchadrezzar at
Riblah in Syria. His sons were executed and Zedekiah himself,
having witnessed their death, was blinded and taken in chains
to Babylon where he died. A few weeks later Nebuzaradan,
captain of Nebuchadrezzar's bodyguard, entered Jerusalem

9

and razed it to the ground and burned down the temple. A further body of Judaeans were now deported to Babylon. Jeremiah, who had been imprisoned in the guard-house during the final stages of the siege, was now released by the Babylonians (cp. 39: 11–14; 40: 1–6).

Judah, now devastated and with the cream of its population either dead or in exile, became a province of the Babylonian empire. Nebuchadrezzar appointed Gedaliah as governor and the centre of his administration was Mizpah. How long he governed it not clear and estimates of anything from a few months to several years have been proposed. He was assassinated by one Ishmael who had the backing of the Ammonites (40: 13 – 41: 3). Fearing reprisals from the Babylonians, the community at Mizpah, though appealed to and warned by Jeremiah to remain in Judah (cp. 42: 7–22), fled to Egypt and forced the prophet to go with them. The last recorded episode of his ministry took place in Egypt and there, we may presume, he died, whether soon after his arrival or later we do not know.

THE BOOK OF JEREMIAH

The book of Jeremiah contains three kinds of literary material. Firstly, there are many poetic oracles and sayings such as we find in most other prophetic books in the Old Testament. Secondly, there are many narratives describing incidents and events in the life and times of Jeremiah. Thirdly, the book contains numerous sayings, some of them lengthy discourses or 'sermons', in prose. The poetic oracles are for the most part from Jeremiah himself, whilst the historical narratives are usually believed to be a biography of the prophet composed by the scribe Baruch. But the many prose sayings and 'sermons' pose the most difficult problem in understanding the composition of the book.

Scholars have long acknowledged that these prose sayings and 'sermons' are closely akin in both style and vocabulary to the Deuteronomic literature which comprises the books

Deuteronomy, Joshua, Judges, Samuel and Kings. So different are these prose sayings and 'sermons' not only in style and language but also in theological content from the poetic oracles that it is very unlikely that both types of material could have come from one and the same author. Some scholars have suggested that a group of disciples gathered round Jeremiah and subsequently recast, so to speak, some of his sayings in the Deuteronomic style and developed them along Deuteronomic lines. But we have no evidence that Jeremiah had such a following of disciples; he appears to have worked alone, accompanied only by his scribe and companion Baruch. More probably, therefore, these prose sayings and 'sermons' were composed by a group of Deuteronomic authors. This does not mean that the passages in question are simply Deuteronomic 'inventions'. Some of them (e.g. 11: 1–14; 17: 19–27) are probably not based on anything Jeremiah said. But most appear to be based on his original sayings. The Deuteronomic authors expanded and developed certain of his sayings and oracles and supplemented the prophet's own message so as to relate them to the needs of the nation at a time later than Jeremiah and to draw out their significance for that time. This means that the material in the book of Jeremiah spans a period considerably longer than that covered by Jeremiah's ministry. It embodies the message of Jeremiah and the oracles he uttered over the forty or so years of his ministry. But it also contains much which originated during the period of the exile when the Deuteronomic authors worked and sought to revive and renew the nation's life after the catastrophe which had befallen it in 587 B.C.

In addition to these prose sayings and speeches, however, it is also probable that the narratives in the book derive from the same Deuteronomic group from which the prose sayings and 'sermons' derive. Certainly in style and language they are very similar to the sort of narratives we find in the Deuteronomic literature, especially, say, in the books of Kings. Furthermore, the fact that not a few of these narratives in Jeremiah embody prose sayings and 'sermons', in some instances providing nothing more than a historical framework for such sayings and 'sermons', renders it all the more likely that both the narratives and the sermons come from the same authors. In addition, these narratives, far from being merely biographical, concern for the most part pressing theological issues which can be shown to be of importance in the Deuteronomic literature as well. The traditional view that Baruch composed these narratives must therefore be regarded as improbable, even though some of the information in them dealing with incidents in Jeremiah's life may have come from him.

We have already seen that the book of Deuteronomy in its original form (substantially chs. 5–26 and 28 of the present book) made its appearance in 622 B.C. The style and language of Deuteronomy are, however, also found in the books which follow it in the Hebrew Bible (Joshua, Judges, Samuel and Kings). The view now shared by most scholars is that the corpus of literature Deuteronomy to 2 Kings is one extended work composed by a group of Deuteronomic theologians and authors who, using sources from varying ages and places in Israel's history, have compiled a history of the nation from Moses to the exile.

These Deuteronomic authors lived and worked in the shadow of the catastrophe of 587 B.C. and their main purpose in composing their history of the nation was twofold. First, they sought to explain why Israel, God's chosen people, had suffered the terrible disasters which had befallen them, first in 722 B.C. when the northern kingdom was destroyed, and finally in 587 B.C. when Judah was destroyed and many deported to Babylon. Their explanation, in brief, was that Israel had persistently, and to an ever-increasing degree, disobeyed God's law, forsaking him and worshipping other gods. God had sent prophets through the centuries to succeed Moses, the first and greatest of the prophets (cp. Deut. 18: 15–19), and to exhort the nation to steadfast obedience to God's law. But the nation had stubbornly refused to listen to these prophets (cp. 2 Kings 17: 13–17). Because of this the nation incurred God's judgement. Secondly, however, although the theme of judgement is emphasized throughout the history, the Deuteronomic authors held out hope for the future of the people, now deprived of their land and living in exile. If, notwithstanding their past rebellion against God, they turned again in penitence to him, he would forgive them and restore them to their homeland and reconstitute them as his people (cp. Deut. 4: 29–31; 30: 1–10; 1 Kings 8: 46–53).

For our understanding of the prose sayings and 'sermons' as well as the narratives in the book of Jeremiah several themes or motifs in the Deuteronomic literature must be noted. First, great emphasis is placed throughout this literature on the central importance of the law in the life of the nation. Secondly, the prophets play a very important role: Moses was the first and greatest of the prophets and he was succeeded by a series of prophets to continue his work in proclaiming God's law and word to the nation. Thirdly, the Deuteronomic historians placed great emphasis on the solemn responsibility of the kings in directing and leading the nation's life as God's holy people and in seeing that the divine law was established and observed in the land. In their history of the monarchy they condemn most kings for not having lived up to this responsibility and for thus having been foremost in bringing disaster upon the nation because of its apostasy. Finally, as we have noted, the Deuteronomic historians also announced promises of hope for the nation's future beyond the judgement which had befallen it.

In commenting on the prose sayings and the narratives in the book of Jeremiah attention will be drawn to the presence of these and other Deuteronomic themes and motifs in them. In broad terms the purpose of the Deuteronomic authors and editors in developing and supplementing Jeremiah's words was, as in the Deuteronomic history itself, twofold. First, they sought to explain the catastrophe of 587 B.C.: it befell the nation because of its persistent refusal to obey the law of God or to pay heed to the word of God announced to it by the prophets, in this instance by Jeremiah. But this was not only instruction about the past; it was at the same time exhortation to those now in exile and living in the shadow of judgement to turn again in penitence and obedience to God. In this way these Deuteronomic authors and editors sought to bring about an inner renewal of the nation's relationship to God. Secondly, alongside this they further developed and supplemented Jeremiah's message of hope for the nation's future beyond judgement and they announced, like Jeremiah himself, that the revival and restoration of the nation to be brought about by God was to be effected through the exiles in Babylon.

All this means that a complicated history lies behind the book of Jeremiah, beginning with the individual oracles and sayings of Jeremiah which were recorded by the prophet in the scroll compiled by Baruch in 604 B.C. and subsequently expanded by the addition of later sayings of the prophet. We must assume that these recorded sayings of the prophet got into the hands of a group of Deuteronomic authors and editors who then arranged them further, expanded and developed a number of them to suit their own theological purposes, and composed many narratives alongside them. There thus arose a number of small groupings of material which were ultimately brought together into larger collections which were in turn united to form the book as it now stands.

The present book comprises four major collections which may be classified with regard to their separate main themes as follows:

(A) chs. 1–25, which comprise a number of smaller units of material, centre on the judgement announced against the nation.

(B) chs. 26–36 comprise oracles and sayings for the most part presented within a narrative framework. The section as a whole may be classified as a history of the word of God proclaimed by Jeremiah and rejected by the nation. The opening chapter introduces this theme, which reaches its climax in ch. 36.

(C) chs. 37–45 cover the period of the prophet's life and ministry from the siege and fall of Jerusalem in 587 B.C. down to the last episode in his ministry which took place in Egypt. They describe the suffering endured by the prophet at the hands of his fellow-countrymen and the subsequent vindication of both the prophet and the word he proclaimed (37: 1 – 40: 6). The section 40: 7 – 44: 30 centres on the history of the community left in Judah by the Babylonians after 587 B.C. and its eventual flight to Egypt. The purpose of all this is to show that the hope for the future did not lie either in the land of Judah itself or amongst those who fled to Egypt; the true 'remnant' of the nation through whom renewal was to come was the community in exile in Babylon.

(D) chs. 46–51 clearly comprise a separate section within the book and consist of oracles against foreign nations. In the Septuagint these chapters follow 25: 13 (25: 14 is omitted) and this may have been their original position. Section 25: 15–38 then stands as a concluding comment to them.

The book ends with a historical appendix (ch. 52) which is largely parallel to 2 Kings 24: 18 – 25: 30 but includes some additional information to what is contained in this narrative.

The Septuagint and the Hebrew texts of the book of Jeremiah differ, as has just been noted, in their placing of the oracles against foreign nations. But in addition to this major difference, the Septuagint has at many points a shorter form of the text. In many cases the shorter form amounts to nothing more than the absence of a word or two and often there is no difference in substance between the two texts. But in some passages there are longer sections found in the Hebrew but not in the Septuagint (e.g. 33: 14–26 where the Hebrew has a group of oracles centring mainly on God's promises to David, but the Greek has none of this material). The existence of these differing forms of the text is further illustrated by fragments of the text found among the Dead Sea Scrolls at Qumran. It appears that the book of Jeremiah existed in more than one form and whilst the shorter text of the Septuagint is easily explained in places as being due to nothing more than a scribal error or to the Greek translators, in other places it seems clear that the longer Hebrew text reflects a greater or lesser degree of development or supplementation of the original Jeremiah material. A good example of this is the material in ch. 33 already mentioned. Another example is contained in 29: 16–20 which is not found in the Septuagint. This passage is an announcement of judgement addressed to and against those left in Jerusalem and Judah after the deportation of 597 B.C. and as such it is out of place in this chapter, which records the letter sent by the prophet to the exiles in Babylon. The passage is probably, therefore, a secondary insertion into this chapter and may have been added in order to emphasize further that the future of Israel as the people of God would be brought about through the exiles in Babylon and not through those who remained in Judah itself during the period of the exile (see the comments on the passage on pp. 46f. below).

THE RELIGIOUS IDEAS OF THE BOOK OF JEREMIAH

Only a careful and thoughtful study of the book of Jeremiah itself can reveal fully the religious and theological riches it contains. But some of the main characteristics of its religious teaching and outlook may here be briefly noted to serve as a guide in reading the book.

First and foremost, as we might expect, the book has much to say about God and the predominant features of its teaching in this respect are as follows. Other 'gods' are mentioned, but they are dismissed as empty illusions. In other words the authors of the book were monotheists. Yahweh alone is God. He is creator and sustainer of the world. As a corollary to this and at the same time further evidence of it, the book is 'universalistic' in its teaching about God. Yahweh is Lord not only over Israel but over the other nations of the world and their destinies are in his hands. He controls history and, though men and nations may not acknowledge him as Lord, his sovereign will and purposes will be established. Yahweh is a holy and righteous God who stands in judgement upon all that is evil in the lives of men and nations. He sets his heart on 'justice and right upon the earth' (9: 24) and man's true wisdom is to know and understand him and so to live in accordance with his divine will and thus manifest his holiness and righteousness. He is the God of unfailing love who summons men to respond to him in love and steadfast loyalty.

The book emphasizes the special relationship between Israel and God. Yet Israel's divine election was election not to privilege but to responsibility. Israel was chosen by this holy God to be his holy people so that the holiness and righteousness of God might be manifested in and through Israel to the world. Yet Israel had turned her back on God; she had broken the covenant. Like an unfaithful wife she had forsaken her first love and had gone after other 'lovers', the gods of the land of Canaan. Such behaviour was beyond belief. No other nation had forsaken its gods, even though they were no gods. Yet Israel had forsaken Yahweh, the 'spring of living water' (2: 13). By doing so Israel had incurred judgement: she had been spurned by God and abandoned. The covenant had been terminated.

Yet the book of Jeremiah sees beyond this judgement to a new beginning in the relationship between Israel and God. Though rejected by God and cast out of her homeland, God would take her again to himself and reconstitute her as his people: 'in after time the land shall be peopled as of old . . . and Jacob shall be at rest once more, prosperous and unafraid' (46: 26–7). Yet just at this point and alongside the promise for the future comes one of the deepest insights of the book. For it was now realized that Israel had not merely refused to love and obey God; Israel had been *unable* by her very nature to do so. Jeremiah saw the source of men's rebellion against God to spring from the natural perverseness of their hearts: 'The heart is the most deceitful of all things, desperately sick; who

17

can fathom it?' (17: 9). He came to realize that Israel's sin was so deep-seated as to be part of her very nature: 'Can the Nubian change his skin, or the leopard its spots? And you? Can you do good, you who are schooled in evil?' (13: 23). Hence in the future renewal and revival of the nation to be brought about by God beyond judgement, God would change the hearts of the people. What is perhaps the most famous passage in the book of Jeremiah speaks of a new covenant between God and Israel, a covenant which would both supersede and surpass the former covenant now broken. God would set his law within the people and 'write it on their hearts' so that 'No longer need they teach one another to know the LORD; all of them, high and low alike, shall know me, says the LORD, for I will forgive their wrongdoing and remember their sin no more' (31: 31–4).

A further important feature of the teaching of the book of Jeremiah concerns the relationship between the individual and God. It is wrong to suppose that personal religion and piety and the responsibility of the individual to obey God's will and live in accordance with his divine laws had played no part in the religion of Israel before the time of Jeremiah. There is an abundance of evidence to prove that this was far from the case. Yet nowhere else in the Old Testament is the subtle power of sin over the individual more emphasized than in the book of Jeremiah. This is already obvious from the stress laid by the prophet on the perverseness of the human heart. It is also clear in the teaching of the new covenant passage which looks to the divine grace for the changing of men's hearts. Most of all, however, the relationship between the individual and God reached new depths from Jeremiah's own experiences during his ministry and from the inner struggle in his mind which was brought about by those experiences. His message met with little or no response from the nation. On the contrary, not only was his message rejected; he himself suffered greatly as God's spokesman to Israel. Frustrated and isolated to the point of sheer despair, he was thrown back upon the

God who had commissioned him to his prophetic ministry. The 'confessions' of Jeremiah, to which reference has already been made (p. 8), give us the most vivid and poignant of pictures of the struggle that went on in the prophet's mind and the assault which his bitter experiences and the apparent success of evil mounted upon his faith. Most of all, however, these 'confessions' witness to Jeremiah's intense personal communion with God and, in revealing not merely the doubts which tormented him but the abyss of darkness which at times seems to have engulfed his mind, they speak of the triumph of faith. In this as in so many other ways the book of Jeremiah has still much to say to us today as it has to men down through the centuries.

✳   ✳   ✳   ✳   ✳   ✳   ✳   ✳   ✳   ✳   ✳   ✳   ✳

Jerusalem laid under a curse

✳ Ch. 26 narrates the disturbance which Jeremiah's famous temple sermon (7: 1–15) provoked and the ensuing demand for his execution on the grounds of blasphemy. As such it has been regarded as part of Baruch's biography of the prophet, in this instance recording the abuse, suffering and threat to his life which he had to endure as God's spokesman to his rebellious people. But as with other similar narratives throughout the book, it is a mistake to understand this one as being concerned merely with recording in biographical fashion a particular incident in the prophet's life. It does provide us with reliable historical and biographical information about Jeremiah, but a closer examination of the narrative reveals that this is not its primary purpose. Rather the story is one of a series which record the rejection of the word of God spoken by his 'servants the prophets', in this particular instance by Jeremiah (but see also verses 20–4), and the judgement which this entailed for Israel. (This theme is the central motif in chs. 26–36 and reaches its climax in ch. 36.) The narrative falls naturally into the following sections: verses 1–6, 7–16, 17–19, 20–4.

THE TEMPLE SERMON: A SUMMARY

26 AT THE BEGINNING OF THE REIGN of Jehoiakim son of Josiah, king of Judah, this word came to Jeremiah[a] 2 from the LORD: These are the words of the LORD: Stand in the court of the LORD's house and speak to the inhabitants of all the cities of Judah who come to worship there. You shall tell them everything that I command you to say 3 to them, keeping nothing back. Perhaps they may listen, and every man may turn back from his evil courses. Then I will relent, and give up my purpose to bring disaster 4 on them for their evil deeds. You shall say to them, These are the words of the LORD: If you do not obey me, if you 5 do not follow the law I have set before you, and listen to the words of my servants the prophets, the prophets whom I have taken pains to send to you, but you have 6 never listened to them, then I will make this house like Shiloh and this city an object of ridicule to all nations on earth.

✷ The narrative begins with a brief recapitulation of the occasion of the temple sermon, a statement of the purpose for which it was preached, and a summary of its contents.

1. *At the beginning of the reign of Jehoiakim:* after the death of Josiah in 609 B.C. his son Jehoahaz (Shallum was his name before he came to the throne; cp. 22: 11) was placed on the throne, evidently by a popular rising among the people (cp. 2 Kings 23: 30). But he reigned for only three months and was then deposed by Pharaoh who replaced him on the throne of

[a] to Jeremiah: *so Pesh.; Heb. om.*

Judah by another son of Josiah, Eliakim, whose name as king
was Jehoiakim (cp. 2 Kings 23: 34). If the Hebrew phrase here
translated *At the beginning of the reign of Jehoiakim* refers to
Jehoiakim's accession year (in Babylonian the equivalent
phrase, *resh sharruti*, does refer to a king's accession year), it
would mean that the sermon was preached in 609 B.C. Some
commentators have suggested that the prophet preached on
the occasion of Jehoiakim's coronation. This is not impossible,
but the text itself provides no such precise date.

2. *Stand in the court of the LORD's house:* cp. the comment on
7: 2 in vol. I. *keeping nothing back:* literally, 'do not hold back
a word'.

3. *Perhaps they may listen, and every man may turn back from
his evil courses:* as on other occasions, the nation is given yet
another opportunity to reject its apostasy and repledge its
loyalty to Yahweh (cp. 36: 3).

4-6. The sermon is summarized as a call to obedience to
God's law and to the words of the prophets.

4f. *if you do not follow the law I have set before you:* this reference to the law (*Torah*) and to the preaching of *my servants the
prophets* is strikingly reminiscent of 2 Kings 17: 14 and together
with other indications is evidence that this narrative was
composed by Deuteronomic authors. In Jer. 7: 5-6, 9 specific
laws are mentioned which the nation is called upon to obey.
It is one of the main themes of the book of Jeremiah that
Israel suffered judgement because she had persistently refused
to *obey* God's *law* and to *listen to the words of my servants the
prophets* (cp. the commentary on 7: 1-5; 11: 1-17; 17: 19-27
in the previous volume; also on 34: 8-22; 35).

6. *I will make this house like Shiloh:* Shiloh, an ancient
sanctuary of the Ark (cp. 1 Sam. 1-4), probably recently
destroyed, provides a telling example of God's judgement
(cp. the commentary on 7: 14). *

JEREMIAH'S ARREST AND TRIAL

7 The priests, the prophets, and all the people heard
8 Jeremiah say this in the LORD's house and, when he came
to the end of what the LORD had commanded him to say
to them, priests, prophets, and people seized him and
9 threatened him with death. 'Why', they demanded,
'have you prophesied in the LORD's name that this house
shall become like Shiloh and this city waste and uninhabited?' The people all gathered against Jeremiah in
10 the LORD's house. The officers of Judah heard what was
happening, and they went up from the royal palace to
the LORD's house and took their places there at the
11 entrance of the new gate. Then the priests and the prophets said to the officers and all the people, 'Condemn
this fellow to death. He has prophesied against this city:
12 you have heard it with your own ears.' Then Jeremiah
said to the officers and the people, 'The LORD sent me to
prophesy against this house and this city all that you have
13 heard. If you now mend your ways and your doings and
obey the LORD your God, then he may relent and revoke
14 the disaster with which he has threatened you. But I am
in your hands; do with me whatever you think right and
15 proper. Only you may be certain that, if you put me to
death, you and this city and all who live in it will be
guilty of murdering an innocent man; for in very truth
the LORD has sent me to you to say all this in your hearing.'
16   Then the officers and all the people said to the priests
and the prophets, 'This man ought not to be condemned
to death, for he has spoken to us in the name of the LORD
our God.'

✻ 7–9. The immediate reaction to Jeremiah's sermon is one of fury and indignation on the part of those who heard him in the temple court.

7. *The priests, the prophets, and all the people: The priests* and *the prophets* are to be understood as the cultic personnel of the temple, whilst *all the people* are to be understood as the congregation who heard the prophet's words. We must understand 'the people' referred to in verses 11 and 16 as having belonged to the court as distinct from those who formed the mob who assailed Jeremiah in the temple.

9. '*Why*', they demanded, '*have you prophesied in the LORD's name*': the charge against Jeremiah was, in effect, that he was a false prophet since, for those who accused him, it was inconceivable that any true prophet of Yahweh could announce the destruction of the holy city and the temple where God dwelt. The prophet's claim to speak in the name of Yahweh and the message he announced thus made him doubly blasphemous in the eyes of these people. *The people all gathered against Jeremiah in the LORD's house*: that is, they set upon him there and then and attempted to lynch him.

10. Fortunately for Jeremiah, at this point a number of *The officers of Judah*, that is, state officials, intervened – they may have heard the commotion or someone may have run and told them of what was happening – and convened a court to try Jeremiah. *at the entrance of the new gate*: we know nothing more about this *new gate* than that it was in 'the upper court' (36: 10).

11. '*Condemn this fellow to death. He has prophesied against this city: you have heard it with your own ears*': Jeremiah is formally charged by those who witnessed his sermon; they demand the death penalty, arguing that the case against him is incontrovertible, as the words *you have heard it with your own ears* indicate.

12–15. Jeremiah then makes his defence, in which he does not deny having pronounced disaster upon Jerusalem and the temple but pleads that he has prophesied only what God commanded him and is therefore innocent of the charge brought against him. True to his prophetic calling, he fearlessly reiterates his woeful message.

16. '*This man ought not to be condemned to death, for he has spoken to us in the name of the LORD our God*': The royal officials, acting as judges in the case, accept his defence and acquit him of the charge brought against him: Jeremiah is acknowledged to be a prophet sent by Yahweh. *

THE ELDERS' PLEA

17 Some of the elders of the land also stood up and said
18 to the assembled people, 'In the time of Hezekiah king of Judah, Micah of Moresheth was prophesying and said to all the people of Judah: "These are the words of the LORD of Hosts:

> Zion shall become a ploughed field,
> Jerusalem a heap of ruins,
> and the temple-hill rough heath."

19 Did King Hezekiah and all Judah put him to death? Did not the king show reverence for the LORD and seek to placate him? Then the LORD relented and revoked the disaster with which he had threatened them. Are we to bring great disaster on ourselves?'

* We should probably regard verse 16 as marking the end of the court case proper, since it appears to record the formal acquittal of the prophet by the presiding officials. The narrator now describes how some elders added their support to the decision given in favour of Jeremiah. They cite as a precedent for the prophet's woeful words against the city and the temple the similar judgement proclaimed by Micah a century or more earlier, adding that far from executing Micah, King Hezekiah and the people at that time repented in

response to his preaching and thus gained forgiveness and forestalled the judgement pronounced against them. Thus not only is Jeremiah's innocence further defended, but his appeal for repentance is also endorsed so that, as in the days of Micah, the nation might now once again turn back from its apostasy and thus avoid the judgement which will otherwise befall it.

18. '*In the time of Hezekiah king of Judah*': Hezekiah reigned from 715 to 687 B.C. Apart from David himself, Hezekiah and Josiah are the only two kings of Judah acclaimed in the Bible without qualification to have been faithful to Yahweh. Hezekiah, like Josiah at a later time, carried out a reformation of the nation's religious life (cp. 2 Kings 18: 3 ff.), centralizing worship in Jerusalem and purging the country of idolatrous practices and cults. *Micah of Moresheth:* Micah's prophetic ministry took place during the reigns of Jotham (742–735 B.C.), Ahaz (735–715 B.C.) and Hezekiah (715–687 B.C.) (cp. Mic. 1: 1). The full name of Micah's home town was Moresheth-gath (cp. Mic. 1: 14). As its name suggests, it was near Gath, one of the five cities of the Philistines. Though an Israelite village, Moresheth appears to have been so close to Gath that it was a satellite of this city. The words of Micah here quoted are from Mic. 3: 12.

19. '*Did King Hezekiah and all Judah put him to death? Did not the king show reverence for the LORD and seek to placate him?*': it is here that the intention of the narrative as a whole begins to emerge. For in further emphasizing the vindication of Jeremiah and endorsing his appeal for repentance, the narrator directs attention pointedly to the one who is ultimately responsible for leading the nation to repentance and faithfulness to God: the reigning king, Jehoiakim. Just as in the books of Kings the burden of responsibility for the judgement upon Israel and Judah is laid squarely upon the shoulders of one king after another, so here, writing after the catastrophe of the destruction of Jerusalem and the exile in 587 B.C., the narrator focuses the decision for the rejection of the word of God, spoken by the prophet, on Jehoiakim. Those who listened

to this story would not have failed to see in it a pointed contrast drawn between Hezekiah's humble and penitent response to the word of God spoken by Micah and Jehoiakim's rejection of God's word proclaimed by Jeremiah. Ch. 36 similarly sharply contrasts Jehoiakim with his pious and faithful father Josiah and, as in ch. 26, also places the responsibility for the rejection of the word of God upon Jehoiakim's shoulders. In these narratives, as in the books of Kings, the king is regarded as the personification of the nation. It was the reigning king's solemn function to lead the nation's worship of God and to ensure faithfulness and obedience to the divine will. The king's failure to do so entailed the failure of the nation itself. *

THE EXECUTION OF A PROPHET

20 There was another man who prophesied in the name of the LORD, Uriah son of Shemaiah, from Kiriath-jearim. He also prophesied against this city and this land, just as 21 Jeremiah had done. King Jehoiakim with all his officers and his bodyguard heard what he said and sought to put him to death. When Uriah heard of it, he was afraid and 22 fled to Egypt. King Jehoiakim sent Elnathan son of Akbor 23 with others to fetch Uriah from Egypt, and they brought him to the king. He had him put to death by the sword, and his body flung into the burial-place of the common 24 people. But Ahikam son of Shaphan used his influence on Jeremiah's behalf to save him from death at the hands of the people.

* The narrator's intention to show that it was the reigning monarch who spearheaded the nation's apostasy and was ultimately responsible for it is finally and sharply brought out in this last section of the chapter. Here it is recorded that another prophet, Uriah, 'also prophesied against this city

and this land, just as Jeremiah had done' and was hounded down and executed by Jehoiakim. Thus the hope expressed in verse 3 that the nation on hearing Jeremiah's words would repent and be delivered from the impending judgement was in vain; the word of God spoken to the nation by his true prophets Jeremiah and Uriah was rejected by the nation as personified in its king. Thus judgement became inevitable.

20. *Uriah son of Shemaiah, from Kiriath-jearim:* Uriah is mentioned only here and we know nothing more about him. *Kiriath-jearim* ('town of the forest thickets') was one of the four Gibeonite cities (cp. Josh. 9: 17). It is referred to as Kiriath-baal in Josh. 18: 14 and as Baalah in Josh. 15: 9. It is best known as the place where the Ark was kept after its recovery from the Philistines and before it was brought to Jerusalem by David (cp. 1 Sam. 7: 1ff.; 2. Sam. 6). It has been identified with the modern Tell el-Azhar just over 8 miles (nearly 13 km) north-west of Jerusalem.

22. *Elnathan son of Akbor:* this royal official is mentioned again in 36: 12, 25 where he is one of those who appear to have reacted reverently to the scroll of Jeremiah's oracles. As his name suggests, he may have been the son of the Akbor who was one of Josiah's officials (cp. 2 Kings 22: 12, 14). He is probably also to be identified with the Elnathan mentioned in 2 Kings 24: 8 as the father of Nehushta the mother of Jehoia-chin, king of Judah.

23. *He had him put to death by the sword:* the Old Testament contains only one other record of the execution of a prophet (cp. 2 Chron. 24: 20-2). The biblical record that Israel per-sistently rejected the preaching of the prophets sent to her by God (cp. 2 Kings 17: 13–17), the suffering many of them had to endure (especially Jeremiah) as well as the execution of others eventually gave rise to the legends of the martyrdom of many of the prophets (for example Isaiah). It is all this that forms the background of Jesus' saying 'O Jerusalem, Jerusalem, the city that murders the prophets and stones the messengers sent to her!' (Matt. 23: 37; Luke 13: 34). *the burial-place of the*

common people: in the Kidron valley, outside Jerusalem, there was a common trench, where the bodies of 'stateless persons' and condemned criminals were buried (cp. 2 Kings 23: 6).

24. *Ahikam son of Shaphan:* one of the officials who had served under Josiah (cp. 2 Kings 22: 12, 14) and subsequently under Jehoiakim. It seems that Ahikam and some other state officials used their 'good offices' at times to protect Jeremiah (cp. 38: 7–13). ✻

A rising against Nebuchadrezzar checked

✻ Chs. 27 and 28 obviously belong together and describe Jeremiah's dramatic symbolic enactment, by means of an ox-yoke tied round his neck, of the inevitable Babylonian subjugation of the states of Syria–Palestine including Judah (ch. 27) and the rejection of his words which are countered by an oracle by one Hananiah, evidently a leading prophet who was bitterly opposed to Jeremiah's message (ch. 28). The main theme of these chapters is the conflict which took place between the word of God spoken by his true prophet Jeremiah and the words of false prophets, notably Hananiah. In this way these chapters continue the theme of ch. 26, whilst at the same time recording the way in which the nation was misled by false prophets – a motif found earlier in the book (14: 11–16; 23: 16–40) and taken up again in 29: 15–23. Both chapters were composed by the Deuteronomic editors of the book of Jeremiah, but the historicity of what is recorded in them cannot be questioned. They provide an excellent example of the way in which these editors, working in the shadow of the catastrophe of 587 B.C., sought to explain why the nation had suffered judgement from God. In stressing the role of false prophets in having led the people into a false sense of security, the Deuteronomic authors also sought to warn those living after 587 B.C. against being further deceived by such prophets among them. Ch. 29 records the activity of such prophets among the exiles in Babylon.

Ch. 27 comprises three sections (verses 1–11, 12–15, 16–22) each of which contains an appeal for submission to the Babylonians and a warning not to be deceived by those prophets who have forecast the imminent downfall of the Babylonian power. The first appeal is addressed to certain ambassadors from Edom, Moab, Ammon, Tyre and Sidon, who were evidently in Jerusalem for consultations with Zedekiah about what possible concerted action they could take against the forces of Nebuchadrezzar. The second is addressed to Zedekiah himself, whilst the third is addressed to the priests and people in general. The Septuagint follows the order of the Hebrew text but links the speech to the priests and people with the preceding address to the king (see comment on verse 16). ✼

AN APPEAL AND A WARNING TO FOREIGN
AMBASSADORS

AT THE BEGINNING OF THE REIGN of Zedekiah[a] son **27** of Josiah, king of Judah, this word came from the LORD to Jeremiah: These are the words of the LORD to me: 2 Take the cords and bars of a yoke and put them on your neck. Then send[b] to the kings of Edom, Moab, Ammon, 3 Tyre, and Sidon by the envoys who have come from them to Zedekiah king of Judah in Jerusalem, and give them 4 the following message for their masters: These are the words of the LORD of Hosts the God of Israel: Say to your masters: I made the earth with my great strength and 5 with outstretched arm, I made man and beast on the face of the earth, and I give it to whom I see fit. I now give all 6

[a] *So some MSS.; others* Jehoiakim.   [b] *So Luc. Sept.; Heb. adds* them.

these lands to my servant Nebuchadrezzar[a] king of
Babylon, and I give him also all the beasts of the field to
7 serve him. All nations shall serve him, and his son and his
grandson, until the destined hour of his own land comes,
and then mighty nations and great kings shall use him as
8 they please. If any nation or kingdom will not serve
Nebuchadrezzar king of Babylon or submit to his yoke,
I will punish them with sword, famine, and pestilence,
says the LORD, until I leave them entirely in his power.
9 Therefore do not listen to your prophets, your diviners,
your wise women,[b] your soothsayers, and your sorcerers
when they tell you not to serve the king of Babylon.
10 They are prophesying falsely to you; and so you will be
carried far from your own land, and I shall banish you
11 and you will perish. But if any nation submits to the
yoke of the king of Babylon and serves him, I will leave
them on their own soil, says the LORD; they shall cultivate
it and live there.

* 1. *At the beginning of the reign of Zedekiah son of Josiah:* in the
Hebrew text this verse dates the events recorded in the reign
of Jehoiakim, whilst verse 12 (cp. also 28: 1) places them in the
reign of Zedekiah. Since the events clearly presuppose the
deportation of 597 B.C. when Zedekiah came to the throne,
the text must be changed, as in the N.E.B., to read Zedekiah
instead of Jehoiakim. A further difficulty is that this verse
dates the events at the beginning of the king's reign, that is,
in his first year, whilst 28: 1 dates them in the fourth year.
The N.E.B. emends 'in the fourth year' in 28: 1 to in 'the
first year'. But there are some grounds for believing that 'the

[a] *So usually in Jer., but here and at 27:8, 20; 28: 3, 11, 14; 29: 1, 3 Heb.
has* Nebuchadnezzar.
[b] wise women: *lit.* women who have dreams.

fourth year' is the correct reading (see the comment on verse 3 below). We should therefore emend 27: 1 to conform to this. Note that 27: 1 is omitted in the Septuagint.

2. *Take the cords and bars of a yoke and put them on your neck:* the bars of the yoke were tied by cords (probably leather thongs) to the ox's neck or perhaps lashed around its horns. A symbolic act such as that here performed by Jeremiah was believed to be imbued with power to effect what it portrayed (see the commentary on 19. 10 in vol. 1).

3. *Then send to the kings of Edom, Moab, Ammon, Tyre, and Sidon:* as noted in the N.E.B. footnote, the Hebrew text reads 'send them', thereby suggesting that a yoke was to be sent to each of the kings mentioned. It is clear, however, that Jeremiah used only one yoke which he tied around his own neck. In reporting his words to their respective kings the envoys would have been expected to recount the symbolism with which the prophet accompanied his message. Accordingly, with some ancient versions the N.E.B. correctly omits 'them'. *by the envoys:* the envoys or ambassadors were probably in Jerusalem to consult with Zedekiah about the formation of a coalition to act against the Babylonians. (The fact that they assembled in the Judaean capital may be an indication that Zedekiah was the initiator and ringleader of the plot.) The year was probably 594/593 B.C., for in the previous year there were disturbances in Babylon and these may have fostered the belief among these western vassals of Nebuchadrezzar that successful revolt was now possible. It seems, however, that their joint deliberations came to nothing, perhaps because they could not agree on a strategy or perhaps because further 'intelligence reports' persuaded them that the risks were too great.

5. In the message to the kings of these foreign states the sovereignty and lordship of Israel's God Yahweh is asserted with the obvious implication of the powerlessness, indeed non-existence, of their own gods. At the same time it is obvious that a statement such as this about the universal

dominion of Yahweh would have been a highly apt word for the people of Israel whose land, after 587 B.C. when this narrative was composed, lay desolate and who, exiled in Babylon, must have questioned the power of their God against the apparent might of the gods of their Babylonian victors. As with the message of Deutero-Isaiah, who prophesied among the exiles in Babylon and whose oracles are contained in Isa. 40–55, the authors of this narrative in Jeremiah announced that Yahweh was Lord of creation and sovereign over the nations of the world whose destiny was under his control.

6. *my servant Nebuchadrezzar:* note the comment in the N.E.B. footnote. On *Nebuchadrezzar* see the commentary on 21: 2. The description of Nebuchadrezzar as God's *servant* (literally 'slave') does not of course mean that the Babylonian king worshipped Israel's God or had committed himself to his service, but only that God chose to use him for the fulfilment of his own divine purposes. It thus reinforces the statement in the previous verse concerning Yahweh's universal dominion. He who controls the destiny of the nations demands their submission to his divine will. But whether or not they submit to him, his will in the end will be established. The eventual downfall of Babylon itself is sounded in verse 7. (Verse 7 is not found in the Septuagint and is possibly a later addition in the Hebrew text.)

7. *All nations shall serve him, and his son and his grandson:* Nebuchadrezzar was succeeded by his son Amel Marduk (Evil-merodach is his name in 2 Kings 25: 27; Jer. 52: 31) but not by his grandson. Amel Marduk was succeeded, probably as a result of a *coup d'état*, by his brother-in-law Neriglissar. Either the biblical author did not know this or else the text is to be understood simply as meaning that the *nations* here referred to would be subject to the Babylonians for a long time, that is, during the reigns of several Babylonian kings.

9. *your wise women:* (literally 'those (feminine) who dream') this reading is based upon a slight alteration in the pointing of the Hebrew word, which as it stands means 'your dreams'.

The fact that various titles are used here supports the emendation which is also suggested by the Septuagint. The precise manner in which these various mantic practitioners here referred to worked is unknown. They were banned as 'abominations' in Israel (cp. Deut. 18: 9–13). ✳

AN APPEAL AND A WARNING
TO ZEDEKIAH AND JUDAH

I have said all this to Zedekiah king of Judah: If you 12 will submit to the yoke of the king of Babylon and serve him and his people, then you shall save your lives. Why 13 should you and your people die by sword, famine, and pestilence, the fate with which the LORD has threatened any nation which does not serve the king of Babylon? Do not listen to the prophets who tell you not to become 14 subject to the king of Babylon; they are prophesying falsely to you. I have not sent them, says the LORD; they 15 are prophesying falsely in my name, and so I shall banish you and you will perish, you and these prophets who prophesy to you.

I said to the priests and all the people, These are the 16 words of the LORD: Do not listen to your prophets who tell you that the vessels of the LORD's house will very soon be brought back from Babylon; they are only prophesying falsely to you. Do not listen to them; serve the king of 17 Babylon, and save your lives. Why should this city become a ruin? If they are prophets, and if they have the 18 word of the LORD, let them intercede with the LORD of Hosts to grant that the vessels still left in the LORD's house, in the royal palace, and in Jerusalem, may not be carried off to Babylon. For these are the words of the 19

LORD of Hosts concerning the pillars, the sea, the trolleys,
20 and all the other vessels still left in this city, which
Nebuchadrezzar king of Babylon did not take when he
deported Jeconiah son of Jehoiakim, king of Judah, from
Jerusalem to Babylon, together with all the nobles of
21 Judah and Jerusalem. These indeed are the words of the
LORD of Hosts the God of Israel concerning the vessels
still left in the LORD's house, in the royal palace, and in
22 Jerusalem: They shall be taken to Babylon and stay there
until I recall them, says the LORD; then I will bring them
back and restore them to this place.

* The message sent to the kings of the nations is repeated to
the king of Judah (verses 12–15). He too is summoned to submit to Babylonian rule and is likewise warned not to listen
to the prophets who call for rebellion: these prophets have
not been sent by God; they are impostors. The same message
is in turn proclaimed to the priests and the people at large
(verses 16–22).

15. *and so I shall banish you and you will perish:* this was in
fact the fate of Zedekiah who, after his abortive attempt to
rebel against Babylon, was taken prisoner in 587 B.C. by
Nebuchadrezzar, who blinded him and took him in chains to
Babylon where he died.

16. *I said to the priests and all the people:* the Septuagint links
this address to *the priests* and *the people* with the preceding
address to Zedekiah by inserting at the beginning 'to you'
(Zedekiah). *the vessels of the LORD's house will very soon be
brought back from Babylon:* evidently the false prophets had
announced the imminent return to the temple of various
sacred objects appropriated from it by the Babylonians in
597 B.C. Jeremiah announces against this that even those
which had been left would soon also be carried off (verses
19–20).

19. *the pillars, the sea, the trolleys, and all the other vessels:* these objects were broken up by the Babylonians and carried off because of their value as metal (bronze; cp. 2 Kings 25: 13–17). (On the problem of the use and symbolism of these and other cultic objects in the temple see the commentary on 1 Kings 7 in this series.)

20. *Jeconiah:* also shortened to Coniah in Jer. 22: 24, an alternative name for Jehoiachin (cp. the note on 22: 24 in the previous volume).

22. *then I will bring them back and restore them to this place:* the chapter ends on a note of hope for the future, for though these vessels are to be taken away to Babylon they will eventually be restored by God to Jerusalem. Thus here another theme of chs. 26–36 is struck: the nation stands under judgement but beyond that judgement God will effect a new beginning for his people. Chs. 30–3 comprise oracles and sayings concerning the nation's future revival and renewal. ✳

A REFUTATION OF JEREMIAH'S PROPHECY

That same year,[a] in the fifth month of the first[b] year of **28** the reign of Zedekiah king of Judah, Hananiah son of Azzur, the prophet from Gibeon, said to me in the house of the LORD, in the presence of the priests and all the people, 'These are the words of the LORD of Hosts the 2 God of Israel: I have broken the yoke of the king of Babylon. Within two years I will bring back to this place 3 all the vessels of the LORD's house which Nebuchadrezzar king of Babylon took from here and carried off to Babylon. I will also bring back to this place, says the 4 LORD, Jeconiah son of Jehoiakim, king of Judah, and all the exiles of Judah who went to Babylon; for I will break

[a] *Prob. rdg.; Heb. adds* at the beginning of the reign.
[b] *Prob. rdg.; Heb.* fourth.

35

5 the yoke of the king of Babylon.' The prophet Jeremiah said to Hananiah the prophet in the presence of the priests
6 and all the people standing in the LORD's house: 'May it be so! May the LORD indeed do this: may he fulfil all that you have prophesied, by bringing back the vessels of the LORD's house and all the exiles from Babylon to this place!
7 Only hear what I have to say to you and to all the people:
8 the prophets who preceded you and me from earliest times have foretold war, famine,[a] and pestilence for many
9 lands and for great kingdoms. If a prophet foretells prosperity, when his words come true it will be known that the LORD has sent him.'

✳ Ch. 28 is clearly the continuation of ch. 27, forming a sequel to it and describing the confrontation which took place between Jeremiah and the prophet Hananiah as a result of Jeremiah's prophecy and symbolic act with the ox-yoke. This confrontation must have taken place very shortly after the events recorded in ch. 27, perhaps even on the same day. Like the preceding chapter, this chapter was also composed by Deuteronomic authors (see the notes below and the summary of both chapters on pp. 28–9).

1. *in the fifth month of the first year of the reign of Zedekiah:* since the events recorded in this chapter and the preceding one probably took place in the fourth year of Zedekiah's reign (cp. the commentary on 27: 1, 3), the statement 'at the beginning of the reign' in the Hebrew text is omitted in the N.E.B. as having probably been erroneously inserted under the influence of 27: 1. For the reasons noted in the commentary on 27: 3, however, we should, against the N.E.B. reading, retain 'of the fourth year' in the Hebrew text of 28: 1. It is unlikely that Zedekiah would have been able to organize such a gathering of envoys to plan rebellion against Babylon

[a] *So some MSS.; others* disaster.

36

in his first year as king and so soon after the debacle of 597 B.C. It would certainly have taken him some substantial period of time to reorganize his forces and prepare for possible revolt. For these reasons, therefore, in addition to those mentioned in the commentary on 27: 3, the reading 'of the fourth year' seems the more probable. *Hananiah:* the name means 'Yahweh has been gracious' – a singularly appropriate name for one who announced such a message of restoration as is here recorded, even though it was a false prophecy! We are told that Hananiah was *from Gibeon*, a town about 6 miles (approximately 9½ km) north-west of Jerusalem. Whether this means that he lived in Gibeon and happened to be in Jerusalem at this time, or that he now lived in the capital, perhaps as a (cultic) prophet attached to the temple personnel, is not known.

2. '*I have broken the yoke of the king of Babylon*': Hananiah directly opposes the prophecy of Jeremiah and, using the same metaphor that Jeremiah has employed, announces that God is shortly to bring home from exile those deported in 597 B.C. and to restore the sacred vessels of the temple seized by the Babylonians at that time. In this way Hananiah is portrayed as a specific example of the false prophets referred to in ch. 27.

6. '*May it be so! May the LORD indeed do this: may he fulfil all that you have prophesied*': we are probably to take this as a sarcastic retort to Hananiah's oracle, since the context makes it clear that Jeremiah knew Hananiah's prediction to be false.

7–9. These verses are a 'reasoned argument' against the possibility that Hananiah's words would be vindicated. In announcing the imminent prosperity and renewed well-being for the nation, Hananiah had chosen to stand apart from the great prophets of the past. The characteristic of their preaching was the announcement of God's judgement upon many nations and so far history had done nothing but prove their message to have been true. Should Hananiah's prophecy, which was the very opposite of the message of the great prophets, prove true, then he would all the more be seen to be indeed a prophet sent by God! In all probability, however, these verses, like most of this chapter, derive not from Jeremiah himself but from the Deuteronomic authors. The style of the chapter is typical of the prose material in Jeremiah which owes its present form to these authors. The expression in verse 6 'may he fulfil all that you have prophesied' (literally 'may the LORD establish your word') occurs elsewhere in the prose in Jeremiah (29: 10; 33: 14; the translation of these two differs from 28: 6 but in the Hebrew the same words are employed in all three instances) and frequently in the Deuteronomic literature. In addition, the criterion formulated in 28: 8–9 for discerning the true from the false prophet appears to be based on Deut. 18: 21–2. (See also the commentary on verses 16 and 17 below.) For these authors, writing after the downfall of the nation in 587 B.C., history had vindicated Jeremiah's words and shown Hananiah to have been a false prophet. But at the time of their confrontation, which was the true and which the false prophet was not as easily discerned. For both men spoke in the name of Yahweh and there is no reason for doubting the sincerity of Hananiah's words and actions. But if to all outward appearance there was no way of telling which of the two was the true and which the false prophet, there was, at a deeper level, a great difference between them. For the one 'stood in the council of the LORD' (cp. 23: 18, 22) and the other quite simply did not. The one had a heart and mind sensitive to the challenging word of God, whilst the other, however sincere he may have been, was governed by a misapprehension of the nature of God's relationship with, and purpose for, Israel and the nations of the world. The one had a vision of God which demanded a response from Israel in terms of holiness and humble obedience to his will; the other understood Israel's election to mean privilege and was blind to the solemn responsibility it placed upon Israel. It has been the mistake, frequently the tragic mistake, of 'religious' men down through the centuries that they, like Hananiah, have all too often confused their own beliefs and aspirations with the will of God. It was the characteristic of the great prophets like Jeremiah as it has been and is of all men of faith that they have learned to 'wait upon God'. ✻

THE YOKE OF IRON ON THE NECKS OF THE NATIONS

Then the prophet Hananiah took the yoke from the 10 neck of the prophet Jeremiah and broke it, saying before 11 all the people, 'These are the words of the LORD: Thus will I break the yoke of Nebuchadrezzar king of Babylon; I will break it off the necks of all nations within two years';[a] and the prophet Jeremiah went his way. After 12 Hananiah had broken the yoke which had been on Jeremiah's neck, the word of the LORD came to Jeremiah: Go and say to Hananiah, These are the words of the 13 LORD: You have broken bars of wood; in their place you shall[b] get bars of iron. For these are the words of the 14 LORD of Hosts the God of Israel: I have put a yoke of iron on the necks of all these nations, making them serve Nebuchadrezzar king of Babylon. They shall serve him, and I have given him even the beasts of the field. Then 15 Jeremiah said to Hananiah, 'Listen, Hananiah. The LORD has not sent you, and you have led this nation to trust in false prophecies. Therefore these are the words of the 16 LORD: Beware, I will remove you from the face of the earth; you shall die within the year, because you have preached rebellion against the LORD.' The prophet 17 Hananiah died that same year, in the seventh month.

[a] within two years: *or* while there are still two full years to run.
[b] *Or, with Sept.,* I will.

✻ 10. *Then the prophet Hananiah took the yoke from the neck of the prophet Jeremiah and broke it:* just as Hananiah has countered Jeremiah's prophecy verbally, so now he counters his symbolic act by taking the yoke from his neck and breaking it. It is a mistake to understand what Hananiah did as simply expressing contempt for Jeremiah's prophecy. By his counter prophecy and symbolic act Hananiah sought to render Jeremiah's prophecy powerless (cp. the comment on 27: 2).

12–14. Jeremiah's immediate reaction to his opponent's prophecy was to go away in silence (verse 11). But he subsequently returned to re-proclaim the nation's continued subjugation by the Babylonians. But both the harshness and strength of this subjugation are now even more starkly emphasized; the metaphor of the wooden yoke is replaced by that of an iron yoke: God has *put a yoke of iron on the necks of all these nations.* Though it is not stated in the text, it is possible that Jeremiah had acquired an iron yoke to re-enact the symbolic act of his first prophecy. Whether or not this was the case, however, Hananiah's counter-prophecy was now itself countered.

14. *I have given him even the beasts of the field:* this further emphasizes the total supremacy of Babylonian dominion decreed by God: so established is it that even the wild beasts are to be subject to Nebuchadrezzar!

15–17. Hananiah is now condemned as a false prophet.

16. *you have preached rebellion against the LORD:* Deut. 13: 5 (Hebrew verse 6), using the same terminology as is employed here (cp. also Jer. 29: 32), decrees the death penalty for one who *preached rebellion against the LORD.* This expression occurs only in the three texts here mentioned and nowhere else in the Old Testament.

17. *The prophet Hananiah died that same year, in the seventh month:* it is a feature of the Deuteronomic literature (Deuteronomy to 2 Kings) that its authors record the fulfilment of prophecies. So here the death of Hananiah, in fulfilment of the

curse pronounced upon him by Jeremiah, is exactly recorded
(cp. also, for example, 2 Kings 1: 17; 7: 19–20; 8: 10–15).

Like other prose passages and narratives in the book of
Jeremiah, chs. 27 and 28 were intended by their authors as
more than simply a record of certain events in the life and
ministry of the prophet. Here, as elsewhere, we have an
instance of such events being narrated in such a way as to
draw out for a later generation the lessons of the past. First
of all, these chapters would have provided for the community
living in the shadow of the terrible events of 587 B.C. an
explanation of why that catastrophe had befallen the nation:
the nation had rejected the word of God spoken by his
prophet Jeremiah and had been led astray by false prophets.
At the same time these chapters would have announced to this
community that the God of Israel was the Lord of history
who controlled the destiny of the nations, including Babylon,
and they would thus have summoned the community to
renewed faith in God whose divine purposes were being
worked out in history. In close connection with this, what is
recorded in these chapters would have been intended to put
the community on its guard against false prophets by whom
its life was apparently still threatened (cp. ch. 29). In short,
these chapters, like others in the book, would have offered an
explanation of the tragedy which had overcome the nation,
and given courage for the present and hope for the future. ✳

A MESSAGE OF HOPE TO THE EXILES

✳ Ch. 29 continues the theme of false prophecy, which
dominates the previous two chapters, but combines with it a
message of future deliverance from exile and so serves as an
anticipation of, and introduction to, the succeeding chapters
in which the nation's restoration after judgement is announced
(chs. 30–3). At first glance it would appear that the whole
chapter narrates one letter which is introduced in verses 1–3.
But it is clear that verses 24–32 presuppose a second message

sent by Jeremiah to Babylon in response to a letter sent by one Shemaiah the Nehelamite protesting about Jeremiah's letter reported in verses 4–23.

Though the essential historicity of what is reported in this chapter cannot be doubted, not all of what is related can be regarded as the prophet's own words. Much of the chapter is composed in the characteristic Deuteronomic style of the prose in the book of Jeremiah so that, as in the case of other such reports, we are once again dealing with a narrative which was intended to develop further a message originally announced by Jeremiah and draw out its continuing significance for a later generation. The chapter as it now stands is very probably an expansion of an earlier record in which certain verses, not found in the Septuagint, were not contained (see the commentary on verses 16–20 below). ✷

A LETTER TO THE EXILES

29 Jeremiah sent a letter from Jerusalem to the remaining elders among the exiles, to the priests and prophets, and to all the people whom Nebuchadrezzar had deported
2 from Jerusalem to Babylon, after King Jeconiah had left Jerusalem with the queen mother and the eunuchs, the officers of Judah and Jerusalem, the craftsmen and the
3 smiths.[a] The prophet entrusted the letter to Elasah son of Shaphan and Gemariah son of Hilkiah, whom Zedekiah king of Judah had sent to Babylon to King Nebuchad-
4 rezzar. This is what he wrote: These are the words of the LORD of Hosts the God of Israel: To all the exiles whom
5 I have carried off from Jerusalem to Babylon: Build houses and live in them; plant gardens and eat their
6 produce. Marry wives and beget sons and daughters; take wives for your sons and give your daughters to

[a] the smiths: *or* the harem.

husbands, so that they may bear sons and daughters and
you may increase there and not dwindle away. Seek the 7
welfare of any city to which I have carried you off, and
pray to the LORD for it; on its welfare your welfare will
depend. For these are the words of the LORD of Hosts the 8
God of Israel: Do not be deceived by the prophets or the
diviners among you, and do not listen to the wise women
whom you set to dream dreams. They prophesy falsely 9
to you in my name; I did not send them. This is the very
word of the LORD.

These are the words of the LORD: When a full seventy 10
years has passed over Babylon, I will take up your cause
and fulfil the promise of good things I made you, by
bringing you back to this place. I alone know my purpose 11
for you, says the LORD: prosperity and not misfortune,
and a long line of children after you. If you invoke me[a] 12
and pray to me, I will listen to you: when you seek me, 13
you shall find me; if you search with all your heart, I will 14[b]
let you find me, says the LORD. I will restore your fortunes and gather you again from all the nations and all the
places to which I have banished you, says the LORD, and
bring you back to the place from which I have carried
you into exile.

You say that the LORD has raised up prophets for you in 15
Babylon. These are the words of the LORD concerning 16
the king who sits on the throne of David and all the
people who live in this city, your fellow-countrymen
who have not gone into exile with you. These are the 17
words of the LORD of Hosts: I bring upon them sword,

[a] *So Pesh.; Heb. adds* and walk.
[b] *Verses 14–20 are probably misplaced, cp. 24: 8–10.*

43

famine, and pestilence, and make them like rotten figs,
18 too bad to be eaten. I pursue them with sword, famine,
and pestilence, and make them repugnant to all the
kingdoms of the earth, an object of execration and horror,
of derision and reproach, among all the nations to which
19 I have banished them. Just as they did not listen to my
words, says the LORD, when I took pains to send them
my servants the prophets, so you did not listen, says the
20 LORD. But now, you exiles whom I have sent from Jeru-
21 salem to Babylon, listen to the words of the LORD. These
are the words of the LORD of Hosts the God of Israel
concerning Ahab son of Kolaiah and Zedekiah son of
Maaseiah, who prophesy falsely to you in my name. I will
hand them over to Nebuchadrezzar king of Babylon,
22 and he will put them to death before your eyes. Their
names shall be used by all the exiles of Judah in Babylon
when they curse a man; they shall say, May the LORD
treat you like Zedekiah and Ahab, whom the king of
23 Babylon roasted in the fire! For their conduct in Israel
was an outrage: they committed adultery with other
men's wives, and without my authority prophesied in
my name, and what they prophesied was false. I know;
I can testify. This is the very word of the LORD.

✻ 1. *the remaining elders:* this may be an indication that of the
elders carried into exile some had been executed, possibly
because of the disturbances among the exiles mentioned in
this chapter. Alternatively, since the chapter in fact mentions
the execution of only the two instigators of these disturbances
(verse 21), there is something to be said for the suggestion that
the word *remaining* stood originally before *all the people* to give
the reading 'and to the rest of all the people'.

2. *the eunuchs:* these may have been servants in the royal household, possibly employed as chamberlains for the women's quarters. In some contexts, however, the word here translated eunuchs appears to designate simply a royal official (cp. Gen. 39: 1 where Potiphar, who was married, is so designated).

3. *The prophet entrusted the letter to Elasah son of Shaphan and Gemariah son of Hilkiah:* the royal messengers here mentioned are two further state officials who appear to have either been in sympathy with Jeremiah's preaching or at least showed friendship and regard for him (cp. 26: 24; 36: 25; 38: 7–13). It is sometimes suggested that these two officials were sent by Zedekiah with tribute to reassure Nebuchadrezzar of his loyalty to him after the abortive attempt to plan revolt recorded in ch. 27. Whilst this remains a possibility, the text itself offers no indication that this was their mission and it is just as possible that they were sent to Babylon on routine business between the vassal and his overlord (cp. the note on 51: 59).

5–6. These verses, together with information provided by the book of Ezekiel, indicate that the Judaean exiles in Babylon, though forced of course to remain there, were left free and unmolested to settle down and lead as normal a life as possible. The only exception to this that we know of is the case of the young King Jehoiachin who appears to have been imprisoned. His release from prison is recorded as having taken place in the accession year of Amel Marduk (Evil-merodach, cp. 2 Kings 25: 27–30; Jer. 52: 31–4) in 562 B.C.

7. *Seek the welfare of any city to which I have carried you off:* such advice would not have been easy to accept by people embittered and bewildered in exile far from their homeland. However, it had a twofold basis: firstly, it was practical, for the well-being of the land of their exile would in the end entail their own security and well-being (cp. 1 Kings 8: 50); and secondly, it was given in the knowledge that the exiles were already the object of God's renewed plans for his people which in due course he would carry out.

8. *Do not be deceived by the prophets or the diviners among you:* it is clear from the ensuing narrative that such prophets were agitating for revolt against the Babylonian captors. Such agitation and revolt could bring only further disaster. God himself was in control of the destiny of his people. They must accordingly wait patiently upon his divine purposes.

10–14. The purposes of God are now explicitly stated. The exile will not come to an end immediately; on the contrary, it will last a long time (for this understanding of the *seventy years* here mentioned, see the commentary on 25: 11). Yet God's *purpose* for his people is fixed; their well-being and restoration are assured. They on their part are exhorted to renewed faithfulness and trust in Yahweh. Note that verses 13–14 are markedly Deuteronomic in phraseology (cp. Deut. 4: 29; 30: 1–4) and are a further indication that the chapter as it now stands was composed by Deuteronomic authors. *and a long line of children after you* (verse 11): the gift of children whereby one's family line would be continued was considered one of the greatest blessings a man could have in ancient Israel. Verse 14 as contained in the Hebrew text is not found in the Septuagint which reads simply 'I will manifest myself to you.' Probably we have an instance here of the Septuagint preserving an earlier form of the chapter than that found in the Hebrew text.

15–23. Of these verses, 16–20 are not found in the Septuagint. Almost certainly they are a secondary addition in the Hebrew text where they interrupt the connection between verses 15 and 21–3.

16–20. Zedekiah and those who escaped exile in 597 B.C. stand under judgement. Their dreadful fate is shortly to befall them. The designation of them as *rotten figs, too bad to be eaten* links these verses with ch. 24 and, like it, they were probably composed mainly as polemic against those living in Judah during the actual period of the exile and, by implication, as 'propaganda' asserting the claims of the exiled community in Babylon to be the true recipients of God's promises for the future and those through whom renewal and restoration would come (cp. the commentary on ch. 24). In both style and phraseology these verses are unmistakably Deuteronomic.

15, 21–3. The two prophets here mentioned appear to have been involved, probably as the instigators, in an abortive revolt against the Babylonian authorities. That Jeremiah condemned them and announced judgement against them need not be questioned. But the report of this given here appears to have been composed after their execution, since it knows how this was carried out: they were 'roasted in the fire' (verse 22).

22. *May the LORD treat you like Zedekiah and Ahab:* so horrific was their fate that if a man wished to curse another he could do no better than call down upon him a fate similar to theirs. The condemnation of these prophets and their fate no doubt continued to be used as a warning to the exiles of the dire consequences of being misled by false prophets. ✳

INDIGNATION AT JEREMIAH'S LETTER

To Shemaiah the Nehelamite.[a] These are the words 24, 25 of the LORD of Hosts the God of Israel: You have sent a letter in your own name[b] to Zephaniah son of Maaseiah the priest,[c] in which you say: 'The LORD has appointed 26 you to be priest in place of Jehoiada the priest, and it is your duty, as officer[d] in charge of the LORD's house, to put every madman who sets up as a prophet into the stocks and the pillory. Why, then, have you not re- 27 primanded Jeremiah of Anathoth, who poses as a prophet before you? On the strength of this he has sent to us in 28 Babylon and said, "Your exile will be long; build houses

[a] *Prob. rdg.; Heb. adds* you shall say, saying.
[b] *So Sept.; Heb. adds* to all the people in Jerusalem.
[c] *So Sept.; Heb. adds* and to all the priests.
[d] *So Sept.; Heb.* officers.

and live in them, plant gardens and eat their produce."'
29 Zephaniah the priest read this letter to Jeremiah the
30 prophet, and the word of the LORD came to Jeremiah:
31 Send and tell all the exiles that these are the words of the
LORD concerning Shemaiah the Nehelamite: Because
Shemaiah has prophesied to you, though I did not send
32 him, and has led you to trust in false prophecies, these are
now the words of the LORD: I will punish Shemaiah and
his children. He shall have no one to take his place in this
nation and enjoy the prosperity which I will bestow on
my people, says the LORD, because he has preached
rebellion against me.

* These verses describe the repercussions which Jeremiah's
letter evoked among some of the exiles. The passage is somewhat confused. It begins with what was evidently intended
to be a letter sent by Jeremiah to Shemaiah the Nehelamite,
yet another false prophet at work among the exiles, who had
written to Jerusalem complaining about Jeremiah's letter to
the exiles and demanding that he be silenced. But Jeremiah's
letter to this prophet gets no further than summarizing the
latter's letter (verses 24–8). The letter is interrupted by, and
not continued after, verse 29 where, instead, we read of a
message concerning Shemaiah sent to the exiles in general
(verses 30–2). In their present form, verses 30–2 were composed by the Deuteronomic editors of the book.

24. *Shemaiah the Nehelamite:* whether *Nehelamite* was simply
Shemaiah's family name, or the name of an otherwise un-
attested and unknown town or locality from which he came,
we do not know. It has been suggested that the name is a play
upon the verb 'to dream' (*ḥālam* in Hebrew) and so understood to mean 'Shemaiah the dreamer'. But there is little to
support this suggestion and the particular form of the verb

ḥālam required by it is nowhere else found in the Hebrew Bible.

25. *Zephaniah son of Maaseiah the priest:* he is mentioned in 21: 1 and 37: 3 and is described as deputy priest in 52: 24. He was taken prisoner by the Babylonians after the fall of Jerusalem in 587 B.C. and executed (52: 24–7; 2 Kings 25: 18–21).

32. *because he has preached rebellion against me:* see the note on 28: 16. ✳

Hopes for the restoration of Jerusalem

✳ Up to this point in the book of Jeremiah the dominant theme has been God's judgement upon Israel, though even here notes of hope for the future of the nation have been sounded, as for example in 23: 1–8; 24; 29. But now we come to four chapters (30–3), usually referred to by scholars as 'the book of consolation', which concentrate on God's promises for his people's future renewal and restoration from exile to their homeland. These chapters contain sayings and other literary units of varied origin and composition and by no means all of them derive from Jeremiah himself (see the commentary on the individual units below). Nevertheless, these chapters as a whole dwell on and develop a theme which was integral to his preaching. For Jeremiah, though he unrelentingly announced God's judgement upon his apostate and disobedient people, saw beyond that judgement to a new beginning for Israel as the people of God. In fact it is true to say that his understanding of Israel's standing before God revolved around the two poles of judgement and renewal after judgement, though, given the circumstances of the age in which he ministered, his proclamation of judgement was bound to be at the forefront of his message. But he never saw

49

that judgement as an end in itself, much less as drawing the final curtain on Israel's existence as God's people. Rather he understood that judgement as the very means whereby God could draw his people into a new and lasting relationship with himself, a relationship which would fully express and bring about the divine purposes he had in choosing Israel to be his people. Israel had failed God but God would not forsake Israel. And so Jeremiah and those who transmitted and developed his message perceived that the judgement which befell the nation, though real and deserved, was but the gate to a new beginning for Israel, who would beyond that judgement become truly God's holy people. For God would not merely forgive his people's sins and rebellion against him; he would change their inner nature so that henceforth they would spontaneously love and serve him (cp. 31: 31–4). *

DESPAIR NOT, O ISRAEL, SAYS THE LORD

30 THE WORD WHICH CAME TO JEREMIAH from the
2 LORD. These are the words of the LORD the God of
3 Israel: Write in a book all that I have said to you, for this is the very word of the LORD: The time is coming when I will restore the fortunes of my people Israel and Judah, says the LORD, and bring them back to the land which I gave to their forefathers; and it shall be their possession.
4, 5   This is what the LORD has said to Israel and Judah. These are the words of the LORD:

You shall hear[a] a cry of terror, of fear without relief.
6   Ask and see: can a man bear a child?
    Why then do I see every man
    gripping his sides like a woman in labour,
every face changed, all turned[b] pale?

[a] *So Sept.; Heb.* We have heard.
[b] turned: *so Sept.; Heb.* alas!

50

Awful is that day: 7
    when has there been its like?
A time of anguish for Jacob,
    yet he shall come through it safely.

In that day, says the LORD of Hosts, I will break their   8
yoke off their[a] necks and snap their[a] cords; foreigners
shall no longer use them as they please; they shall serve 9
the LORD their God and David their king, whom I will
raise up for them.

And you, Jacob my servant, have no fear;   10
    despair not, O Israel, says the LORD.
For I will bring you back safe from afar
and your offspring from the land where they are
        captives;
and Jacob shall be at rest once more,
    prosperous and unafraid.
For I am with you and will save you, says the LORD.   11
    I will make an end of all the nations
    amongst whom I have scattered you,
but I will not make an end of you;
    though I punish you as you deserve,
    I will not sweep you clean away.

* Ch. 30 contains a number of separate oracles brought
together by an editor. Some commentators have claimed that
none of the material in this chapter comes from Jeremiah.
But whilst much of it bears signs of deriving from an author
or authors other than the prophet himself, some of it can
confidently be attributed to him. The section comprising
verses 1–11 is itself composite.

[a] *So Sept.; Heb.* your.

1–3. These verses form an editorial preface and also provide a summary of the message of renewal and restoration which follows in chs. 30–3. *Write in a book:* it is this that has prompted commentators to designate chs. 30–3 as 'the book of consolation'. We know from ch. 36 that Jeremiah took the initiative in having his oracles and sayings committed to writing by his scribe Baruch in the year 605/604 B.C. and there is no reason to question that the message he delivered in the years after this was similarly written down by Baruch at the prophet's behest. (For the reasons why the prophet's message was written down see the commentary on ch. 36.) *Israel and Judah:* the nation as a whole, that is, both the people of the former northern kingdom (Israel) and the people of Judah, are the subject of the ensuing divine promises for the future. *and bring them back to the land which I gave to their forefathers:* though many people were deported from the northern kingdom in 722 B.C. and from Judah in 597 B.C. and 587 B.C., the bulk of the nation remained in the homeland. Why then talk of bringing back *Israel and Judah* to the homeland when only a small section, numerically speaking, of the nation as a whole had been exiled? The reason is that those who had been exiled to Babylon were believed to be the only true and proper heirs of God's purposes for his people's future. Those who remained in the land or who had gone into exile elsewhere (cp. the commentary on 24: 8) were either ignored by those who proclaimed the future to lie with the exiles in Babylon or were actually written off as apostate and still under God's judgement (cp. in addition to the commentary on ch. 24 the comments on 29: 16–20 and the comments on the main theme of 40: 7 – 44: 30 on pp. 132–3 below). Thus, for the Deuteronomic authors of the corpus of literature Deuteronomy to 2 Kings, for Jeremiah and those who developed his preaching, as well as for Ezekiel and Deutero-Isaiah, God's people, properly understood, were in exile; these people alone were the object of Yahweh's plans for the future of his chosen people; they alone could be referred to as *Israel and Judah.*

4–7. Of the material in verses 1–11, these verses alone may with confidence be regarded as coming from Jeremiah. The metaphor here employed to describe the anguish and suffering of the coming day of Yahweh is the same as in 4: 31. *Awful is that day:* the announcement of the coming day of Yahweh as a day of judgement upon his people is a characteristic of the preaching of Jeremiah's predecessors (cp. e.g. Amos 5: 18–20; Isa. 2: 12–21; Zeph. 1: 7–11). *yet he shall come through it safely:* the oracle ends with a note of hope: though it would suffer judgement, the nation would have a future beyond judgement. This promise, here tersely stated, has provided the cue for an editor to append two further sayings which more fully express this promise.

8–9. These verses, which are in prose, are commonly agreed to come from an editor. The terminology employed in verse 8 links this verse unmistakably with the contents of chs. 27 and 28. Indeed, strange as it may seem, the author has used in part the words attributed to Hananiah in 28: 11 'Thus *will I break the yoke* of Nebuchadrezzar king of Babylon; *I will break it off the necks* of all nations.' But whereas the promise in 30: 8 is prefaced by *In that day*, Hananiah announced that deliverance was to take place 'within two years' and in this way failed to perceive the nature, extent and purpose of the judgement which was to befall the nation (see the commentary on 28: 7–9). One further point must be emphasized here. It is true of this short passage in ch. 30 (cp. verse 9) as it is true of 'the book of consolation' as a whole that the promised restoration of the nation is devoid of any merely national-istically motivated aspirations. Israel's restoration had for its real goal the nation's faithfulness to, and true service of, God, faithfulness and service which had been conspicuous by their absence in Israel's past history. That those who had oppressed Israel were themselves to be punished was not intended as a means of establishing Israel's national supremacy over against the nations but was merely the means whereby God could renew Israel as his people, dedicated and faithful to him and

3   53

his divine purposes. *they shall serve the LORD their God and David their king, whom I will raise up for them:* here and elsewhere in the book of Jeremiah only in 23: 5–6; 33: 14–16; 33: 17–26 do we find reference to the special relationship between God and the Davidic dynasty and the messianic hopes to which they gave rise. But with the possible exception of 23: 5–6 (see, however, the commentary on this passage), none of these passages can be attributed to Jeremiah. We know that in the immediate period after the exile King Jehoiachin's grandson Zerubbabel, who was appointed governor of Judah by the Persians, became the focus of hopes for the re-establishment of the Davidic kingship in Jerusalem (cp. Hag. 2: 21–3; Zech. 3: 8; 4: 6–7; 6: 12). But it is possible that hopes for the re-establishment of the Davidic dynasty sprang up already in the later period of the exile, perhaps prompted by the release of Jehoiachin from prison in exile in 562 B.C. (cp. the commentary on 52: 31–4), and it is not unlikely that these few passages in the book of Jeremiah which concern God's promises to David and his dynasty derive from this period.

10–11. These verses are also found, with only minor differences in the text, in 46: 27–8. Their proper context is here in ch. 30 (cp. the note on 46: 27–8). Verse 10 shows unmistakably the influence of Deutero-Isaiah (cp., for example, Isa. 41: 8-9, 13–14; 43: 1, 5; 44: 1–2) and is widely accepted as coming from an author later than Jeremiah. ✻

ZION'S WOUNDS WILL BE HEALED

12 For these are the words of the LORD to Zion:

> Your injury is past healing,
>> cruel was the blow you suffered.

13   There can be no[a] remedy for your sore,
>> the new skin cannot grow.

14   All your lovers have forgotten you;
>> they look for you no longer.

[a] *Prob. rdg.; Heb. adds* one judging your case.

54

I have struck you down
as an enemy strikes, and punished you cruelly;
for your wickedness is great and your sins are many.
Why complain of your injury,   15
    that your sore cannot be healed?[a]
I have done this to you,
because your wickedness is great and your sins are many.
Yet all who devoured you shall themselves be devoured, 16
all your oppressors shall go into captivity.
Those who plunder you shall be plundered,
    and those who despoil you I will give up to be
        spoiled.
I will cause the new skin to grow   17
    and heal your wounds, says the LORD,
although men call you the Outcast,
    Zion, nobody's friend.

✻ This passage falls into two contrasting parts, verses 12–15
and verses 16–17. Verses 12–15 are most probably to be understood as a description of the terrible judgement which befell
Judah and Jerusalem in 587 B.C. though it is not impossible
that they were an announcement of it by Jeremiah. The only
question that arises is whether verses 16–17 are a later addition
to verses 12–15. There is nothing in verses 16–17 to suggest
that they are not from Jeremiah himself. Nor is the coupling
of a description or announcement of judgement with a
promise of salvation a basis for questioning the unity of the
two parts, for the basic scheme of judgement and renewal
after judgement was a characteristic of the prophet's message
as a whole. Some commentators, however, believe that the
word at the beginning of verse 16 marking the transition
between the two sections is awkward and that therefore the

[a] Why...healed?: *or* Cry not for help in your injury. Your sore
cannot be healed.

second section is a later appendix to the first. But the word in question, though most often having the meaning 'therefore', can be translated as 'yet', as in the N.E.B., that is, as an adversative, so that there is a perfectly smooth connection and transition between the two sections.

14. *All your lovers have forgotten you:* this is probably a reference to Judah's allies, especially Egypt, in her final and ill-fated rebellion against Babylon in 589 B.C. which ended with the destruction of Judah and Jerusalem in 587 B.C. Though an Egyptian army did engage the Babylonians in 588 B.C., it was quickly routed and withdrew. Jerusalem was captured and destroyed a few months later (cp. 37: 1 ff.). ✻

THE RESTORATION OF JACOB

18   These are the words of the LORD:

> Watch; I will restore the fortunes of Jacob's clans
>   and show my love for all his dwellings.
> Every city shall be rebuilt on its mound of ruins,
>   every mansion shall have its familiar household.

19   From them praise shall be heard
>   and sounds of merrymaking.
> I will increase them, they shall not diminish,
> I will raise them to honour, they shall no longer
>   be despised.

20   Their sons shall be what they once were,
>   and their community shall be established in my
>   sight.
> I will punish all their oppressors;

21   a ruler shall appear, one of themselves,
>   a governor shall arise from their own number.
> I will myself bring him*a* near and so he*b* shall
>   approach me;

[a] *Or* them.   [b] *Or* they.

56

for no one ventures of himself to approach me,
    says the LORD.
So you shall be my people,   22
and I will be your God.

✻ Up to this point in the chapter the promises of renewal have
been of a somewhat general nature: God would restore the
fortunes of Israel and Judah, he would break the yoke of
bondage from their necks, he would bring them back from
exile and deliver them from those who plunder them. In
verses 18–21 the promises are more concrete: the cities which
had been left heaps of ruins by their enemies would be rebuilt
complete with mansions; once more the sound of people
making merry would echo through the streets; their numbers,
no doubt severely reduced by death at the hands of those who
invaded the land, would increase again. In short there would
once again be a community leading a normal and prosperous
life. Opinion is divided as to whether this passage comes
from Jeremiah.

18. *Jacob's clans:* the word here translated *clans* is literally
'tents'. By extension, however, the word can designate those
who dwell together in tents, that is, a clan (a collection of
interrelated families). *mound of ruins:* the Hebrew word here
translated is identical with the Arabic word 'tell' found in so
many place-names in Palestine today (e.g. Tell ed-Duweir =
Lachish). The word means 'hill' or 'mound'. But often such
mounds, though originally a natural mound or hillock, have
been further built up by the destruction and rebuilding of the
town on it over many centuries (see in this series *Understanding
the Old Testament,* pp. 37f.) – hence the N.E.B. translation
mound of ruins.

21. *a ruler shall appear...a governor shall arise:* the author
appears to wish to avoid using the word 'king' and for this
reason the passage is probably not to be understood as concerned with a coming king. In addition the saying *I will myself*

bring him near and so he shall approach me appears to indicate that the ruler in question is to be a priest. Though perhaps not impossible for the period in which Jeremiah lived, the idea of a ruler–priest is best understood as coming from a later time.

22. This verse sums up the goal of all the promises of restoration and renewal: they are to the intent that Israel would realize her true calling to be God's holy and elect people. Note, however, that the Septuagint omits this verse and since the phrase *So you shall be my people, and I will be your God* occurs elsewhere in the book only in prose passages, it is probably an addition here (cp. the comment on 31: 33). *

THEY SHALL BECOME MY PEOPLE

23 See what a scorching wind has gone out from the
        LORD,
        a sweeping whirlwind.
    It whirls round the heads of the wicked;
24   the LORD's anger is not to be turned aside,
    till he has finished and achieved his heart's desire.
    In days to come you will understand.

31 At that time, says the LORD, I will become God of all the families of Israel, and they shall become my people.

* Verses 23–4 occur also in 23: 19–20 where they are to be understood as emphasizing the true nature of what God has declared as against the message of imminent prosperity announced by the false prophets. No doubt because of their last line, *In days to come you will understand*, an editor has incorporated them in 'the book of consolation'. He has, however, supplemented this somewhat vague promise with the explicit promise of salvation in 31: 1. At the same time this verse also forms an apt introduction to the material in ch. 31 as a whole.

31: 1 *all the families of Israel:* the promises of restoration and renewal in these chapters concern all Israel, that is, the people of the former northern kingdom as well as of Judah (cp. 30: 3. For a similar expression see Amos 3: 1: N.E.B. 'nation'). ✻

FURTHER PROMISES TO EPHRAIM AND JUDAH

✻ Ch. 31, like ch. 30, comprises a number of separate sayings and once again not all of them derive from Jeremiah himself. But there can be no doubt that the chapter as a whole conforms entirely to a basic feature of the prophet's message, that is, his announcement that beyond the judgement which God would visit upon his people would come renewed salvation. Furthermore, again as in the case of ch. 30, all Israel, both north and south, are the object of the promises in ch. 31. Thus the sayings in verses 2–6, 7–9, 10–14, 27–30, 31–4, 35–7 refer to the people of both northern Israel and Judah, whilst the passage in verses 15–22 which concerns the people of the northern kingdom is matched by the sayings in verses 23–6 and 38–40 which concern Judah and Jerusalem respectively. ✻

I WILL BUILD YOU UP AGAIN, O VIRGIN ISRAEL

These are the words of the LORD: 2

> A people that survived the sword
>   found favour in the wilderness;
>   Israel journeyed to find rest;
>   long ago[a] the LORD appeared to them:[b]   3
> I have dearly loved you from of old,
> and still I maintain my unfailing care for you.
> I will build you up again, O virgin Israel,   4
>   and you shall be rebuilt.
>   Again you shall adorn yourself with jingles,
>   and go forth with the merry throng of dancers.

[a] long ago: *or* from afar.   [b] *So Sept.; Heb.* me.

59

5   Again you shall plant vineyards on the hills of
          Samaria,
       vineyards which those who planted them defiled;
6   for a day will come when the watchmen on
          Ephraim's hills cry out,
       Come, let us go up to Zion, to the LORD our God.

* Because this passage refers to the restoration of northern
Israel (see verse 5) many commentators believe that it derives
from an early period in Jeremiah's ministry and understand it
as indicating the prophet's concern with the restoration of
northern Israel. But the Israel referred to in verse 2 must
clearly be understood as referring to all Israel and not just the
people of the former northern kingdom and there is no reason
for believing that 'O virgin Israel' in verse 4 is to be taken in
any other sense. The point of the passage is that all Israel, both
north and south, is the object of God's 'unfailing care', that
the nation as a whole is to be restored, 'rebuilt' by God,
and that the old division between north and south will be
forgotten and Zion acknowledged as the focal point for all
Israel.

  2. *A people that survived the sword found favour in the wilderness:* a reference to Israel's escape from bondage in Egypt,
perhaps specifically to the deliverance from Pharaoh's troops
at the Red (properly 'reed') Sea, and to God's gracious
dealings with them during the years of wandering in the
wilderness as they *journeyed to find rest*, that is, to the promised
land of Canaan.

  3f. *long ago the LORD appeared to them:* this is probably to
be understood as referring to God's appearance (the usual
word employed is 'theophany') to his people at Mount Sinai.
Such an interpretation certainly fits the context suggested by
the preceding verse. *still I maintain my unfailing care for you:*
just as of old God had revealed his love for his chosen people,
so also he would act again: Israel would be *rebuilt. unfailing*

care translates the same word (*ḥesed*) translated 'unfailing devotion' in 2: 2 (see the comment on this verse).

5. *vineyards which those who planted them defiled:* it is not clear what this means, but it is possible that it refers to the worship of the Canaanite god Baal by Israelites in northern Israel. Baal was the god of fertility in Canaanite religion and was worshipped as the one who ensured the produce of field, flock and herd. Hosea ch. 2 indicates that Israelites in northern Israel engaged in this worship.

6. *Come, let us go up to Zion, to the LORD:* under David and his successor Solomon who built the temple in Jerusalem, Zion became the most holy place in Israelite religion. It was the place where Yahweh dwelt, enthroned above the Ark which David had brought to the city and which Solomon housed in the 'holy of holies' in the temple. At the break-up of the kingdom, when the northern tribes rebelled against the Davidic dynasty and formed a state of their own under their first king, Jeroboam I (922–901 B.C.), the sanctuaries of Bethel and Dan in the north were elevated to rival Jerusalem and to be the central shrines of pilgrimage and worship for the people of the northern kingdom (cp. 1 Kings 12: 25–33). This saying in Jeremiah announces the future re-unification of the people of Israel when the people of the old northern kingdom would once again acknowledge Zion as the sacred dwelling-place of God. ✵

ISRAEL WILL BE REDEEMED

For these are the words of the LORD: 7

> Break into shouts of joy for Jacob's sake,
>   lead the nations, crying loud and clear,
> sing out your praises and say,
>   The LORD has saved his[a] people,
>   and preserved a remnant of Israel.

[a] *So Sept.; Heb.* your

8   See how I bring them from the land of the north;
      I will gather them from the ends of the earth,
      their blind and lame among them,
          women with child and women in labour,
          a great company.

9   They come home, weeping as they come,
          but I will comfort them[a] and be their escort.
      I will lead them to flowing streams;
    they shall not stumble, their path will be so smooth.
      For I have become a father to Israel,
      and Ephraim is my eldest son.

10   Listen to the word of the LORD, you nations,
    announce it, make it known to coasts and islands
            far away:
          He who scattered Israel shall gather them again
          and watch over them as a shepherd watches his
              flock.

11   For the LORD has ransomed Jacob
      and redeemed him from a foe too strong for him.

12   They shall come with shouts of joy to Zion's
              height,
      shining with happiness at the bounty of the LORD,
      the corn, the new wine, and the oil,
          the young of flock and herd.
    They shall become like a watered garden
      and they shall never want again.

13   Then shall the girl show her joy in the dance,
      young men and old shall rejoice;
    I will turn their mourning into gladness,
    I will relent and give them joy to outdo their sorrow.

[a] I will comfort them: *so Sept.; Heb.* prayers for favour.

I will satisfy the priests with the fat of the land   14
and fill my people with my bounty.
    This is the very word of the LORD.

＊ There are really two separate sayings in this passage, verses
7–9 and 10–14. But they have it in common that a shout of
joy at the imminent return of the exiles predominates in both
and, in addition, they both show the strong influence, in both
style and content, of the preaching of Deutero-Isaiah. It is
probable that they were composed by an author late in the
period of the exile. There is no compelling reason for dating
them, as do some commentators, in the period after the exile.

7. *Break into shouts of joy for Jacob's sake:* the summons to
break forth in song because of Israel's deliverance from exile
occurs frequently in Deutero-Isaiah, for example, 'Shout for
joy, you heavens, rejoice, O earth, you mountains, break into
songs of triumph, for the LORD has comforted his people and
has had pity on his own in their distress' (Isa. 49: 13).

9. *I will lead them to flowing streams:* for the same thought see
Isa. 41: 18; 43: 20; 49: 10. The imagery in this verse, like the
similar imagery in Deutero-Isaiah, presents a picture of Israel's
return home from bondage in Babylon which would trans-
cend the exodus of old from Egypt. The imminent journey
back to the homeland would not be fraught with the same
hazards as the journey through the wilderness when Israel left
Egypt under Moses' guidance (cp., for example, Isa. 43: 16–20
and see the commentary on Jer. 16: 14–15).

10. *and watch over them as a shepherd watches his flock:* with
this we may compare Isa. 40: 11 'He will tend his flock like a
shepherd.' Note that the word in this verse translated *coasts
and islands* occurs frequently in Deutero-Isaiah.

11. *and redeemed him from a foe too strong for him:* the word
here translated *redeemed* is characteristic of the preaching of
Deutero-Isaiah. Both this word and the word translated
ransomed in the first line of the verse were employed in the

63

secular sphere in ancient Israel in the laws governing the redemption of property or persons. For example, if a man has fallen into debt and is forced to sell some of his property, his next of kin must purchase it back for him, that is, 'redeem' it (cp. Lev. 25: 25). Or again, if a poor man is forced to sell himself into slavery, he may subsequently buy back his freedom, that is, 'redeem' himself or, if he is unable to do so, a kinsman may do so on his behalf (cp. Lev. 25: 47–55). In ch. 32 Jeremiah himself is involved in an act of redemption of a field at Anathoth owned by his cousin Hanamel. Both words were taken up into the 'theological' sphere to describe God's redemption of his people. They were used to describe Israel's deliverance from slavery in Egypt (cp. Exod. 6: 6; 15: 13; Deut. 7: 8; 9: 26). Most especially, however, Deutero-Isaiah employed the word 'redeem' as a basic concept in his message of Israel's deliverance from bondage in Babylon: Yahweh would be 'redeemer' of his people, acting as their 'kinsman', lovingly concerned with their freedom.

14. *I will satisfy the priests with the fat of the land:* a reference to the share received by the priests from the offerings of the people at the altar. ✳

CEASE YOUR LOUD WEEPING

15 These are the words of the LORD:

> Hark, lamentation is heard in Ramah, and bitter
> weeping,
>> Rachel weeping for her sons.
>> She refuses to be comforted: they are no more.

16 These are the words of the LORD:

> Cease your loud weeping,
>> shed no more tears;
> for there shall be a reward for your toil,[a]
>> they shall return from the land of the enemy.

[a] *So Sept.; Heb. adds* says the LORD.

You shall leave descendants after you;[a] [b]   17
your sons shall return to their own land.
I listened; Ephraim was rocking in his grief: 18
'Thou hast trained me to the yoke like an unbroken
        calf,
    and now I am trained;
        restore me, let me return,
    for thou, LORD, art my God.
Though I broke loose I have repented: 19
now that I am tamed I beat my breast;[c]
    in shame and remorse
I reproach myself for the sins of my youth.'
Is Ephraim still my dear son,   20
a child in whom I delight?
    As often as I turn my back on him
    I still remember him;
and so my heart yearns[d] for him,
    I am filled with tenderness towards him.
    This is the very word of the LORD.
Build cairns to mark your way,   21
set up sign-posts;
make sure of the road,
    the path which you will tread.
    Come back, virgin Israel,
    come back to your cities.
How long will you twist and turn, my wayward child?   22
For the LORD has created a new thing in the earth:
    a woman turned into a man.

[a] *So Sept.; Heb. adds* says the LORD.
[b] You shall. . .you: *or* There shall be hope for your posterity.
[c] *Lit.* thigh.   [d] heart yearns: *lit.* bowels rumble.

✻ This poem announces the return of the people of northern Israel who had been taken into exile in 722 B.C. Because of this some commentators believe that it comes from an early period in Jeremiah's ministry, probably from the reign of Josiah who sought to extend his political and religious reformation into northern Israel. But the poem itself contains no hint that the promise of restoration it announces to the people of northern Israel is in any way linked to this king's activities. It is just as possible that the prophet delivered it at a late stage in his ministry when his message concerning the future renewal and restoration of God's people would have intensified. The fact that this poem refers only to the people of northern Israel and does not mention Judah is no argument against this. For both Jeremiah and those who supplemented and developed his message of hope for the future had all God's people in mind, both those of the former northern kingdom and those of the southern kingdom, and it is in every way likely that the promise of restoration would be addressed now to the northerners (as in this poem), now to Judah (as in verses 23–5), whilst in other places in this chapter both are referred to together.

15. *Ramah:* the word means 'a height'. The town here referred to was situated in the territory of the tribe of Benjamin and on the boundary between the kingdoms of Israel and Judah. It has been identified with er-Ram about 5 miles (approximately 8 km) north of Jerusalem. *Rachel:* one of Jacob's wives and mother of Joseph and Benjamin and hence ancestress of the two tribes who bore these names (cp. Gen. 30: 22–4; 35: 16–18). The reference to Rachel and to the northern town Ramah as well as to Ephraim (verses 18, 20) indicates that this poem concerns northern Israel. The saying is quoted in Matt. 2: 18 where it is understood in connection with Herod's slaughter of the children of Bethlehem after the birth of Jesus.

18–19. These verses contain a penitential confession placed on the lips of the northern exiles.

20. With this verse compare Hos. 11: 1ff., 8f.

22. *a woman turned into a man:* though many suggestions have been made, we simply do not know what this strange saying means. It is possibly an ancient proverbial saying or a fragment of such a saying, perhaps used to describe something so unusual or unexpected as to be incomprehensible. But this is only one of many guesses. *

THE RESTORATION OF JUDAH

These are the words of the LORD of Hosts the God of 23
Israel: Once more shall these words be heard in the land of
Judah and in her cities, when I restore their fortunes:

> The LORD bless you,
> the LORD, your true goal,[a] your holy mountain.
> Ploughmen and shepherds who wander with their   24
>   flocks
> shall live together there.[b]
> For I have given deep draughts to the thirsty,   25
> and satisfied those who were faint with hunger.

Thereupon I woke and looked about me, and my dream[c] 26
had been pleasant.

* This is a short saying portraying the restoration of Judah and Jerusalem. Once again Yahweh, the LORD, would dwell among his people to bless them. Both farmers and shepherds would once again go about their livelihood.

26. *Thereupon I woke and looked about me, and my dream had been pleasant:* this very enigmatic saying is probably a gloss inserted here by an editor. There have been numerous suggestions as to what it means but none has found general acceptance. But glancing back at the promises for the future of the nation contained thus far in this 'book of consolation',

[a] the LORD. . .goal: *or* O home of righteousness.
[b] *Prob. rdg.; Heb. adds* Judah and all his cities.   [c] *Or* sleep.

it is clear that, whilst there was indeed a return to the homeland from exile, the promises for the glorious future of God's people were by no means fully realized. The nation was still subject to foreign dominion; there was no reconstitution of the monarchy with a Davidic king reigning in prosperity over the nation; far from the people of the north returning in loyalty to acknowledge Jerusalem as the cultic centre of the nation, the division between north and south simply increased. Indeed for many years after the return life was harsh and difficult for the restored community. That many were disillusioned can scarcely be doubted and it is possible that this saying in verse 26 is an expression of disillusion. Alternatively, however, it is equally possible that the editor or glossator believed tenaciously in the ultimate fulfilment of all the promises of old: though they now were like a dream when compared with the harsh facts of life, the dream would one day be realized. ✻

TWO SHORT SAYINGS

27 The time is coming, says the LORD, when I will sow Israel and Judah with the seed of man and the seed of
28 cattle. As I watched over them with intent to pull down and to uproot, to demolish and destroy and harm, so now will I watch over them to build and to plant. This is the very word of the LORD.

29   In those days it shall no longer be said,

'The fathers have eaten sour grapes
and the children's teeth are set on edge';

30 for a man shall die for his own wrongdoing; the man who eats sour grapes shall have his own teeth set on edge.

✻ Two short sayings are contained in this passage. The first, verses 27-8, announces the repopulation of the land; the second, verses 29-30, concerns individual retribution.

27. *I will sow Israel and Judah with the seed of man and the seed of cattle:* the aftermath of the Babylonian invasion and destruction of Palestine was that the land lay desolate, its population diminished and its wonted herds and flocks decimated. But God would break up the fallow ground and repopulate the land with both man and beast so that both would once again abound.

28. For the terminology of this verse see the commentary on 1: 10. It centres on one of the main themes of the book, the theme of judgement and renewal after judgement.

29f. The proverb here quoted occurs again in Ezek. 18: 2, whilst the same sentiment is expressed in Lam. 5: 7. Whilst it is an oversimplification to say that whenever a man committed an offence in ancient Israel his whole family suffered the penalty imposed upon him, it is true that this frequently happened (cp. for example the case of Achan reported in Josh. 7). Deut. 24: 16 is clearly aimed at banning such a practice. The belief that God would punish the innocent because of the guilt of their fathers is cynically attacked in the proverb quoted here in Jer. 31: 29 and Ezek. 18: 2, for the natural effects of a man eating sour grapes are that his teeth alone are set on edge; it is impossible for his children to share his unpleasant experience. Here in Jer. 31: 29-30, as in the long discussion of it in Ezek. 18, such a belief is repudiated: *a man shall die for his own wrongdoing* or, as Ezekiel puts it, 'The soul that sins shall die', it and no other. ✻

THE NEW COVENANT

The time is coming, says the LORD, when I will make 31
a new covenant with Israel and Judah. It will not be like 32
the covenant I made with their forefathers when I took
them by the hand and led them out of Egypt. Although
they broke my covenant, I was patient with them, says
the LORD. But this is the covenant which I will make with 33

Israel after those days, says the LORD; I will set my law within them and write it on their hearts; I will become
34 their God and they shall become my people. No longer need they teach one another to know the LORD; all of them, high and low alike, shall know me, says the LORD, for I will forgive their wrongdoing and remember their sin no more.

* This short passage is one of the most important in the book of Jeremiah. Indeed it represents one of the deepest insights in the entire prophetic literature in the Old Testament. It became of supreme importance in the New Testament the very title of which ('The New Testament *or* Covenant') derives from it. The new covenant promised in this passage is believed by Christians to have found its fulfilment in the life and passion of Jesus (cp. Heb. 8: 8–12; 9; 2 Cor. 3: 5–18) who at the 'last supper' announced the imminent inauguration of the new covenant in his self-offering on the cross (cp. Mark 14: 23–5).

The background to this announcement of a new covenant in Jer. 31: 31-4 is of course the covenant believed to have been inaugurated between God and Israel at Sinai (Exod. 19: 1 – 24: 11). Integral to the covenant and its continued existence was Israel's obedience to the laws it laid down, 'the terms of the covenant' (cp. Jer. 11: 1–8). Failure to obey the covenant laws would entail judgement upon the nation, and the book of Deuteronomy contains a long list of the curses which would befall Israel if it failed to obey these laws (cp. Deut. 28). The Deuteronomic history (Deuteronomy to 2 Kings) records how down through the centuries Israel had persistently failed to live in accordance with the terms of the covenant and so incurred judgement, first the northern kingdom in 722 B.C. and finally Judah in 587 B.C. Central to the whole issue and to the very existence of Israel as God's people was thus the question of her obedience to the law. What became apparent, however, to those who looked back over Israel's past was that the nation had not merely refused to obey the law but in fact was quite simply incapable of obeying it. It was the realization of this that produced one of the greatest crises for Israel's faith: how could Israel be God's holy people if by her very nature she was incapable of being holy? Jeremiah expressed the problem aptly: 'Can the Nubian change his skin, or the leopard its spots? And you? Can you do good, you who are schooled in evil?' (13: 23).

The new covenant passage here in 31: 31-4 announces that God himself will graciously bring about the necessary change in his people's inner nature so that their past failure to obey his laws will be replaced by both the will and the ability to do so. He will set his law within them and write it on their hearts so that henceforth they will each and everyone 'know' him, that is, spontaneously love and obey him: *No longer need they teach one another to know the LORD; all of them, high and low alike, shall know me, says the LORD* (verse 34).

The passage is composed in the characteristic style of the prose in the book of Jeremiah and very probably comes from a Deuteronomic author. The phrase *I will become their God and they shall become my people* (verse 33) occurs frequently elsewhere in the prose in the book (7: 23; 11: 4; 24: 7; 32: 38. It is probably a secondary addition in 30: 22 where the Septuagint omits it). In addition, the notion of the law being in Israel's heart is found in such passages as Deut. 6: 6 and 30: 14, whilst the statement that God would place his *law within them and write it on their hearts* is clearly closely akin to Deut. 30: 6 where indeed the same message is in essence set out: 'The LORD your God will bring you into the land which your forefathers occupied, and you will occupy it again... The LORD your God will circumcise your hearts and the hearts of your descendants, so that you will love him with all your heart and soul and you will live' (Deut. 30: 5-6). *

THE INSEPARABLE BOND BETWEEN
GOD AND ISRAEL

35 These are the words of the LORD, who gave the sun
for a light by day and*ᵃ* the moon and stars for a light by
night, who cleft the sea and its waves roared; the LORD
of Hosts is his name:

36   If this fixed order could vanish out of my sight,
              says the LORD,
       then the race of Israel too could cease for evermore
              to be a nation in my sight.

37   These are the words of the LORD: If any man could
measure the heaven above or fathom the depths of the
earth beneath, then I could spurn the whole race of Israel
because of all they have done. This is the very word of the
LORD.

✳ The two sayings contained in this passage (verses 35-6 and
37) announce the impossibility of Israel being forsaken for
ever by God. They are self-explanatory.
    35. *who cleft the sea and its waves roared:* the same expression
is found in Isa. 51: 15. ✳

THE REBUILDING OF JERUSALEM

38 The time is coming, says the LORD, when the city shall
be rebuilt in the LORD's honour from the Tower of
39 Hananel to the Corner Gate. The measuring line shall
then be laid straight out over the hill of Gareb and round
40 Goath.*ᵇ* All the valley*ᶜ* and every field as far as the gorge

[a] So Sept.; Heb. adds the ordered movements of.   [b] Or Goah.
[c] So Sept.; Heb. adds the corpses and the buried bodies.

of the Kidron to the corner by the Horse Gate eastwards shall be holy to the LORD. It shall never again be pulled down or demolished.

✻ The city of Jerusalem devastated by the Babylonians would be rebuilt never again to be demolished.

38. *the Tower of Hananel:* this tower stood on the north side of Jerusalem. It is mentioned in Neh. 3: 1; 12: 39 and in Zech. 14: 10. The person after whom it was named is unknown. *the Corner Gate:* a gate somewhere near the north-west corner of the city. 2 Chron. 26: 9 records that its towers were built by Uzziah (783–742 B.C.).

39. *The measuring line shall then be laid straight out:* similar imagery is employed of the future restoration of Jerusalem in, for example, Ezek. 40–8 and Zech. 2. Not unnaturally the rebuilding of the city figured prominently in the hopes for the future of God's people. As in the past, so again in the future Jerusalem would become the centre of God's dwelling among his people. *the hill of Gareb:* a part of Jerusalem, possibly on the south-west hill. *Goath* may also have been a quarter or suburb of the city, possibly in the south-east. Neither of these two places is mentioned elsewhere in the Old Testament.

40. *as far as the gorge of the Kidron:* this gorge or valley is east of Jerusalem, between the city and the Mount of Olives. *the Horse Gate:* this gate was probably in the south-east corner of the city and led to the Kidron Valley. ✻

THE FUTURE RETURN TO THE HOMELAND

✻ Ch. 32 continues the theme of the future restoration of Israel and Judah prophesied in the sayings in chs. 30–1. It differs from them, however, in that it does not contain a series of separate sayings and oracles but is concerned with an event in the prophet's life which, at God's command, he used as a means of announcing the future renewal and restoration of the land beyond judgement. The chapter is composed entirely in prose and is widely recognized to come from a Deuteronomic author, though the historicity of what is recorded cannot be doubted.

The chapter falls into two parts, verses 1-15 and 16-44. The first section records that during the Babylonian siege of Jerusalem in 588-587 B.C. Jeremiah, exercising his right as 'redeemer' of a field belonging to a kinsman at Anathoth, purchases, at the command of God, the field in question and proclaims it to be a sign of the future restoration of the land after the judgement which is about to befall the nation and the devastation and exile this is to bring. This 'acted prophecy' takes place in the presence of various witnesses in the guard-house where the prophet has been imprisoned. The second section is a dialogue in private between Jeremiah and God. The prophet asks whether in view of the nation's sin and the terrible judgement which is about to come upon it, such a prophecy of restoration is really credible (verses 16-25). Verses 26-44 contain God's reply: nothing is impossible for God (verses 26-7); the nation has indeed rebelled against him and for this it is about to be handed over to the Babylonians (verses 28-35), but beyond this God will bring his people home from exile and will make an eternal covenant with them. As Jeremiah's 'acted prophecy' had declared, the land would be restored again (verses 36-44). ✳

JEREMIAH BUYS A FIELD AT ANATHOTH

32 The word which came to Jeremiah from the LORD in the tenth year of Zedekiah king of Judah (the eighteenth year
2 of Nebuchadrezzar). At that time the forces of the Babylonian king were besieging Jerusalem, and the prophet Jeremiah was imprisoned in the court of the
3 guard-house attached to the royal palace. Zedekiah king of Judah had imprisoned him after demanding what he

meant by this prophecy: 'These are the words of the
LORD: I will deliver this city into the hands of the king of
Babylon, and he shall take it. Zedekiah king of Judah will 4
not escape from the Chaldaeans but will be surrendered
to the king of Babylon; he will speak with him face to
face and see him with his own eyes. Zedekiah will be 5
taken to Babylon and will remain there until I turn my
thoughts to him, says the LORD. However much you
fight against the Chaldaeans you will have no success.'

Jeremiah said, The word of the LORD came to me: 6
Hanamel son of your uncle Shallum is coming to see 7
you and will say, 'Buy my field at Anathoth; you have
the right of redemption, as next of kin, to buy it.' As the 8
LORD had foretold, my cousin Hanamel came to the
court of the guard-house and said, 'Buy my field at
Anathoth in Benjamin. You have the right of redemption
and possession as next of kin: buy it.' I knew that this
was the LORD's message; so I bought the field at Anathoth 9
from my cousin Hanamel and weighed out the price,
seventeen shekels of silver. I signed and sealed the deed 10
and had it witnessed; then I weighed out the money on
the scales. I took my copies of the deed of purchase, both 11
the sealed[a] and the unsealed, and gave them to Baruch 12
son of Neriah, son of Mahseiah, in the presence of
Hanamel my cousin,[b] of the witnesses whose names were
on the deed of purchase, and of the Judaeans sitting in the
court of the guard-house. In the presence of them all I gave 13
my instructions to Baruch: These are the words of the 14
LORD of Hosts the God of Israel: Take these copies of the

[a] *So Sept.; Heb. adds* the command and the statutes.
[b] *So some MSS.; others* uncle.

deed of purchase, the sealed and the unsealed, and deposit them in an earthenware jar so that they may be preserved
15 for a long time. For these are the words of the LORD of Hosts the God of Israel: The time will come when houses, fields, and vineyards will again be bought and sold in this land.

* 1-5. These verses describe the historical setting for Jeremiah's 'acted prophecy' recorded in this section. He was imprisoned in the tenth year of Zedekiah's reign (588/587 B.C.) and during the final siege of Jerusalem by the Babylonians. But the account is wrong in attributing the prophet's imprisonment directly to Zedekiah. It appears to have been instigated by certain royal officials and probably took place during the short period when the Babylonians were forced to abandon the siege on Jerusalem in order to engage an Egyptian army which had advanced to help Judah (cp. 37: 5, 11 and the commentary on ch. 38).

2. *imprisoned in the court of the guard-house:* he had initially been imprisoned in an underground dungeon where he would certainly have perished had he not been removed to the court of the guard-house (cp. 37: 18–21; 38: 7–13).

7. *Hanamel son of your uncle Shallum:* here and in verses 8 and 9 Hanamel is referred to as Jeremiah's cousin. The N.E.B. correctly emends the text in verse 12 where the Hebrew reads 'Hanamel my uncle'. *Buy my field at Anathoth; you have the right of redemption, as next of kin, to buy it:* here and in what follows we have an example of the law governing the right of redemption to which reference was made in the commentary on 31: 11. The law in question is set out in Lev. 25: 25–31. Probably Hanamel had fallen into debt and now was liable to lose his land or part of it to a creditor. He came to his kinsman Jeremiah who had the necessary financial resources to 'redeem' it. By purchasing it from Hanamel, Jeremiah kept the field within the family or clan circle. The

land owned by a family or clan in ancient Israel was regarded as a sacred inheritance. There was thus a close bond between a family or clan and the land it owned. This was the central reason why Naboth would not give up his vineyard to Ahab: 'The LORD forbid that I should let you have the land which has always been in my family' (1 Kings 21: 3).

9. *and weighed out the price, seventeen shekels of silver:* the *shekel* was originally, as here, a weight and only later a coin. In ancient Israel a shekel weighed about 0·4 of an ounce (about 11·5 grams). Jeremiah thus paid just under 7 ounces of silver for the field.

11. *both the sealed and the unsealed:* there were two copies of the deed of purchase. This appears to have been standard procedure in such transactions. One copy was rolled up and sealed, whilst the other was left unsealed and attached to the sealed copy. The contents of the deed could thus be read or consulted without breaking the seal. This ensured that the deed was protected from forged additions or alterations. If a dispute arose or there was suspicion of any fraudulent tampering with the unsealed copy, the sealed copy could be opened.

12. *Baruch son of Neriah:* this is the first mention of Baruch in the book. He was Jeremiah's faithful scribe and companion. Cp. the commentary on ch. 45.

14. *deposit them in an earthenware jar so that they may be preserved for a long time:* the storage of documents in jars is well attested in ancient Israel. Some of the famous Dead Sea scrolls discovered in 1947 had been stored in jars.

15. *houses, fields, and vineyards will again be bought and sold in this land:* by his purchase of the field Jeremiah betokens and declares the future restoration of the land and his own faith in God's promises. ✳

THE PROMISE IS SURE

16 After I had given the deed of purchase to Baruch son of
17 Neriah, I prayed to the LORD: O Lord GOD, thou hast
made the heavens and the earth by thy great strength and
with thy outstretched arm; nothing is impossible for thee.
18 Thou keepest faith with thousands and thou dost requite
the sins of fathers on to the heads[a] of their sons. O great
19 and mighty God whose name is the LORD of Hosts, great
are thy purposes and mighty thy actions. Thine eyes
watch all the ways of men, and thou rewardest each
20 according to his ways and as his deeds deserve. Thou
didst work signs and portents in Egypt and hast continued
them to this day, both in Israel and amongst all men, and
21 hast won for thyself a name that lives on to this day. Thou
didst bring thy people Israel out of Egypt with signs and
portents, with a strong hand and an outstretched arm, and
22 with terrible power. Thou didst give them this land
which thou didst promise with an oath to their fore-
23 fathers, a land flowing with milk and honey. They came
and took possession of it, but they did not obey thee or
follow thy law, they disobeyed all thy commands; and
24 so thou hast brought this disaster upon them. Look at the
siege-ramps, the men who are advancing to take the city,
and the city given over to its assailants from Chaldaea, the
victim of sword, famine, and pestilence. The word thou
25 hast spoken is fulfilled and thou dost see it. And yet thou
hast bidden me buy the field, O Lord GOD, and have the
deed witnessed, even though the city is given to the
Chaldaeans.

[a] requite. . .on to the heads: *lit.* repay. . .into the bosoms.

✻ There follows a long section, which for convenience sake we shall divide into three parts (verses 16–25, 26–35, 36–44), describing an alleged dialogue between Jeremiah and God concerning the promised restoration of the land recorded in verses 1–15. But this dialogue is so thoroughly Deuteronomic in both style and phraseology as well as in content that it is very improbable that it is based upon anything deriving from the prophet. Most modern commentators regard it as entirely a Deuteronomic composition prompted by the prophecy recorded in verses 1–15.

In the first part of this dialogue the prophet is represented as addressing God, extolling him as creator, omnipotent and merciful, the deliverer of his people and their sustainer and preserver down through the centuries. But Israel had rebelled against him and now faced imminent judgement justly inflicted upon them. Can it really be that the nation has a future, as God's promise recorded in verse 15 declares?

When it is borne in mind that the Deuteronomic authors who composed this dialogue worked in the period of the exile, it will be readily recognized that the question here posed must have been asked by many a person, whether living in the homeland, amidst the devastation wrought by the Babylonians in 587 B.C., or in exile.

17. *nothing is impossible for thee:* the very way in which the question is posed in these verses already anticipates the answer to come from God. Here already his omnipotence as well as his love for his people is the centre of emphasis: nothing is impossible for him (cp. verse 27).

23. *they did not obey thee or follow thy law:* the main indictment of Israel in the Deuteronomic theology was that the nation had not obeyed God's law (see pp. 12f. above and the commentary on 7: 1–15 and 11: 1–17 in vol. I). ✻

79

GOD'S REPLY – I

26,27 These are the words of the LORD to Jeremiah: I am the
LORD, the God of all flesh; is anything impossible for me?
28 Therefore these are the words of the LORD: I will deliver
this city into the hands of the Chaldaeans and of Nebu-
29 chadrezzar king of Babylon, and he shall take it. The
Chaldaeans who are fighting against this city will enter it,
set it on fire and burn it down, with the houses on whose
roofs sacrifices have been burnt to Baal and drink-
offerings poured out to other gods, by which I was provoked to anger.

30 From their earliest days Israel and Judah have been
doing what is wrong in my eyes, provoking me to anger
31 by their actions, says the LORD. For this city has so roused
my anger and my fury, from the time it was built down
32 to this day, that I would rid myself of it. Israel and Judah,
their kings, officers, priests, prophets, and everyone living
in Jerusalem and Judah have provoked me to anger by
33 their wrongdoing. They have turned their backs on me
and averted their faces; though I took pains to teach
34 them, they would not hear or learn their lesson. They set
up their loathsome idols in the house which bears my
35 name and so defiled it. They built shrines to Baal in the
Valley of Ben-hinnom, to surrender their sons and
daughters to Molech. It was no command of mine, nor
did it ever enter my thought to do this abominable thing
and lead Judah into sin.

✻ In this first part of God's reply the judgement to befall the nation is unrelentingly emphasized (verses 26-9) and the justice of it spelled out in the description of the people's rebellion against God (verses 30-5).

27. *is anything impossible for me?* the statement in verse 17 is here taken up again and once more anticipates God's affirmation that the promise of restoration is sure (verses 36-44).

34. *the house which bears my name:* cp. the commentary on 7: 10.

35. *to surrender their sons and daughters to Molech:* the cult of Molech involved offering children as sacrifices. The Valley of Ben-hinnom was the main location of this cult (cp. the commentary on 2: 23 and 7: 30 – 8: 3.). ✻

GOD'S REPLY - II

Now, therefore, these are the words of the LORD the 36
God of Israel to this city of which you say, 'It is being
given over to the king of Babylon, with sword, famine,
and pestilence': I will gather them from all the lands to 37
which I banished them in my anger, rage, and fury, and
I will bring them back to this place and let them dwell
there undisturbed. They shall become my people and I 38
will become their God. I will give them one heart and 39
one way of life so that they shall fear me at all times, for
their own good and the good of their children after them.
I will enter into an eternal covenant with them, to follow 40
them unfailingly with my bounty; I will fill their hearts
with fear of me, and so they will not turn away from me.
I will rejoice over them, rejoice to do them good, and 41
faithfully with all my heart and soul I will plant them in
this land. For these are the words of the LORD: As I 42
brought on this people such great disaster, so will I bring

43 them all the prosperity which I now promise them. Fields shall again be bought and sold in this land of which you now say, 'It is desolate, without man or beast; it is given
44 over to the Chaldaeans.' Fields shall be bought and sold, deeds signed, sealed, and witnessed, in Benjamin, in the neighbourhood of Jerusalem, in the cities of Judah, of the hill-country, of the Shephelah, and of the Negeb; for I will restore their fortunes. This is the very word of the LORD.

✳ The main point of the dialogue is now reached. Israel has rebelled against God and justly deserved the judgement inflicted upon her. Yet God will not abandon his people. We can now appreciate what this dialogue as a whole was intended to impart to those living in the shadow of 587 B.C. to whom it was addressed by its authors. It would have reminded them of their divine election and of their rebellion against God and the disaster this entailed for them. In this way it would have provided an explanation for their present plight. At the same time it declared to them the omnipotence of God and so his control of their destiny: for God nothing is impossible. Finally it re-affirmed God's promise of their eventual restoration and so gave them sure hope for the future.

37. *I will gather them from all the lands to which I banished them:* cp. Deut. 30: 1–5.

38. *They shall become my people and I will become their God:* cp. the comment on this on p. 71 above.

39. *I will give them one heart and one way of life so that they shall fear me at all times:* the promise is the same as that given in 31: 33.

40. *I will enter into an eternal covenant with them:* in content the promise here given is obviously parallel to the new covenant passage in 31: 31–4. God would so change the hearts of his people, so imbue their hearts with love and reverence

(fear) for him, that they would spontaneously obey and serve him alone.

42. This verse sums up God's intentions for his people: as he had punished them so would he forgive and restore them and the glory of their restoration and renewal would match the suffering of their punishment.

43. *Fields shall again be bought and sold in this land:* this brings us back to the 'acted prophecy' recorded in verses 1–15 which prompted the ensuing dialogue in verses 16–44. The promise there announced by Jeremiah stood firm; Israel's restoration to the homeland is assured.

44. On the places here mentioned see the note on 17: 25–6. The list of areas stresses the total restoration of the land. *I will restore their fortunes:* that is, reverse their present state. ✻

PROMISES CONCERNING RESTORATION, THE DAVIDIC DYNASTY AND THE LEVITICAL PRIESTS

✻ Ch. 33, the final chapter in 'the book of consolation', comprises two separate complexes of sayings. The first (verses 1–13) contains three sayings (verses 1–9, 10–11, 12–13), all in prose, concerning the restoration of Israel and Judah with a return to normal life and peace and prosperity. The second (verses 14–26) contains four sayings (verses 14–16, 17–18, 19–22, 23–6), again all in prose, announcing promises concerning the Davidic dynasty and the levitical priesthood. Verses 14–26 are not found in the Septuagint (on the differences between the Septuagint and the Massoretic Text see pp. 15f.). Most modern commentators consider these verses to have been added secondarily to this chapter so that the text of the Septuagint represents here, as in places elsewhere in the book, a different and probably earlier form of the book than the Massoretic Text. ✻

AN AGE OF PEACE AND PROSPERITY

33 The word of the LORD came to Jeremiah a second time
while he was still imprisoned in the court of the guard-
2 house: These are the words of the LORD who made the
earth,[a] who formed it and established it; the LORD is his
3 name: If you call to me I will answer you, and tell you
great and mysterious things which you do not under-
4 stand. These are the words of the LORD the God of Israel
concerning the houses in this city and the royal palace,
which are to be razed to the ground, concerning siege-
5 ramp and sword, and attackers[b] who fill the houses with
the corpses of those whom he struck down in his furious
rage: I hid my face from this city because of their wicked
6 ways, but now I will bring her healing; I will heal and
cure Judah and Israel, and will let my people see an age
7 of peace and security. I will restore their fortunes and
8 build them again as once they were. I will cleanse them
of all the wickedness and sin that they have committed;
I will forgive all the evil deeds they have done in rebellion
9 against me. This city will win me a name[c] and praise and
glory before all the nations on earth, when they hear of all
the blessings I bestow on her; and they shall be moved
and filled with awe because of the blessings and the peace
which I have brought upon her.

10   These are the words of the LORD: You say of this place,
'It is in ruins, and neither man nor beast lives in the cities
of Judah or in the streets of Jerusalem. It is all a waste,

[a] the earth: *so Sept.; Heb.* it.
[b] *Prob. rdg.; Heb. adds* the Chaldaeans.
[c] *Prob. rdg.; Heb. adds* of joy.

inhabited by neither man nor beast.' Yet in this place shall be heard once again the sounds of joy and gladness, 11 the voice of the bridegroom and the bride; here too shall be heard voices shouting, 'Praise the LORD of Hosts, for he is good, for his love endures for ever', as they offer praise and thanksgiving in the house of the LORD. For I will restore the fortunes of the land as once they were. This is the word of the LORD.

These are the words of the LORD of Hosts: In this place 12 and in all its cities, now ruined and inhabited by neither man nor beast, there shall once more be a refuge where shepherds may fold their flocks. In the cities of the hill- 13 country, of the Shephelah, of the Negeb, in Benjamin, in the neighbourhood of Jerusalem and the cities of Judah, flocks will once more pass under the shepherd's hand as he counts them. This is the word of the LORD.

* The three sayings contained in these verses have it in common that they look beyond the devastation which has been wrought upon the land to a new beginning to be inaugurated by God, who is to restore its waste places and usher in a new age of peace and prosperity for his people. All three passages are composed in the characteristic style of the prose in the book and were probably composed by a Deutero-nomic author. Once again, however, what is herein contained must be seen as a development of Jeremiah's own belief in the restoration of the nation at God's hands.

1. *The word of the LORD came to Jeremiah a second time:* this verse clearly links the sayings which follow with the previous chapter.

2. *who made the earth, who formed it and established it; the LORD is his name:* a further link between this passage and the previous chapter (cp. 32: 17).

6. *I will heal and cure Judah and Israel:* the word *cure* translates a phrase which is literally 'I will cause new skin to grow.' The authors have borrowed the phrase in question from 30: 17 where it is more literally translated. *Judah and Israel:* once again we note that the message of hope for the future concerns all God's people, both those of the former northern kingdom and those of Judah.

9. *before all the nations on earth:* this expresses the universal significance of Israel's standing before God and at the same time the universal dominion of God over all the nations. It is also by implication an expression of the monotheistic teaching of the book (see pp. 16f.).

11. *the sounds of joy and gladness, the voice of the bridegroom and the bride:* a precise reversal of the judgement announced in 7: 34; 16: 9; 25: 10. *Praise the LORD of Hosts, for he is good, for his love endures for ever:* a closely similar expression of praise is found in Pss. 106; 107; 118; 136.

12. *a refuge where shepherds may fold their flocks:* cp. 31: 24 for a similar promise.

13. See the note on 32: 44. ✻

THE DAVIDIC DYNASTY AND THE LEVITICAL PRIESTS

14 Wait, says the LORD, the days are coming when I will bestow on Israel and Judah all the blessings I have
15 promised them. In those days, at that time, I will make a righteous Branch of David spring up; he shall maintain
16 law and justice in the land. In those days Judah shall be kept safe and Jerusalem shall live undisturbed; and this shall be her[a] name: The LORD is our Righteousness.

17 For these are the words of the LORD: David will never
18 lack a successor on the throne of Israel, nor will the levitical priests lack a man who shall come before me

[a] Or, *with Pesh.*, his.

86

continually to present whole-offerings, to burn grain-offerings and to make other offerings.

This word came from the LORD to Jeremiah: These are 19, 20 the words of the LORD: If the law that I made for the day and the night could be annulled[a] so that they fell out of their proper order, then my covenant with my servant 21 David could be annulled so that none of his line should sit upon his throne; so also could my covenant with the levitical priests who minister to me. Like the innumerable 22 host of heaven or the countless sands of the sea, I will increase the descendants of my servant David and the Levites who minister to me.

The word of the LORD came to Jeremiah: Have you 23, 24 not observed how this people have said, 'It is the two families whom he chose that the LORD has spurned'? So others will despise my people and no longer regard them as a nation. These are the words of the LORD: If I had not 25 made[b] my law for day and night nor established a fixed order in heaven and earth, then I would spurn the 26 descendants of Jacob and of my servant David, and would not take any of David's line to be rulers over the descendants of Abraham, Isaac and Jacob. But now I will restore their fortunes and have compassion upon them.

* As already noted, these verses are not found in the Septuagint and most modern commentators regard them as a later addition to this chapter. They are widely believed to have been composed in the period after the exile, on the grounds that they reflect a situation in which both national and religious zeal had waned and when therefore the emphasis here placed

[a] could be annulled: *so Vulg.; Heb.* you annul.
[b] If. . .made: *prob. rdg., cp. Targ.; Heb.* If not.

upon the divine promises to David and upon the eternal ministry of the levitical priesthood would have been called for. But there is no need to date these sayings as late as this and they are just as plausibly understood as having been composed late in the period of the exile itself when, after the edict of Cyrus allowing the exiles to return home (538 B.C.; cp. Ezra 1: 1–4; 6: 3–5), the possibility of rebuilding the temple and the renewal of the sacrificial cult which this would obviously have entailed became a reality, and when also the hope of the restoration of the Davidic dynasty in Jerusalem would very probably have been asserted.

14–16. Verses 15–16 are a prose parallel to 23: 5–6. Verse 14 is a general statement of God's promises concerning Israel and Judah. But whereas in 23: 6 the name *The LORD is our Righteousness* is applied to the promised *Branch of David*, in 33: 16 it is applied to Judah and Jerusalem or perhaps just to Jerusalem, the text here being *this shall be her name* as against 23: 6 which reads 'This is the name to be given to him.' The meaning of 33: 16 may be that because of the law and justice to be established in the land by the righteous Branch of David, the whole nation would be known as *The LORD is our Righteousness* or, if the name applies to Jerusalem, that the city will so manifest the qualities of righteousness that it will be named in such a manner.

17–18. Obviously closely attached to verses 14–16 is this further saying concerning the Davidic dynasty. Here also the levitical priesthood is the object of God's promises for his people's future.

17. *David will never lack a successor on the throne of Israel:* this phrase is found elsewhere only in 1 Kings 2: 4; 8: 25 (= 2 Chron. 6: 16); 9: 5 (= 2 Chron. 7: 18) and is thus evidence that the passage derives from a Deuteronomic editor. Note that it is the throne of *Israel* which is referred to and not just Judah. The Davidic dynasty was always believed in Judah and Jerusalem to be the divinely appointed kingship over all God's people. The establishment of a separate mon-

archy in northern Israel was regarded in Judah as not merely political rebellion against the house of David but as rebellion against God who had chosen David and his successors alone to rule over his people.

18. *the levitical priests:* literally 'the priests the Levites'. This is the way the Levites are designated in the Deuteronomic literature. In Deuteronomy, as here in Jer. 33: 18, any Levite may officiate at the altar. The right to do so is not limited to any one priestly family such as the Aaronites or the Zadokites. *whole-offerings:* in this particular type of sacrifice the whole victim is burnt without any of it being given back to either the worshipper or the priest. *grain-offerings:* for this particular kind of offering (the word here translated probably means 'a gift') see Lev. 2.

19-22. God's promises to David and to the levitical priesthood are as fixed and unalterable as the order of nature itself (for a similar thought see 31: 36).

21. *my covenant with my servant David:* on the special relationship, the covenant, between God and David, see the commentary on 21: 11-12. *my covenant with the levitical priests:* for this covenant see Num. 25: 12f.; Neh. 13: 29; Mal. 2: 4-9.

23-6. The same promise as in the previous verses is expressed again but is extended to include the whole nation in addition to the line of David.

24. *It is the two families whom he chose that the LORD has spurned:* the *two families* are probably the people of northern Israel and those of Judah rather than the family of David and that of the Levites. Many people living after the tragedy of 587 B.C. must have believed that Yahweh had completely rejected his people. These verses are best understood as a direct response to such pessimism (cp. also the commentary on 32: 16-25). *

Events under Jehoiakim
and Zedekiah

✳ Ch. 34 comprises two separate sections both of which, however, concern events during the period leading up to the final destruction of Jerusalem by the Babylonians in 587 B.C. The first (verses 1–7) reports words spoken by Jeremiah to Zedekiah at a stage when the Babylonian invasion of the country was well advanced and when the Babylonians were attacking Jerusalem itself. The second (verses 8–22) concerns an occasion when, at the instigation and command of Zedekiah, those who owned slaves who were Hebrews agreed to release them as required by law, but subsequently revoked their decision and re-imposed servitude upon those who had been released. ✳

A MESSAGE TO ZEDEKIAH

34 THE WORD WHICH CAME TO JEREMIAH from the LORD when Nebuchadrezzar king of Babylon and his army, with all his vassal kingdoms and nations, were 2 fighting against Jerusalem and all her towns: These are the words of the LORD the God of Israel: Go and say to Zedekiah king of Judah, These are the words of the LORD: I will give this city into the hands of the king of Babylon 3 and he will burn it down. You shall not escape, you will be captured and handed over to him. You will see him face to face, and he will speak to you in person; and you 4 shall go to Babylon. But listen to the LORD's word to you,

Zedekiah king of Judah. This is his word: You shall not die by the sword; you will die a peaceful death, and they 5 will kindle fires in your honour like the fires kindled in former times for the kings your ancestors who preceded you. 'Alas, my lord!' they will say as they beat their breasts in mourning for you. This I have spoken. This is the very word of the LORD. The prophet Jeremiah re- 6 peated all this to Zedekiah king of Judah in Jerusalem when the army of the king of Babylon was attacking 7 Jerusalem and the*a* remaining cities of Judah, namely Lachish and Azekah. These were the only fortified cities left in Judah.

* 1. *with all his vassal kingdoms and nations:* among the terms of the treaties between a suzerain and his vassals there was frequently one requiring the vassals to provide military support for their overlord against an enemy. The suzerain on his part usually protected and defended his vassals against attack by an enemy.

4–5. *You shall not die by the sword; you will die a peaceful death:* the apparent assurance here given to Zedekiah that he would have *a peaceful death* is in sharp contrast to the harrowing fate which actually befell the king (cp. 39: 4–7; 52: 7–11. See also 2 Kings 25: 4–7). Probably, therefore, we should understand this assurance as having been conditional in nature: Babylonian victory was inevitable, decreed by God; only by acknowledging this and surrendering forthwith to Nebuchadrezzar could the day be saved and peace ensured (cp. 21: 8–10). Failing this, the fate of both king and people was sealed.

6–7. More precise information is here given than in

[a] *So Sept.; Heb. adds* all.

verse 1 of how advanced the Babylonian invasion of Judah was when Jeremiah delivered this message to Zedekiah.

7. *Lachish and Azekah. These were the only fortified cities left in Judah:* it is interesting to note in connection with the mention of Lachish and Azekah as the last remaining fortified cities in Judah, apart from Jerusalem, that Azekah is mentioned in one of the Lachish letters. These letters were written on pieces of broken pottery and belong to the period immediately before the fall of Lachish and Jerusalem in 587 B.C. There are eighteen letters in all among a group of twenty-one such ostraca, as they are called; they were found in a room filled with ashes from the fire which destroyed the city in 587 B.C. In letter 4 the writer, who was probably an officer in charge of a military outpost between Lachish and Azekah, in a message to the garrison commander at Lachish states that he can no longer see Azekah: 'And let (my lord) know that we are watching for the signals of Lachish, according to all the indications which my lord hath given, for we cannot see Azekah' (translated in J. B. Pritchard, *Ancient Near Eastern Texts Relating to the Old Testament* (third edition, Princeton 1969), p. 322). This probably indicated that Azekah had by now already fallen to the Babylonian armies. Lachish has been identified with the modern Tell ed-Duweir about 23 miles (37 km) south-west of Jerusalem. Azekah has been identified with the modern Tell ez-Zakariyeh about 11 miles (nearly 18 km) north of Lachish and 18 miles (nearly 29 km) west-south-west of Jerusalem. ✳

TREACHERY AGAINST SLAVES

8 The word that came to Jeremiah from the LORD after Zedekiah had made a covenant with all the people in
9 Jerusalem to proclaim an act of freedom for the slaves. All who had Hebrew slaves, male or female, were to set them free; they were not to keep their fellow Judaeans in

servitude. All the officers and people, having made this 10
covenant to set free their slaves, both male and female,
and not to keep them in servitude any longer, fulfilled its
terms and let them go. Afterwards, however, they 11
changed their minds and forced back again into slavery
the men and women whom they had freed. Then this 12
word came from the LORD to Jeremiah: These are the 13
words of the LORD the God of Israel: I made a covenant
with your forefathers on the day that I brought them out
of Egypt, out of the land of slavery. These were its terms:
'Within seven years each of you shall set free any Hebrew 14
who has sold himself to you as a slave and has served you
for six years; you shall set him free.' Your forefathers
did not listen to me or obey me. You, on the contrary, 15
recently proclaimed an act of freedom for the slaves and
made a covenant in my presence, in the house that bears
my name, and so have done what is right in my eyes. But 16
you too have profaned my name. You have all taken
back the slaves you had set free and you have forced them,
both male and female, to be your slaves again. Therefore 17
these are the words of the LORD: After you had proclaimed an act of freedom, a deliverance for your kins-
men and your neighbours, you did not obey me; so I will
proclaim a deliverance for you, says the LORD, a deliverance over to sword, to pestilence, and to famine, and I
will make you repugnant to all the kingdoms of the earth.
You have disregarded my covenant and have not fulfilled 18
the terms to which you yourselves had agreed; so I will
make you like the calf of the covenant when they cut it
into two and passed between the pieces. Those who 19
passed between the pieces of the calf were the officers of

Judah and Jerusalem, the eunuchs and priests and all the
20 people of the land. I will give them up to their enemies
who seek their lives, and their bodies shall be food for
21 birds of prey and wild beasts. I will deliver Zedekiah king
of Judah and his officers to their enemies who seek their
lives and to the army of the king of Babylon, which is
22 now raising the siege. I will give the command, says the
LORD, and will bring them back to this city. They shall
attack it and take it and burn it down, and I will make the
cities of Judah desolate and unpeopled.

✻ We do not know precisely what prompted Zedekiah to
rebel against the Babylonians, but it is evident that a major
factor in his decision was the promise of help from the
Egyptians. As a result of his revolt the Babylonians launched
an offensive against Judah in 589 B.C. and it was probably in
this situation, when prospects for the success of the rebellion
looked precarious if not bleak, that the release of the slaves
here recorded took place. Verse 21 is probably to be interpreted as a reference to the advance of Egyptian troops in
588 B.C. which forced the Babylonians to raise the siege of
Jerusalem in order to engage the Egyptian army (cp. 37: 5).
In this situation there may have been renewed optimism in
Jerusalem and this would have prompted the slave-owners to
revoke their decision and so the slaves who had gained their
freedom were forced back into bondage.

That Jeremiah attacked such heinous behaviour on the part
of these slave-owners cannot be doubted. The passage as it
now stands, however, is composed in the characteristic prose
style of the book and contains a number of typical Deuteronomic words and expressions. The 'sermon' also follows the
same form as we have already found in several such 'sermons'
and passages in the book: after an introduction in verses 8-12,

94

the passage contains (a) a proclamation of God's law (verses 13–14); (b) a description of Judah's disobedience to this law (verses 15–16); and (c) the announcement of judgement upon the nation (verses 17–22).

The main theme of the passage is one with which we have already seen the Deuteronomic authors to have been particularly concerned, the nation's disobedience to God's law (cp. the commentary on 7: 1 – 8: 3; 11: 1–17), in this case a specific instance of such disobedience being described (cp. also 17: 19–27 where breach of the law relating to the Sabbath is recorded). As in other similar 'sermons', the purpose of its author was twofold: first, to offer an explanation of why judgement had befallen the nation in 587 B.C. and, second, at the same time to exhort those now living in the shadow of that catastrophe to live according to the requirement of God's law which their fathers had so failed to obey.

8–12. In initiating this reform Zedekiah was possibly seeking to placate God and gain his favour and blessing in the struggle for independence from Babylon. But the shallowness of this apparent desire to obey God's law was soon to be seen. How often men in a crisis perceive what is right and just, only to revert to complacency and injustice when the crisis has passed!

8. *after Zedekiah had made a covenant with all the people in Jerusalem to proclaim an act of freedom for the slaves:* on the manner in which this covenant was made see the comments on verses 18–19 below.

13. *I made a covenant with your forefathers on the day that I brought them out of Egypt, out of the land of slavery:* we are not of course meant to understand that the law governing the release of slaves was the sole content of the terms of the covenant. But it was, the author is declaring, one of the terms of the covenant, so that breach of this law was breach of the covenant. The reference to the exodus is very pointed here: those whose ancestors had once been slaves in Egypt and had been graciously brought out of bondage by God were now

ruthlessly exploiting people in bondage under them. We recall that in the law concerning the release of slaves in Deut. 15: 12–18 the people of Israel are reminded that they had once been slaves in Egypt.

14. *Within seven years each of you shall set free any Hebrew who has sold himself to you as a slave and has served you for six years:* the law requiring the release of Hebrew slaves who had been in service six years is formulated in both Exod. 21: 2–6 and Deut. 15: 12–18. The former does not extend the release to female slaves. But Deut. 15: 12 reads: 'When a fellow-Hebrew, man or woman, sells himself to you as a slave, he shall serve you for six years and in the seventh year you shall set him free.' Since in Jer. 34: 9, 16 both male and female slaves are included it is clear that the author of this passage had the Deuteronomic law in mind. The reason the release of slaves was stipulated for the seventh year was of course because the last year of a seven-year cycle was a sabbatical year, that is, it stood in relation to the previous six years as the seventh day stood in relation to the previous six in the week. In agriculture a farmer had to let his land lie fallow every seventh year. He was not permitted to till his fields in that year or to reap any produce which grew in them during that year (cp. Exod. 23: 10–11; Lev. 25: 3–7). Note also that Deut. 15: 1–4 legislates for the remission of debts of the poor every seven years.

15. *in the house that bears my name:* the covenant in question was made in the temple. It is probably wrong to understand the terms of this covenant to have been limited specifically to the law concerning the release of slaves. No doubt we are to think instead of a ceremony of covenant renewal such as had been carried out by Josiah in 622 B.C. (2 Kings 23: 1 ff.). That is, Zedekiah and the people in general in a solemn ceremony in the temple re-pledged themselves to serve God and obey his laws, of which that demanding the septennial release of slaves was one. On the temple as the place where God's name was believed to dwell see the comment on 7: 10.

17. *I will make you repugnant to all the kingdoms of the earth:* this expression is peculiar, as we have already seen, to Deuteronomy and the prose passages in Jeremiah (cp. the comment on 15: 1–4).

18. *so I will make you like the calf of the covenant when they cut it into two and passed between the pieces:* the method of ratifying the covenant was of very ancient origin. A similar rite is described in the story of the making of the covenant between God and Abraham in Gen. 15. It seems that when the terms of the covenant were proclaimed, animals were slain and halved and placed opposite each other. The people would then have passed between these pieces and in this way expressed a curse upon themselves in the event of the covenant subsequently being broken by them. What had happened to the animals would happen to them. It is possible that the act of walking between the two rows of dismembered animals was accompanied by some such declaration as 'So may the Lord do to us if we do not abide with the terms of this covenant.'

20. *their bodies shall be food for birds of prey and wild beasts:* yet another expression peculiar to Deuteronomy and the prose in Jeremiah (cp. the comment on 7: 33).

21. *which is now raising the siege:* as noted above, the coming of the Egyptian army in 588 B.C. forced the Babylonians to withdraw temporarily from Jerusalem. But this relief for the city was short-lived. ✳

THE EXAMPLE OF THE RECHABITES

The word which came to Jeremiah from the LORD in **35** the days of Jehoiakim son of Josiah, king of Judah: Go and 2 speak to the Rechabites, bring them to one of the rooms in the house of the LORD and offer them wine to drink. So I fetched Jaazaniah son of Jeremiah, son of Habaziniah, 3 with his brothers and all his sons and all the family of the

4 Rechabites. I brought them into the house of the LORD
to the room of the sons of Hanan[a] son of Igdaliah, the
man of God; this adjoins the officers' room above that of
Maaseiah son of Shallum, the keeper of the threshold.
5 I set bowls full of wine and drinking-cups before the
6 Rechabites and invited them to drink wine; but they said,
'We will not drink wine, for our forefather Jonadab son
of Rechab laid this command on us: "You shall never
7 drink wine, neither you nor your children. You shall
not build houses or sow seed or plant vineyards; you shall
have none of these things. Instead, you shall remain tent-
dwellers all your lives, so that you may live long in the
8 land where you are sojourners." We have honoured all
the commands of our forefather Jonadab son of Rechab
and have drunk no wine all our lives, neither we nor our
9 wives, nor our sons, nor our daughters. We have not
built houses to live in, nor have we possessed vineyards
10 or sown fields. We have lived in tents, obeying and
observing all the commands of our forefather Jonadab.
11 But when Nebuchadrezzar king of Babylon invaded the
land we said, "Come, let us go to Jerusalem before the
advancing Chaldaean and Aramaean armies." And we
have stayed in Jerusalem.'

12, 13   Then the word of the LORD came to Jeremiah: These
are the words of the LORD of Hosts the God of Israel:
Go and say to the men of Judah and the inhabitants of
Jerusalem, You must accept correction and obey my
14 words, says the LORD. The command of Jonadab son of
Rechab to his descendants not to drink wine has been
honoured; they have not drunk wine to this day, for

[a] *Or, with one MS.*, the son of Hanan.

they have obeyed their ancestor's command. But I have taken especial pains to warn you and yet you have not obeyed me. I sent my servants the prophets especially to 15 say to you, 'Turn back every one of you from his evil course, mend your ways and cease to follow other gods and worship them; then you shall remain on the land that I have given to you and to your forefathers.' Yet you did not obey or listen to me. The sons of Jonadab son of 16 Rechab have honoured their ancestor's command laid on them, but this people have not listened to me. There- 17 fore, these are the words of the LORD the God of Hosts, the God of Israel: Because they did not listen when I spoke to them, nor answer when I called them, I will bring upon Judah and upon all the inhabitants of Jerusalem the disaster with which I threatened them. To the Rechabites 18 Jeremiah said, These are the words of the LORD of Hosts the God of Israel: Because you have kept the command of Jonadab your ancestor and obeyed all his instructions and carried out all that he told you to do, therefore these 19 are the words of the LORD of Hosts the God of Israel: Jonadab son of Rechab shall not want a descendant to stand before me for all time.

* Like the preceding chapter, this chapter also is primarily concerned with the theme of Israel's disobedience to God's law. The narrative contrasts the loyalty and obedience of the sect of the Rechabites to the laws and 'rule of life' laid down by its founder with Israel's faithlessness to God and wanton disregard for his laws and commands. It cannot be doubted that the narrative is based upon an event in Jeremiah's ministry and that the prophet himself drew the contrast here described between the Rechabites and Israel. By its very nature, however, such a contrast would clearly have been of central significance and pertinence to the Deuteronomic authors, concerned as they were with Israel's disobedience to the law of God. Not surprisingly, therefore, we find that this chapter also has been composed in the typical prose style of the book and provides another example of the manner in which a Deuteronomic author has taken up and described an event in the life of Jeremiah, as well as something the prophet had declared, in order to stress the continued relevance for the nation of the prophet's message on a particular issue. As with other such passages, the Deuteronomic author was concerned with providing an explanation of the catastrophe of 587 B.C., whilst at the same time exhorting the later generation to which he addressed himself to be faithful to God's law which their fore-fathers, as this narrative relates, had so stubbornly disobeyed.

1–11. Jeremiah brings the Rechabites into a room in the temple and offers them wine. Since, however, their rule of life forbade the drinking of wine, they refused the offer.

1. *in the days of Jehoiakim son of Josiah:* the fact that this chapter concerns an event in the reign of Jehoiakim whilst the previous chapter relates events in the reign of his successor Zedekiah is a further indication that the authors and redactors of the book of Jeremiah were not always concerned to arrange the material in chronological order. Where it suited their purposes best, they arranged the oracles, speeches and narra-tives according to themes and motifs which they wished to emphasize and inculcate upon the minds of those to whom they addressed themselves in composing and compiling the different sections and sub-sections of the book. No precise date within Jehoiakim's reign is given. But verse 11 indicates that the event described took place at a time when Babylonian and Aramaean army-units were rampaging through Judah. The attack by these raiding-parties is briefly recorded in 2 Kings 24: 1–2 and took place as a result of a rebellion by Jehoiakim against Nebuchadrezzar after the Babylonians had suffered a temporary set-back at the hands of the Egyptians

late in 601 B.C. Nebuchadrezzar appears to have deployed a number of raiding-parties – 2 Kings 24: 1–2 states that Moabite and Ammonite as well as Babylonian and Aramaean troops were involved – to contain the Judaean rebellion until he had reorganized his forces and could deal decisively with Jehoiakim's revolt. Since he was not able himself to move against Judah until 598 B.C. we can date the activities of these raiding-parties in the period between about 600 and 598 B.C. This in turn provides a date for the event narrated in this chapter.

2. *the Rechabites:* the Hebrew text reads literally 'go to the house of the Rechabites'. But 'house' here does not mean a dwelling but designates the clan or community of the Rechabites. This community was founded by Jonadab son of Rechab who was involved in Jehu's bloody extermination of the house of Ahab in 842 B.C. and the subsequent purge of the worship of Baal which had flourished under the patronage of Ahab's Tyrian wife Jezebel (2 Kings 10: 15–17). From 1 Chron. 2: 55 we learn that the Rechabites were a branch of the Kenites, a semi-nomadic clan which had relations with Israel's ancestors in the desert after the exodus from Egypt. Jonadab represented an ultra-conservative tradition in Israel which refused to adopt or participate in the sedentary, organized Canaanite way of life which the Israelite clans and tribes had gradually and increasingly taken over after their settlement in the land. Instead they regarded themselves as 'sojourners' in the land (Jer. 35: 7) and refused to drink wine or even to engage in the cultivation of grapes (verses 6–7). They also refused to live in houses, continuing instead to be tent-dwellers as their semi-nomadic ancestors had been (verse 7). We must suppose that they also continued to be shepherds, since they refused to engage in any agricultural activity (verse 7). We may note that there were others too in Israel who in some respects shared the Rechabites' rejection of Canaanite life, the Nazirites. These also, as we learn from Num. 6, were pledged to desist from drinking wine and indeed from eating any other produce of the vine.

4. *to the room of the sons of Hanan son of Igdaliah:* we do not know anything about this man Hanan. He is referred to as *the man of God* and since this term was used to describe a prophet it might mean that Hanan had been a prophet, perhaps a prophet who had functioned in the temple cult. If this is so, the *sons of Hanan* may have been his disciples who worked in the temple as a sort of 'guild' of cultic prophets. From the fact that they evidently placed their room at the disposal of Jeremiah we may assume that they were in sympathy with his message. *Maaseiah son of Shallum:* probably to be identified with the father of Zephaniah the priest (cp. 21: 1; 29: 26; 37: 3). *the keeper of the threshold:* from 2 Kings 12: 9 we learn that certain priests were 'keepers of the threshold' of the temple and had duties to perform there. In 2 Kings 25: 18 (= Jer. 52: 24) three such priests are mentioned and it is possible that they were each responsible for one of the three principal entrances to the temple. In ancient Israel, as elsewhere in the ancient Near East generally, sanctuaries and temples had rules and laws governing admission to them. A priest was assigned to the entrance of the shrine or temple and it was his duty to instruct the worshippers and pilgrims of the conditions of admission to the cult in the holy place. It has been suggested that Pss. 15 and 24 were composed as 'entrance liturgies' recited or sung by a procession of worshippers as they approached the entry to the temple in Jerusalem.

5. *I set bowls full of wine and drinking-cups before the Rechabites and invited them to drink wine:* Jeremiah did not simply ask the Rechabites if they would drink wine. He heightened the drama of the occasion and further emphasized the point he wished to make by actually setting a quantity of wine, together with cups with which to drink it, before them. By so doing he graphically symbolized what he wished to declare.

6–10. The Rechabites briefly recite the essentials of their 'rule of life' to which for more than two-and-a-half centuries after their founder Jonadab they had remained, and continued to remain, faithful. Notice how their faithfulness to Jonadab's commands is emphasized by the statement in verse 8 as well as by their declaration in verses 9–10 of obedience to each individual rule of their community. The author in this way further heightens the contrast subsequently to be drawn between the faithfulness of the Rechabites and the disobedience of Israel to God's laws and commands.

11. *And we have stayed in Jerusalem:* the Rechabites explain why they are now in the city, contrary to their normal way of life (cp. verse 10). Their presence in a place which they would normally never have gone to was due to the danger they would be exposed to in the open country at this time.

12–19. The purpose of the exercise with the Rechabites is now stated: their obedience is contrasted with the apostasy and faithlessness of Israel. Needless to say, Jeremiah himself did not subscribe to the Rechabites' 'rule of life' and mode of existence. But that was beside the point for what he wished to do on the occasion here described. Clearly, he held them up to the people as an example of integrity and steadfast obedience to their particular beliefs and code of behaviour; that was nothing but praiseworthy and to be admired, and was a vivid condemnation of the wanton faithlessness and disobedience of Israel to the law and commandments laid down for them by God.

15. *I sent my servants the prophets especially to say to you:* here as elsewhere (cp. 7: 25; 25: 4; 26: 5; 29: 19; 44: 4) the Deuteronomic author of the prose in the book of Jeremiah points to the work of the prophets down through the centuries (cp. 2 Kings 17: 13), sent by God to warn and exhort his people but rejected by them.

19. *Jonadab son of Rechab shall not want a descendant to stand before me for all time:* we cannot be sure that the Rechabites survived the upheaval in Judah brought about by the disaster of 587 B.C. and its aftermath. In Neh. 3: 14 we read of one Malchiah son of Rechab who is said to have repaired the Dung Gate. But this very fact together with the statement in the

same verse that he was ruler of the district of Beth-hakkerem ('the house of the vineyard'!) is already an indication that he certainly no longer lived according to the Rechabite rule of life. We may surmise from this that sheer force of circumstances in later times compelled many Rechabites to abandon or at least modify their ancient and traditional way of life. The expression 'to stand before the Lord' was used to describe priestly service in the temple and there is a Jewish tradition that the Rechabites became engaged in the service of the temple through the marriage of their daughters to priests. But this tradition may well have been prompted by the prophecy in this verse. *

A SCROLL OF JEREMIAH'S ORACLES

* Ch. 36 is usually regarded as being of great importance for our understanding of the origin and growth of the book of Jeremiah, for this narrative is believed to have been written by Baruch as a record of how the earliest 'draft' of the book came into existence. But though the narrative provides us with authentic historical information, it is a mistake to interpret it merely as biographical. Rather, as with other narratives in the book, the main purpose of this one also is theological. The story moves with increasing intensity to its climax in the destruction of the scroll of Jeremiah's oracles by the king, Jehoiakim, the immediate consequence of which is a pronouncement of inevitable judgement upon both king and nation. Thus the central theme of this narrative is one with which we are already familiar (cp. the commentary on ch. 26): the story tells how the word of God spoken by his prophet Jeremiah was rejected by the nation as led by its king. There are a number of striking indications that this narrative was composed by a Deuteronomic author. *

THE SCROLL IS WRITTEN

In the fourth year of Jehoiakim son of Josiah, king of **36**
Judah, this word came to Jeremiah from the LORD: Take 2
a scroll and write on it every word that I have spoken to
you about Jerusalem[a] and Judah and all the nations, from
the day that I first spoke to you in the reign of Josiah down
to the present day. Perhaps the house of Judah will be 3
warned of the calamity that I am planning to bring on
them, and every man will abandon his evil course; then
I will forgive their wrong-doing and their sin. So Jere- 4
miah called Baruch son of Neriah, and he wrote on the
scroll at Jeremiah's dictation all the words which the LORD
had spoken to him. He gave Baruch this instruction: 'I am 5
prevented from going to the LORD's house. You must go 6
there in my place on a fast-day and read the words of the
LORD in the hearing of the people from the scroll you have
written at my dictation. You shall read them in the hearing
of all the men of Judah who come in from their cities.
Then perhaps they will present a petition to the LORD and 7
every man will abandon his evil course; for the LORD
has spoken against this people in great anger and wrath.'
Baruch son of Neriah did all that the prophet Jeremiah 8
had told him to do, and read the words of the LORD in the
LORD's house out of the book.

* Jeremiah is commanded by God to write in a scroll the
oracles he had announced during his ministry up to this time.
The prophet engages the scribe Baruch not only to write the
oracles down, at Jeremiah's dictation, but also to read them in
the temple.

1. *In the fourth year of Jehoiakim:* that is 605/604 B.C. The

[a] *So Sept.; Heb.* Israel.

year 605 B.C. was of momentous significance on the inter-
national scene in the ancient Near East, for in that year the
Babylonians established their supremacy by their crushing
defeat of the Egyptians at Carchemish on the Euphrates.
Subsequently they began their advance into Syria–Palestine.
Almost certainly there was a connection between these events
and the writing of the scroll of Jeremiah's early oracles. For
although we can no longer determine the precise contents of
this scroll, we know that its general nature was one of divine
judgement against Jerusalem and Judah and that it announced
that the instrument of God's judgement was to be the Babylonians (cp. verse 29). From this it becomes clear why the
prophet had his scrolls written down and reproclaimed: the
message of judgement addressed to the nation by Jeremiah
hitherto was on the point of fulfilment: the 'foe from the
north' was on Judah's very doorstep!

2. *Take a scroll:* the scroll was made from either papyrus or
leather. Sheets of papyrus were pasted together to form a long
strip which, like leather, could then be rolled up and easily
stored or carried. Since Jeremiah began his ministry in the
thirteenth year of Josiah (627 B.C.), the scroll would have
contained his oracles delivered over a period of just over
twenty years. *Jerusalem:* the N.E.B. follows the reading of the
Septuagint against the Hebrew text which reads 'Israel'.

3. Cp. the comment on 26: 3.

5. *I am prevented from going to the LORD's house:* we are not
told why Jeremiah himself could not go to the temple to read
the scroll. Perhaps it was because he was for some reason or
other regarded as ritually impure at this time. Probably,
however, it was quite simply because the temple authorities
had banned him as a trouble-maker (cp. 20: 1–6; 26: 7–16).

6. *on a fast-day:* fasts were frequently held in times of crisis.
In choosing a fast-day for the reading of the scroll in the
temple, Jeremiah obviously had in mind the large crowd
which would have assembled there on such an occasion (cp.
verse 9). ✳

THE READING OF THE SCROLL

In the ninth month of the fifth year of the reign of 9
Jehoiakim son of Josiah, king of Judah, all the people in
Jerusalem and all who came there from the cities of
Judah proclaimed a fast before the LORD. Then Baruch 10
read Jeremiah's words in the house of the LORD out of the
book in the hearing of all the people; he read them from
the room of Gemariah son of the adjutant-general
Shaphan in the upper court at the entrance to the new
gate of the LORD's house. Micaiah son of Gemariah, son 11
of Shaphan, heard all the words of the LORD out of the
book and went down to the palace, to the adjutant- 12
general's room where all the officers were gathered –
Elishama the adjutant-general, Delaiah son of Shemaiah,
Elnathan son of Akbor, Gemariah son of Shaphan,
Zedekiah son of Hananiah and all the other officers. There 13
Micaiah repeated all the words he had heard when
Baruch read out of the book in the people's hearing. Then 14
the officers sent Jehudi son of Nethaniah, son of Shelemiah,
son of Cushi, to Baruch with this message: 'Come here
and bring the scroll from which you read in the people's
hearing.' So Baruch son of Neriah brought the scroll to
them, and they said, 'Sit down and*a* read it to us.' When 15, 16
they heard what he read, they turned to each other trembling and said,*b* 'We must report this to the king.' They 17
asked Baruch to tell them how he had come to write all
this.*c* He said to them, 'Jeremiah dictated every word of 18
it to me, and I wrote it down in ink in the book.' The 19

[a] Sit down and: *or* This time.
[b] *So Sept.; Heb. adds* to Baruch.
[c] *So Sept., Heb. adds* at his dictation.

officers said to Baruch, 'You and Jeremiah must go into
20 hiding so that no one may know where you are.' When
they had deposited the scroll in the room of Elishama the
adjutant-general, they went to the court and reported
everything to the king.

✻ Baruch reads the scroll in the temple on the chosen occasion.
The reaction of the congregation is not mentioned (contrast
26: 7–9). Instead, our attention is immediately focused on one
Micaiah who goes to the palace and reports what he has heard
to some of his fellow state-officials. By this means the narrative acquires increased urgency and our anticipation of the
ensuing events is heightened.

9. *In the ninth month of the fifth year:* we may surmise that the
scroll had been completed some time before this in readiness
for such an occasion as the fast now being held. There is some
evidence that in this month the Babylonians captured Ashkelon, a city on the coastal plain and one of the five cities of
the Philistines, and we may assume that it was the alarm caused
by this in Jerusalem and throughout Judah which led to the
proclamation of a day of national fasting.

10. *Gemariah:* evidently yet another son of Shaphan who
played such a prominent part in Josiah's reformation in 622
B.C. Verse 24 indicates that Gemariah was probably in
sympathy with Jeremiah's message. Another son of Shaphan,
Ahikam, is mentioned in 26: 24 and also appears to have been
well disposed towards Jeremiah. *at the entrance to the new gate:*
cp. the note on 26: 10.

11–16. Micaiah hears the scroll and brings a report of it to
various state officials in the palace. They give orders for
Baruch to be brought before them and, having heard the
contents of the scroll for themselves, *turned to each other
trembling.* They thereupon decide to bring the issue before the
king.

18. *Jeremiah dictated every word of it to me:* the prophetic

authority for the words and message of the scroll is affirmed and stressed.

19. *You and Jeremiah must go into hiding:* evidently these officials had little confidence that Jehoiakim would share their convictions about the prophet's message and in the knowledge of how he was likely to react to it (cp. 26: 20–4) caution Baruch, and through him Jeremiah, to go into hiding. It was a caution which turned out to have been well advised (cp. verse 26). By recording this, the narrator again heightens our anticipation of what is to follow; we sense already what Jehoiakim's reaction is to be. ✷

JEHOIAKIM DESTROYS THE SCROLL

The king sent Jehudi to fetch the scroll. When he had 21 fetched it from the room of Elishama the adjutant-general, he read it to the king and to all the officers in attendance. It was the ninth month of the year, and the king was 22 sitting in his winter apartments with a fire burning in a brazier in front of him. When Jehudi had read three or 23 four columns of the scroll, the king cut them off with a penknife and threw them into the fire in the brazier. He went on doing so until the whole scroll had been thrown on the fire. Neither the king nor any of his 24 courtiers who heard these words showed any fear or rent their clothes; and though Elnathan, Delaiah, and Gemariah 25 begged the king not to burn the scroll, he would not listen to them. The king then ordered Jerahmeel, a royal prince,[a] 26 Seraiah son of Azriel, and Shelemiah son of Abdeel to fetch the scribe Baruch and the prophet Jeremiah; but the LORD had hidden them.

[a] a royal prince: *or* the king's deputy.

✻ The climax of the narrative is now reached: the king destroys the scroll and so rejects the word of God announced by Jeremiah.

21. *The king sent Jehudi to fetch the scroll:* that the officials did not bring the scroll with them for their audience with the king is a further anticipatory indication of what Jehoiakim was about to do with it.

22. *his winter apartments:* state rooms in the palace which afforded warmth during the winter. We may presume that during the hot summer, other state rooms which afforded shade and cool from the heat of the sun were used by the king.

23. *the king cut them off with a penknife and threw them into the fire:* in destroying the scroll, Jehoiakim must not be thought of as merely expressing his contempt for Jeremiah and his message. What he sought to do was to nullify the power of the prophet's woeful words. Jeremiah's subsequent rewriting of the scroll (cp. verses 27-32) was to ensure that they remained in force. The action of both the king and the prophet were 'symbolic actions' (cp. the commentary on 19: 10 and 28: 10).

24. It seems likely that the narrative in this chapter was consciously composed as a parallel to 2 Kings 22 with the primary intention of pointing to the contrast between the reaction of Jehoiakim to the word of God and that of his revered father Josiah whose humble obedience to 'the book of the law' is recorded there. (Note the contrast drawn between these two kings in Jer. 22: 13-17.) The broad outline of both narratives is strikingly similar. In both of them we read of a scroll, in the one a scroll of the law and in the other a scroll of prophetic oracles, which began its public history, so to speak, in the temple (2 Kings 22: 8; Jer. 36: 10). In both instances the scroll first comes into the hands of a state official (2 Kings 22: 9f.; Jer. 36: 10f.). Both narratives record the reaction of the king (2 Kings 22: 11-13; Jer. 36: 23-6) and both give a prominent place to a prophetic oracle which followed that reaction (2 Kings 22: 15-20; Jer. 36: 28-31). There appears to be a very deliberate contrast drawn between

Josiah and Jehoiakim, for we read in 2 Kings 22: 11 (cp. verse 19) 'When the king heard what was in the book of the law, *he rent his clothes*', whilst Jer. 36: 24 records 'Neither the king nor any of his courtiers who heard these words showed any fear or *rent their clothes*.'

26. What the fate of both Jeremiah and Baruch would have been at the hands of Jehoiakim may be gathered from 26: 20–3. ✻

THE SCROLL IS RE-WRITTEN

After the king had burnt the scroll with all that Baruch 27 had written on it at Jeremiah's dictation, the word of the LORD came to Jeremiah: Now take another scroll and 28 write on it all the words that were on the first scroll which Jehoiakim king of Judah burnt. You shall say to 29 Jehoiakim king of Judah, These are the words of the LORD: You burnt this scroll and said, Why have you written here that the king of Babylon shall come and destroy this land and exterminate both men and beasts? Therefore these are the words of the LORD about Jehoia- 30 kim king of Judah: He shall have no one to succeed him on the throne of David, and his dead body shall be exposed to scorching heat by day and frost by night. I will punish 31 him and also his offspring and his courtiers for their wickedness, and I will bring down on them and on the inhabitants of Jerusalem and on the men of Judah all the calamities with which I threatened them, and to which they turned a deaf ear. Then Jeremiah took another scroll 32 and gave it to the scribe Baruch son of Neriah, who wrote on it at Jeremiah's dictation all the words of the book which Jehoiakim king of Judah had burnt; and much else was added to the same effect.

* By destroying the scroll Jehoiakim has rejected the word of God and, since he is king and leader of the nation, his rejection, as understood in this narrative, betokens and epitomizes the nation's rejection of it. There is now no hope and the purpose for which the scroll was compiled in the first place (cp. verse 3) has not been achieved. Both king and nation are now faced with inevitable doom.

32. *Then Jeremiah took another scroll:* as a sign and witness to the judgement declared against the nation, Jeremiah has his oracles rewritten: God's word stands and will find fulfilment. *and much else was added to the same effect:* we may understand this as a reference to Jeremiah's oracles and sayings in the years after the events recorded in this chapter. *

THE LAST YEARS OF JUDAH

* Chs. 37–45 form a further major section of the book of Jeremiah. They record the history of the last years of Judah from the reign of Zedekiah to the flight to Egypt of the 'remnant' left in the land after the catastrophe of 587 B.C. As such these chapters cover the same period as the narrative in 2 Kings 24: 18 – 25: 26 but provide much more information than the latter. In particular, whereas the narrative in Kings makes no mention of Jeremiah, these chapters describe the part played by him during the last years of Judah and the period in the land immediately following 587 B.C.

These chapters form the sequel to chs. 26–36. In the latter the main theme is the nation's rejection of the word of God proclaimed by Jeremiah. This rejection is confirmed in chs. 37-8 by the attempt to kill the prophet himself, the bearer of God's word. But both the word of God and his messenger are vindicated; the judgement decreed by God through Jeremiah is violently realized in the downfall of Judah and the destruction of Jerusalem and the prophet is released from prison (ch. 39). Chs. 40-4 centre on the history of the community left in Judah by the Babylonians after 587 B.C. and its eventual

flight to Egypt. The purpose of these chapters is to show that
the hope for the future of the nation did not lie either in the
land of Judah itself or amongst those who fled to Egypt; the
true 'remnant' of the nation through whom renewal was to
come was the community in exile in Babylon. Ch. 45 is an
'appendix' recording the promise of divine protection given
to Jeremiah's faithful scribe Baruch. ✳

INEVITABLE DISASTER

King Zedekiah son of Josiah was set on the throne of **37**
Judah by Nebuchadrezzar king of Babylon, in succession
to Coniah son of Jehoiakim. Neither he nor his courtiers 2
nor the people of the land listened to the words which the
LORD spoke through the prophet Jeremiah.

King Zedekiah sent Jehucal[a] son of Shelemiah and the 3
priest Zephaniah son of Maaseiah to the prophet Jeremiah
to say to him, 'Pray for us to the LORD our God.' At the 4
time Jeremiah was free to come and go among the people;
he had not yet been thrown into prison. Meanwhile, 5
Pharaoh's army had marched out of Egypt, and when the
Chaldaeans who were besieging Jerusalem heard of it
they raised the siege. Then this word came from the 6
LORD to the prophet Jeremiah: These are the words of the 7
LORD the God of Israel: Say to the king of Judah who sent
you to consult me, Pharaoh's army which marched out to
help you is on its way back to Egypt, its own land, and 8
the Chaldaeans will return to the attack. They will capture
this city and burn it to the ground. These are the words 9
of the LORD: Do not deceive yourselves, do not imagine
that the Chaldaeans will go away and leave you alone.

[a] Jucal in 38: 1

10 They will not go; for even if you defeated the whole Chaldaean force with which you are now fighting, and only the wounded were left lying in their tents, they would rise and burn down the city.

⁎ Zedekiah consults Jeremiah and asks him to pray for the deliverance of the nation from the Babylonians. But the prophet's reply is that the defeat and subjugation of Judah by the Babylonians is inevitable, irrevocably decreed by God. Nothing can prevent it now.

1-2. These two verses form a superscription to the narrative contained in chs. 37-45. Zedekiah's appointment as king by Nebuchadrezzar (cp. 2 Kings 24: 17) is noted and followed by a summary of the new king's response and that of the nation to the word of God announced by Jeremiah. This serves to link this new section with chs. 26-36 and at the same time acts as an anticipation of what is recorded in the ensuing chapters.

3-10. What is here described may be based upon the same event as is recorded in 21: 1-7, though there are a number of differences between the two passages. The inevitability and vehemence of the judgement announced against Judah are here fully brought out. The raising of the siege of Jerusalem by the Babylonians was merely temporary. Nothing can prevent the overthrow of Jerusalem; even if, as the result of battle, the Babylonians were left with nothing more than wounded troops, a situation which in any other circumstances would lead to the withdrawal of the army (cp. 2 Kings 19: 35-7), they would be sufficient to take and destroy Jerusalem.

4. *At the time Jeremiah was free to come and go among the people:* after his arrest and imprisonment recorded subsequently in this chapter, Jeremiah remained confined until the downfall of Jerusalem in 587 B.C.

5. *Meanwhile, Pharaoh's army had marched out of Egypt:* this was probably in the summer of 588 B.C. But the relief of

Jerusalem which it brought was short-lived. The Babylonians quickly dealt with the Egyptian threat and were soon again attacking Jerusalem.

8. *They will capture this city and burn it to the ground:* at a time when morale would probably have been boosted, if only a little, by the withdrawal of the Babylonians from Jerusalem, a message such as this delivered by Jeremiah would assuredly have raised bitter and violent antagonism against him. The record of his arrest and imprisonment which follows (verses 11–21) is scarcely surprising. ✳

JEREMIAH'S LIFE IN PERIL

When the Chaldaean army had raised the siege of 11 Jerusalem because of the advance of Pharaoh's army, Jeremiah was on the point of leaving Jerusalem to go into 12 Benjamite territory and take possession of his patrimony in the presence of the people there. Irijah son of Shele- 13 miah, son of Hananiah, the officer of the guard, was in the Benjamin Gate when Jeremiah reached it, and he arrested the prophet, accusing him of going over to the Chaldaeans. 'It is a lie,' said Jeremiah; 'I am not going 14 over to the Chaldaeans.' Irijah would not listen to him but arrested him and brought him before the officers. The 15 officers were indignant with Jeremiah; they flogged him and imprisoned him in the house of Jonathan the scribe, which they had converted into a prison; for Jeremiah 16 had been put into a vaulted pit beneath the house, and here he remained for a long time.

King Zedekiah had Jeremiah brought to him and con- 17 sulted him privately in the palace, asking him if there was a word from the LORD. 'Indeed there is,' said Jeremiah; 'you shall fall into the hands of the king of Babylon.'

18 Then Jeremiah said to King Zedekiah, 'What wrong have I done to you or your courtiers or this people? Why have 19 you thrown me into prison? Where are your prophets who prophesied that the king of Babylon would not 20 attack you or your country? I pray you now, my lord king, give me a hearing and let my petition be presented: do not send me back to the house of Jonathan the scribe, 21 or I shall die there.' Then King Zedekiah gave the order and Jeremiah was committed to the court of the guard-house and was granted a daily ration of one loaf from the Street of the Bakers, until the bread in the city was all gone. So Jeremiah remained in the court of the guard-house.

* The events here recorded must have taken place very shortly after what is reported in verses 1-10, especially since it is probable that the Babylonians routed the Egyptian army in a matter of a few weeks.

12. *and take possession of his patrimony: patrimony* translates an obscure Hebrew word which the N.E.B. understands as a technical term relating to the legal rights of one claiming inheritance of ancestral property. Since, as the context indicates, the attempt of the prophet to journey to his native town took place before his imprisonment, the patrimony in question cannot have been connected with the event recorded in ch. 32 which took place after his imprisonment and at a time when the Babylonian siege of Jerusalem had been renewed.

13. *the Benjamin Gate* (cp. 38: 7): this gate was probably in the north wall of the city and was possibly so called simply because it led to the territory of the tribe of Benjamin north of Jerusalem. *and he arrested the prophet, accusing him of going over to the Chaldaeans:* in view of Jeremiah's own message of certain victory for the Babylonians, as well as the fact that

a number of Judaeans did defect to the enemy (cp. 38: 19; 52: 15), Irijah's accusation was understandable. Other grounds for his arrest and imprisonment are recorded in ch. 38 (see the commentary on this chapter).

15. *in the house of Jonathan the scribe:* why it was necessary to convert this man's house into a prison is not known. It has been suggested that it was because other places of detention were already full or, alternatively, that this house was being used as a 'maximum-security' prison.

16. *a vaulted pit beneath the house:* the Hebrew is literally 'to the house of the pit (*or* cistern) and to the vaults'. What the precise meaning of the phrase is is obscure, but it is clear that Jeremiah was imprisoned in an underground dungeon. Evidently the chances of survival in it were slender (cp. verse 20).

17. *and consulted him privately in the palace:* there are indications that Zedekiah was convinced, at least at times, of the truth of Jeremiah's message and counsel (cp. 38: 14–28). Here he reveals his deep anxiety about the situation and privately consults the prophet, only to receive the terse, sharp reply that his fate was sealed.

18–21. Jeremiah makes a successful plea to the king not to be sent back to the prison in the house of Jonathan. He is sent instead to 'the court of the guard-house' where conditions were better. (This was probably more a place of detention than a prison.) At the same time provision is made for his food.

21. *the Street of the Bakers:* probably this is an indication that in ancient Jerusalem individual streets were allocated to, or taken over as places of business by, people engaged in the same trade, an arrangement still to be found in modern cities such as Athens. *until the bread in the city was all gone:* that is, until the collapse of Jerusalem to the Babylonians (cp. 38: 28). *

ANOTHER NARRATIVE OF JEREMIAH'S IMPRISONMENT

✻ The major problem in ch. 38 concerns the relationship between the events there recorded and those narrated in 37: 11–21, which are strikingly similar: the prophet is arrested and imprisoned in an underground pit or cistern where conditions are such that anyone confined there would perish; some time later, however, he is released and privately consulted by Zedekiah, the content of the conversation between the king and the prophet being substantially the same in both narratives; subsequently Jeremiah is not sent back to the underground prison but is detained henceforth in the court of the guard-house where, it seems, he remained in relative safety until the city fell to the Babylonians (cp. 37: 21; 38: 28). So similar is the broad pattern as well as some of the details of what is recorded in these two narratives that it is probable that they are both, in spite of some obvious differences, based upon one and the same course of events. This probability is further strengthened by the fact that 37: 21, with its implication that Jeremiah having been rescued from certain death was henceforth detained apparently without further serious threat or danger to his life, is surely contradicted by what is then narrated in ch. 38. In addition, although the underground prison in which Jeremiah was confined is described in 38: 6 (Hebrew text; see the note on this verse below) as the pit or cistern of Malchiah the king's son and to have been located in the court of the guard-house, 38: 26 clearly implies that it was the same as in 37: 11–16, that is, the house of Jonathan. On balance, therefore, it seems best to regard ch. 38 and 37: 11–21 to be divergent accounts of one and the same course of events. ✻

ARREST AND IMPRISONMENT

Shephatiah son of Mattan, Gedaliah son of Pashhur, **38** Jucal son of Shelemiah, and Pashhur son of Malchiah heard what Jeremiah was saying to all the people: These 2 are the words of the LORD: Whoever remains in this city shall die by sword, by famine, or by pestilence, but whoever goes out to surrender to the Chaldaeans shall survive; he shall survive, he shall take home his life and nothing more.[a] These are the words of the LORD: This city will 3 fall into the hands of the king of Babylon's army, and they will capture it. Then the officers said to the king, 4 'The man must be put to death. By talking in this way he is discouraging the soldiers and the rest of the people left in the city. He is pursuing not the people's welfare but their ruin.' King Zedekiah said, 'He is in your hands; 5 the king is powerless against you.' So they took Jeremiah 6 and threw him into the pit,[b] in the court of the guardhouse, letting him down with ropes. There was no water in the pit, only mud, and Jeremiah sank in the mud.

✳ The most significant difference between ch. 38 and 37: 11–21 lies in their descriptions of the circumstances of Jeremiah's arrest. In this respect the two narratives are irreconcilable and any attempt to 'harmonize' them is futile. Nor is it possible to determine which of the two descriptions of the prophet's arrest here recorded is historically authentic, since either is perfectly plausible.

2. *he shall take home his life and nothing more:* cp. the comment on 21: 9.

4. *he is discouraging the soldiers:* literally translated, the Hebrew is 'he is weakening the hands of the soldiers'. One

[a] See note on 21: 9.
[b] Prob. rdg.; Heb. adds Malchiah son (or deputy) of the king.

of the Lachish letters (cp. the note on 34: 7) makes the same accusation against certain defeatist elements among the officials in Jerusalem. Since the death penalty is demanded by Jeremiah's accusers, it is clear that the charge brought against him was, in effect, treason.

5. *the king is powerless against you:* a further indication that affairs were no longer, if indeed they ever had been, under the control of Zedekiah who here, as elsewhere, weakly yields to a power group among his state officials (see pp. 7–8. Cp. the note on verses 25–6 below).

6. *So they took Jeremiah and threw him into the pit:* the Hebrew text describes this pit as the pit of Malchiah the king's son (cp. N.E.B. footnote). This appears to be contradicted by verse 26. Either we should omit, with the N.E.B., the reference to Malchiah in verse 6 and understand the pit here mentioned to be the same as that referred to in 37: 11–16, on the grounds that the house of Jonathan possibly belonged to the same complex of buildings as the guard-house; or, alternatively, it may be that the cistern referred to was located in the house of Jonathan, but was popularly known, for some reason or other, as the cistern of Malchiah. ✳

THE TIMELY INTERVENTION OF A JUST MAN

7-8 Now Ebed-melech the Cushite, a eunuch, who was in the palace, heard that they had thrown Jeremiah into the pit and went to tell the king, who was seated in the

9 Benjamin Gate. 'Your majesty,' he said, 'these men have shown great wickedness in their treatment of the prophet Jeremiah. They have thrown him into the pit, and when there is no more bread in the city he will die of hunger

10 where he lies.' Thereupon the king told Ebed-melech the Cushite to take three[a] men with him and hoist

[a] *So one MS.; others* thirty.

Jeremiah out of the pit before he died. So Ebed-melech 11
went to the palace with the men and took some tattered,
cast-off clothes from the wardrobe[a] and let them down
with ropes to Jeremiah in the pit. Ebed-melech the Cushite 12
said to Jeremiah, 'Put these old clothes under your arm-
pits to ease the ropes.' Jeremiah did this, and they pulled 13
him up out of the pit with the ropes; and he remained in
the court of the guard-house.

* Another royal official, in this instance an Ethiopian named
Ebed-melech, takes quick action to rescue Jeremiah from
certain death. For this, Ebed-melech is subsequently promised
safety and deliverance from the coming destruction of Jerusalem (cp. 39: 15–18). Nothing of this rescue is mentioned in
37: 17–21 where it is simply stated that the king sent for the
prophet, who was brought from the dungeon to Zedekiah,
who then acceded to Jeremiah's plea not to be sent back to the
dungeon.

7–8. *Ebed-melech:* the name means literally 'servant of the
king' but is here a proper name. *the king, who was seated in the
Benjamin Gate:* it is possible that the king was here to hear and
adjudicate in law cases – law suits were regularly conducted
in the city gate (cp. 2 Sam. 15: 2–4) – or quite simply to inspect
the defences of the city. On *the Benjamin Gate* cp. the note on
37: 13.

11. *the wardrobe:* the Hebrew means literally 'to beneath the
treasury'. By omitting the word for treasury and slightly
emending the Hebrew word 'to beneath', the obviously more
suitable reading *the wardrobe* is achieved. The word, as
emended, is found in 2 Kings 10: 22. *

[a] the wardrobe: *prob. rdg.; Heb.* underneath the treasury.

THE KING AND THE PROPHET

14 King Zedekiah had the prophet Jeremiah brought to him by the third entrance to the LORD's house and said to him, 'I want to ask you something; hide nothing from
15 me.' Jeremiah answered, 'If I speak out, you will certainly put me to death; if I offer you any advice, you will not
16 take it.' But King Zedekiah swore to Jeremiah privately, 'By the life of the LORD who gave us our lives, I will not put you to death, nor will I hand you over to these men
17 who are seeking to take your life.' Jeremiah said to Zedekiah, 'These are the words of the LORD the God of Hosts, the God of Israel: If you go out and surrender to the officers of the king of Babylon, you shall live and this city shall not be burnt down; you and your family shall
18 live. But if you do not surrender to the officers of the king of Babylon, the city shall fall into the hands of the Chaldaeans, and they shall burn it down, and you will not
19 escape them.' King Zedekiah said to Jeremiah, 'I am afraid of the Judaeans who have gone over to the enemy. I fear the Chaldaeans will give me up to them and I shall
20 be roughly handled.' Jeremiah answered, 'They will not give you up. If you obey the LORD in everything I tell
21 you, all will be well with you and you shall live. But if you refuse to go out and surrender, this is what the LORD
22 has shown me: all the women left in the king of Judah's palace will be led out to the officers of the king of Babylon and they will say:

> Your own friends have misled you
> and have been too strong for you;

they have let your feet sink in the mud
and have turned away and left you.

All your women and children will be led out to the 23
Chaldaeans, and you will not escape; you will be seized
by the king of Babylon and this city will be burnt down.'
Zedekiah said to Jeremiah, 'Let no one know about this, 24
and you shall not be put to death. If the officers hear that 25
I have been speaking with you and they come to you and
say, "Tell us what you said to the king and what he said
to you; hide nothing from us, and we will not put you
to death", then answer, "I was presenting a petition to 26
the king not to send me back to the house of Jonathan to
die there."' The officers all came to Jeremiah and 27
questioned him, and he said to them just what the king
had told him to say; so their talk came to an end and
they were none the wiser. Jeremiah remained in the court 28
of the guard-house till the day Jerusalem fell.[a]

✻ In spite of the peril into which his preaching has brought
him, Jeremiah unrelentingly announces again to Zedekiah that
only immediate surrender to the Babylonians can save the
nation.

19. *I am afraid of the Judaeans who have gone over to the enemy:*
such defectors are mentioned in 39: 9 and 52: 15. Zedekiah's
fear implies that not a few had deserted to the Babylonians.

22. This short poetic fragment has all the appearance of
having been part of a psalm. The motif of being betrayed by
friends is found, for example, in Ps. 41: 9 (cp. also Jer. 20: 10),
whilst the imagery of sinking in mud is found in Ps. 69: 14.
Almost certainly the author of this chapter intends us to see a
connection between the fate of Zedekiah described in this

[a] *So Sept.; Heb. adds* when Jerusalem was captured.

verse and the rescue of Jeremiah described in verses 7-13. Verse 6 records that Jeremiah was imprisoned in a waterless pit and that he 'sank in the mud'. In other places in the Old Testament 'the pit' is used as a symbol of the place of the dead from which only divine protection can deliver one (cp. for example Ps. 28: 1; Isa. 38: 18). Hence God through Ebed-melech delivers his servant Jeremiah from the pit and from death, whilst on the other hand and by contrast the fate that might have been Jeremiah's is applied to Zedekiah in verse 22.

25–6. Zedekiah's evident fear lest certain of his officials should hear that he had conferred with Jeremiah about what to do in the face of the Babylonian siege is further evidence that this king was not now, if he ever had been, master of his own house (cp. the note on 38: 5). ✻

THE FALL OF JERUSALEM

39 ₁ᵃ In the tenth month of the ninth year of the reign of Zedekiah king of Judah, Nebuchadrezzar advanced with all his army against Jerusalem, and they laid siege to it.

2 In the fourth month of the eleventh year of Zedekiah, on the ninth day of the month, the city was thrown open.

3 All the officers of the king of Babylon came in and took their seats in the middle gate: Nergalsarezer of Simmagir, Nebusarsekimᵇ the chief eunuch,ᶜ Nergalsarezer the commander of the frontier troops,ᵈ and all the other

4 officers of the king of Babylon. When Zedekiah king of Judah saw them, he and all his armed escort left the city and fled by night by way of the king's garden through the gate called Between the Two Walls. They escaped

[a] *Verses 1–10: cp. 52: 4–16 and 2 Kgs. 25: 1–12.*
[b] *Probably a different form of Nebushazban (verse 13).*
[c] the chief eunuch: *or* Rab-saris.
[d] the commander. . .troops: *or* Rab-mag.

towards the Arabah, but the Chaldaean army pursued 5
them and overtook Zedekiah in the lowlands of Jericho.
The king was seized and brought before Nebuchadrezzar
king of Babylon at Riblah in the land of Hamath, and he
pleaded his case before him. The king of Babylon slew 6
Zedekiah's sons before his eyes at Riblah; he also put to
death the nobles of Judah. Then Zedekiah's eyes were put 7
out, and he was bound in fetters of bronze to be brought
to Babylon. The Chaldaeans burnt the royal palace and 8
the house of the LORD and the houses[a] of the people, and
pulled down the walls of Jerusalem. Nebuzaradan captain 9
of the bodyguard deported to Babylon the rest of the
people left in the city, those who had deserted to him and
any remaining artisans.[b] At the same time the captain of 10
the guard left behind the weakest class of the people, those
who owned nothing at all, and made them vine-dressers
and labourers.

☀ Ch. 39: 1–14 records the downfall of Jerusalem in 587 B.C.,
the fate of Zedekiah as well as of his sons and those who fled
with the king from the city as the Babylonians invaded it, and
the release of Jeremiah from prison in the court of the guard-
house. Verses 1–10 are substantially the same as 52: 4–16 (see
the commentary on this passage) and 2 Kings 25: 1–12. But
its position here in Jer. 39 is obviously apt. The nation had
rejected the word of God proclaimed to it by Jeremiah (chs.
26–36) and had sought to destroy the prophet himself (chs.
37–8). The judgement declared against Judah and Jerusalem
was now violently realized.

Verse 3, which is not found in either 52: 4–16 or 2 Kings
25: 1–12, is out of place in its present context. This verse has all

[a] of the LORD and the houses: *prob. rdg.; Heb. om.*
[b] artisans: *prob. rdg., cp. 52: 15; Heb.* people who were left.

the appearance of having originally come immediately before verse 14, both verses thus providing a brief record of the release of Jeremiah from prison after which he joined the community left in Judah by the Babylonians under the newly appointed governor, Gedaliah, at Mizpah. It is also probable that the last part of 38: 28 – 'when Jerusalem was captured' (cp. the N.E.B. footnote on this verse) – was originally the introduction to this brief record. Taken together in this way 38: 28*b* + 39: 3, 14 read: 'When Jerusalem was captured, all the officers of the king of Babylon came in and took their seats in the middle gate: Nergalsarezer of Simmagir, Nebusarsekim the chief eunuch, Nergalsarezer the commander of the frontier troops, and all the other officers of the king of Babylon. They fetched Jeremiah from the court of the guard-house and handed him over to Gedaliah son of Ahikam, son of Shaphan, to take him out to the residence. So he stayed with his own people.' It is best to understand 39: 11–12 in connection with 40: 1–6. The command given by Nebuchadrezzar to Nebuzaradan in 39: 12 to 'do for him (Jeremiah) whatever he says' is carried out in 40: 4–5 but not in 39: 14 where Jeremiah is not consulted about his future. We should then probably understand 39: 13 as having been composed to form a connection between verses 11–12 and 14 when these were combined to form the passage as it now stands.

2. *In the fourth month of the eleventh year of Zedekiah*: if the last year of Zedekiah's reign was 587 B.C. (it is disputed whether it was this year or 586 B.C.), the details here given indicate that Jerusalem was occupied by the Babylonians and destroyed in July of that year.

3. *Nergalsarezer of Simmagir*: the Hebrew text understands the word here translated *Simmagir* together with the first part of the next name (*nebu*) as a personal name (cp. the Authorized Version translation of it as Samgar-nebo). We now know, however, that Simmagir was the name of a district in Babylon over which Nergalsarezer was governor. It is possible that the two Nergalsarezers mentioned in this verse are one and the

same person, since there is no mention of *Nergalsarezer of Simmagir* in verse 13. But the name Nergalsarezer was not uncommon in Babylon and it is equally possible, as the text indicates, that they were two separate officials. On the other hand, since *Nebusarsekim* in this verse and *Nebushazban* in verse 13 are both designated as *the chief eunuch*, it is probable that they are simply different names of the same individual, or perhaps the first is a corruption of the second. Amel-Marduk, Nebuchadrezzar's son and successor (562–560 B.C.), was replaced, probably by a *coup d'état*, by his brother-in-law Neriglissar (= Nergalsarezer) and it is possible that this king is to be identified with *Nergalsarezer the commander of the frontier troops*.

4. *When Zedekiah king of Judah saw them:* the *them* here refers to the officials mentioned in verse 3. If, as seems likely (see above), verse 3 was not originally here, the *them* would have referred to Nebuchadrezzar and his army mentioned in verse 1. But by a slight change in the Hebrew *them* can be read as 'it' or 'this', so that before the insertion of verse 3, verse 4 would have begun 'When Zedekiah saw *it* (or *this*)', i.e. when he saw that the city had now finally collapsed. *They escaped towards the Arabah:* that is, to the Jordan valley. Whether Zedekiah was going into hiding here or was intending to go further east across the Jordan is impossible to say.

5. *Riblah in the land of Hamath:* Riblah was an ancient Syrian town to the south of Kadesh on the river Orontes. Being situated where the military highways between Egypt and Mesopotamia crossed, it was a convenient and strategic halting-place and base for Nebuchadrezzar.

6–7. Zedekiah's horrific fate of having his eyes put out as punishment for his crimes against the Babylonians was made all the more horrific by the fact that the last sight he saw was the execution of his sons. The king was taken to prison in Babylon where he died (cp. 52: 11). In view of the physical and mental torture inflicted upon him, we may surmise that his death came soon.

8. *the royal palace and the house of the LORD and the houses of the people:* the Hebrew text reads 'the royal palace and the house of the people' and it has been suggested that 'the house of the people' may refer to a general assembly hall or council building. But the reading proposed and adopted by the N.E.B. is to be preferred and is supported by 52: 13.

9. *any remaining artisans:* this reading is based upon 52: 15 and makes better sense than the repetition in the Hebrew text of 'the people who were left' (cp. the N.E.B. footnote). *

THE RELEASE OF JEREMIAH FROM PRISON

11 Nebuchadrezzar king of Babylon sent orders about
12 Jeremiah to[a] Nebuzaradan captain of the guard. 'Take him,' he said; 'take special care of him, and do him no
13 harm of any kind, but do for him whatever he says.' So Nebuzaradan captain of the guard sent Nebushazban the chief eunuch, Nergalsarezer the commander of the frontier troops, and all the chief officers of the king of
14 Babylon, and they fetched Jeremiah from the court of the guard-house and handed him over to Gedaliah son of Ahikam, son of Shaphan, to take him out to the Residence. So he stayed with his own people.

15 The word of the LORD had come to Jeremiah while he
16 was under arrest in the court of the guard-house: Go and say to Ebed-melech the Cushite, These are the words of the LORD of Hosts the God of Israel: I will make good the words I have spoken against this city, foretelling ruin and not prosperity, and when that day comes you will be there
17 to see it: But I will preserve you on that day, says the LORD, and you shall not be handed over to the men you
18 fear. I will keep you safe and you shall not fall a victim

[a] So *Vulg.*; *Heb.* by.

to the sword; because you trusted in me you shall escape, you shall take home your life and nothing more.[a] This is the very word of the LORD.

✻ As already noted, 38: 28b + 39: 3, 14 and 39: 11–12 + 40: 1–6 are best understood as originally two separate accounts of Jeremiah's release from prison. As now arranged, 39: 11–14 provides a record of the vindication of Jeremiah's words: God has been true to his promise to protect the prophet's life (cp. 1: 8). The section 40: 1–6 now provides an introduction to the story of Gedaliah.

14. *to take him out to the Residence:* the Hebrew text 'to bring him out to the house' is ambiguous. The 'house' obviously cannot refer to either the temple, which is sometimes referred to simply as 'the house', or to the palace. Furthermore, since it is 'the house' and not 'his house' it is unlikely that it refers to either Jeremiah's own house or Gedaliah's. Perhaps therefore we should think in terms of a building designated by the Babylonians as the headquarters of the new administration under Gedaliah and thus a sort of 'Governor's Residence' which formed the focal point of the community under his governorship at Mizpah.

15–18. This promise to Ebed-melech that he would survive the coming destruction of Jerusalem probably originally followed immediately after 38: 13. It was possibly placed at the end of ch. 39 as an indication that Ebed-melech, like Jeremiah himself (cp. 39: 11–14), survived the fall of Jerusalem recorded in 39: 1–10.

18. *because you trusted in me:* Ebed-melech must have been yet another of those state officials who sympathized with Jeremiah's message. ✻

[a] *See note on 21: 9.*

Jeremiah after the capture of Jerusalem

* The N.E.B. marks off chs. 40–5 under the above subtitle. But this is not entirely appropriate, for although this section does tell us what happened to the prophet after the fall of the city and his release from prison, he himself is not the centre of attention in these chapters. He is not mentioned in 40: 7 – 41: 18, which concern the governorship and assassination of Gedaliah at Mizpah, and 41: 17 and 42: 1 imply that he had moved to Bethlehem. It is incorrect, therefore, to classify these chapters as 'biographical'. They are best understood as being concerned primarily with the question where and amongst which group of Israelites are God's promises of future deliverance and restoration for his people to be realized and fulfilled. *

ANOTHER RECORD OF JEREMIAH'S RELEASE
FROM PRISON

40 THE WORD WHICH CAME FROM THE LORD concerning Jeremiah: Nebuzaradan captain of the guard had taken him in chains to Ramah along with the other exiles from Jerusalem and Judah who were being deported
2 to Babylon; and there he set him free, and took it upon himself to say to Jeremiah, 'The LORD your God threat-
3 ened this place with disaster, and has duly carried out his threat that this should happen to all of you because you
4 have sinned against the LORD and not obeyed him. But as for you, Jeremiah, today I remove the fetters from your wrists. Come with me to Babylon if you wish, and

I will take special care of you; but if you prefer not to
come, well and good. The whole country lies before
you; go wherever you think best.' Jeremiah had not yet 5
answered when Nebuzaradan went on,[a] 'Go back to
Gedaliah son of Ahikam, son of Shaphan, whom the king
of Babylon has appointed governor of the cities of Judah,
and stay with him openly; or else go wherever you
choose.' Then the captain of the guard granted him an
allowance of food, and gave him a present, and so took
leave of him. Jeremiah then came to Gedaliah son of 6
Ahikam at Mizpah and stayed with him among the
people left in the land.

☆ The record here of Jeremiah's release by the Babylonians
is at variance with that contained in 38: 28*b*; 39: 3, 14 (see the
commentary on 39: 1–10), though it is not impossible that
38: 28*b*; 39: 3, 14 form a shorter, if somewhat misleading,
version of what is more fully reported in 39: 11–12; 40: 1–6.
As already noted, 40: 1–6 now forms an introduction to the
narrative about Gedaliah.

  1. *Ramah:* cp. the note on 31: 15.

  5. *Jeremiah had not yet answered when Nebuzaradan went on:*
the Hebrew text reads literally 'and he was not yet returning'.
It is possible that this is a corruption of an original 'and he
(Jeremiah) had not yet returned (answer) when Nebuzaradan
went on', as the N.E.B. suggests. Alternatively, the Hebrew
text could be emended to give a reading 'if it is your wish to
remain [in the land rather than go to Babylon (cp. verse 4)]
go back to Gedaliah.'

  6. *Mizpah:* this is probably to be identified with the modern
Tell en-Nasbeh about 8 miles (nearly 13 km) north of Jerusalem, though another site known as Nebi Samwil (Samuel)
about 5 miles (approximately 8 km) north of Jerusalem has

[a] Jeremiah. . .went on: *prob. rdg.; Heb. unintelligible in context.*

also been suggested. But of these two proposed identifications, the former is the more probable. Though this verse records that Jeremiah went to Mizpah, 41: 17; 42: 1 imply that he subsequently moved to Bethlehem. ✻

THE REMNANT OF ISRAEL

✻ Chs. 40: 7 – 44: 30 may be subdivided into two sections, 40: 7 – 43: 7 and 43: 8 – 44: 30. The former deals with the period in the land of Judah immediately following the destruction of Jerusalem in 587 B.C. It narrates the appointment of Gedaliah as governor of the community left by the Babylonians (40: 7–12) and the conspiracy and rebellion of Ishmael by whom Gedaliah was assassinated (40: 13 – 41: 3, 4–15). It reaches its climax in a description of the community's rejection of the word of God spoken by Jeremiah exhorting them to remain in the land and not to flee to Egypt (41: 16 – 43: 7). This further act of disobedience is described in the darkest colours and is reinforced by the second section of this group of chapters, 43: 44 – 44: 30. The latter describes Jeremiah's ministry among those who fled to Egypt in defiance of God's command. It begins with an oracle of doom against Egypt; there will be no refuge there for those who have fled to it from the Babylonians, for Egypt also will be destroyed by the Babylonians (43: 8–13). Ch. 44 is a long discourse or 'sermon' in prose, abounding in Deuteronomic words and expressions, which describes the apostasy of the community living in Egypt. In spite of all that has happened and the catastrophe which had befallen Judah and Jerusalem because of the nation's rebellion against God, idolatry persists (44: 1–10). Not only does it persist, it is now openly defended by those who engage in it (44: 15–19). Because of this, the people who have fled to Egypt are condemned (44: 11–14, 24–8).

Coming as they do after the description of the destruction of Jerusalem and the ensuing exile to Babylon, 40: 7 – 44: 30 focus attention not on Jeremiah but on the community which was left in Judah at that time. The question with which they are primarily concerned is whether this community constituted the 'remnant' (the word occurs frequently in these few chapters) with whom the future of Israel as God's people lay. As in the case of 29: 16–20 but even more so ch. 24, the answer given is uncompromisingly 'No'; the continued disobedience of those who were left in the land, their eventual flight to Egypt and the idolatry which they enthusiastically practised there render this impossible. They are condemned in language which is amongst the most vehement in the whole book; apart from a few fugitives, they are quite simply written off without hope for the future.

Accordingly, just as chs. 24 and 29 announce that the promises for the future of God's people are directed towards those in exile in Babylon and at the same time denounce those who remained in the homeland as well as those who fled to Egypt (cp. 24: 8), so also the section 40: 7 – 44: 30, though it nowhere mentions those in captivity in Babylon, by a process of elimination, so to speak, asserts that the future of Israel as God's people lies with the Babylonian exiles. It is therefore a mistake to understand these chapters in terms of a biography of Jeremiah or as merely a chronicle of events in Judah after 587 B.C. Their central concern is theological. ✳

GEDALIAH AND THE COMMUNITY IN JUDAH AFTER 587 B.C.

When all the captains of the armed bands in the 7 country-side and their men heard that the king of Babylon had appointed Gedaliah son of Akiham governor of the land, and had put him in charge of the weakest class of the population, men, women, and children, who had not been deported to Babylon, they came to him at Mizpah; Ishmael son of Nethaniah came, and Johanan

and Jonathan sons[a] of Kareah, Seraiah son of Tanhumeth,
the sons of Ephai[b] from Netophah, and Jezaniah[c] of
9 Beth-maacah, with their men. Gedaliah son of Ahikam,
son of Shaphan, gave them all this assurance: 'Have no
fear of the Chaldaean officers.[d] Settle down in the land
and serve the king of Babylon; and then all will be well
10 with you. I am to stay in Mizpah and attend upon the
Chaldaeans whenever they come, and you are to gather
in the summer-fruits, wine, and oil, store them in jars,
11 and settle in the towns you have taken over.' The
Judaeans also, in Moab, Ammon, Edom and other
countries, heard that the king of Babylon had left a
remnant in Judah and that he had set over them Gedaliah
12 son of Ahikam, son of Shaphan. The Judaeans, therefore,
from all the places where they were scattered, came back
to Judah and presented themselves before Gedaliah at
Mizpah; and they gathered in a considerable store of
fruit and wine.

* A good beginning was made under the governorship of
Gedaliah after the Babylonian subjugation of Judah and
Jerusalem. His headquarters at Mizpah became the rallying
point for the population remaining in the land and the news
that Babylonian military operations had ceased in Judah and
that peace was being restored prompted many who had fled
the country to return home. Gedaliah urged all concerned to
settle down and assured them that they had nothing further
to fear from the Babylonian troops garrisoned in the country.

7. *the captains of the armed bands in the country-side:* a refer-

[a] Johanan. . .sons: *or, with Sept.,* Johanan son.
[b] *Or* Ophai.   [c] Jaazaniah *in* 2 Kgs. 25: 23.
[d] of the Chaldaean officers: *so one MS., cp.* 2 Kgs. 25: 24; *others* to serve
the Chaldaeans.

ence to groups of Judaean troops who had managed to escape the Babylonian forces and had gone into hiding throughout the country. The terrain of the land, especially the Judaean hills, would have afforded numerous safe hideouts. *Gedaliah son of Ahikam:* Gedaliah may have been a son of the Ahikam mentioned in 26: 24 who had saved Jeremiah's life on the occasion there described. A contemporary seal from Lachish is inscribed 'Gedaliah who is over the house'. Why Gedaliah was chosen by the Babylonians to be governor is not known, but it is possible that he had belonged to a body of Judaean state officials who had opposed Zedekiah's rebellion against Nebuchadrezzar and was known by the Babylonian authorities to have done so. But it would be a mistake to understand this to mean that he had been a traitor. He no doubt opposed the rebellion not because of any loyalty to Babylon, but because he believed that such rebellion could bring only disaster upon Judah. Like some other state officials, Gedaliah had also probably lent support to Jeremiah's message and counsel.

9. *gave them all this assurance:* the Hebrew is literally 'he swore to them'. *Have no fear of the Chaldaean officers:* the Hebrew text reads 'Do not be afraid to serve the Chaldaeans.' The parallel text in 2 Kings 25: 24 reads literally 'Do not fear the servants (i.e. officers) of the Chaldaeans.' This reading is that adopted by the N.E.B. in the present context and is preferable. It requires only a slight emendation in the text of Jer. 40: 9. *

THE ASSASSINATION OF GEDALIAH

Johanan son of Kareah and all the captains of the armed 13 bands from the country-side came to Gedaliah at Mizpah and said to him, 'Do you know that Baalis king of the 14 Ammonites has sent Ishmael son of Nethaniah to assassinate you?' But Gedaliah son of Ahikam did not believe them. Then Johanan son of Kareah said in private to 15

Gedaliah, 'Let me go, unknown to anyone else, and kill Ishmael son of Nethaniah. Why allow him to assassinate you, and so let all the Judaeans who have rallied round
16 you be scattered and the remnant of Judah lost?' Gedaliah son of Ahikam answered him, 'Do no such thing. Your story about Ishmael is a lie.'

41   In the seventh month Ishmael son of Nethaniah, son of Elishama, who was a member of the royal house,[a] came with ten men to Gedaliah son of Ahikam at Mizpah.
2 While they were at table with him there, Ishmael son of Nethaniah and the ten men with him rose to their feet and assassinated Gedaliah son of Ahikam, son of Shaphan, whom the king of Babylon had appointed governor of
3 the land. They also murdered the Judaeans with him in Mizpah and the Chaldaeans who happened to be there.[b]

✳ We do not know why Ishmael assassinated Gedaliah. Since Ishmael was 'a member of the royal house' (41: 1) it might seem that he planned to seize power and lay claim to the throne. But this is very unlikely, for he does not appear to have followed up his assassination of the governor with any military movement or to have attempted a *coup d'état*. Instead, he fled to Ammon. More probably, therefore, he was motivated by nothing more than a fanatical hatred for the Babylonians and was determined to create as much trouble for them as possible. He probably regarded Gedaliah as nothing less than a collaborator with the enemy. The encouragement Ishmael received from Baalis, king of Ammon, may have sprung from the latter's desire to frustrate and prevent any return to normality in Judah, perhaps because he believed that he would in due course be able to take possession of some Judaean territory.

[a] *So Sept.; Heb. adds* and the chief officers of the king.
[b] *So Sept.; Heb. adds* it was the fighting men whom Ishmael murdered.

13–16. We do not know why Gedaliah refused to believe that Baalis and Ishmael had conspired to assassinate him. It was possibly due to nothing more than his own good nature or because he refused to become engaged in, and even sought to rid the new community of, the sort of intrigue and counter-intrigue to which the unstable and precarious situation of the time would have given rise. Alternatively, it is possible that Gedaliah, having been a state official under Zedekiah, knew Ishmael personally and so rebuffed Johanan's allegations, quite tersely and sharply as described in verse 16.

15. *and the remnant of Judah lost:* the ominous consequences of Gedaliah's imminent assassination are here sounded. Subsequent chapters describe how the chain of events started by Ishmael's treachery eliminated any possibility of a new beginning for the nation being founded upon the *remnant of Judah* left in the land.

41: 1. *In the seventh month:* the year is not mentioned and the implication is thus that Gedaliah was assassinated in the same year that Jerusalem was destroyed, in fact barely three months after this event and his appointment as governor (cp. 39: 2 'in the fourth month'). This is not impossible, though some commentators have questioned whether such a short period would have allowed enough time for the events recorded in 40: 7–12 to have taken place, and have suggested that Gedaliah's murder took place a year later. Others suggest that the governor's murder is to be seen in connection with a third deportation of Judaeans into exile in Babylon in 582 B.C. (cp. 52: 30), that is, about five years later. If the latter is the case, then the record here of Gedaliah's governorship is very truncated, telling us only of the beginning and end of it. *While they were at table with him:* this might lend some support to the suggestion made above that Gedaliah and Ishmael were personally known to each other for some time, perhaps years, before the events here narrated took place.

3. *and the Chaldaeans who happened to be there:* these may have been a number of Babylonians who were staying

temporarily at Mizpah, though it may well be that they formed a Babylonian garrison attached to the governor's residence. The fact that they were murdered with Gedaliah would have obviously heightened the fear of stern reprisals on the community by the Babylonians. ✳

FURTHER TREACHERY COMMITTED BY ISHMAEL

4 The second day after the murder of Gedaliah, while it
5 was not yet common knowledge, there came eighty men from Shechem, Shiloh, and Samaria. They had shaved off their beards, their clothes were rent and their bodies gashed, and they were carrying grain-offerings and
6 frankincense to take to the house of the LORD. Ishmael son of Nethaniah came out weeping from Mizpah to meet them and, when he met them, he said, 'Come to
7 Gedaliah son of Ahikam.' But as soon as they reached the centre of the town, Ishmael son of Nethaniah and his men murdered them and threw their bodies into a pit,
8 all except ten of them who said to Ishmael, 'Do not kill us, for we have a secret hoard in the country, wheat and barley, oil and honey.' So he held his hand and did not
9 kill them with the others. The pit into which he threw the bodies of those whose death he had caused by using Gedaliah's name was the pit which King Asa had made when threatened by Baasha king of Israel; and the dead
10 bodies filled it. He rounded up the rest of the people in Mizpah, that is the king's daughters and all who remained in Mizpah when Nebuzaradan captain of the guard appointed Gedaliah son of Ahikam governor; and with
11 these he set out to cross over into Ammon. When Johanan son of Kareah and all the captains of the armed bands

heard of the crimes committed by Ishmael son of Nethaniah, they took all the men they had and went to attack 12
him. They found him by the great pool in Gibeon. The 13
people with Ishmael were glad when they saw Johanan
son of Kareah and the captains of the armed bands with
him; and all whom Ishmael had taken prisoner at Mizpah 14
turned and joined Johanan son of Kareah. But Ishmael 15
son of Nethaniah escaped from Johanan with eight men,
and they made their way to the Ammonites.

Johanan son of Kareah and all the captains of the armed 16
bands took from Mizpah the survivors whom he had
rescued from Ishmael son of Nethaniah after the murder
of Gedaliah son of Ahikam – men, armed and unarmed,
women, children, and eunuchs, whom he had brought
back from Gibeon. They started out and broke their 17
journey at Kimham's holding near Bethlehem, on their
way into Egypt to escape the Chaldaeans. They were 18
afraid because Ishmael son of Nethaniah had assassinated
Gedaliah son of Ahikam, whom the king of Babylon had
appointed governor of the country.

✻ For no apparent reason, Ishmael, having murdered Gedaliah and others at Mizpah, now murders some pilgrims on
their way from northern Israel to worship in Jerusalem.

5. *there came eighty men from Shechem, Shiloh, and Samaria:*
that these pilgrims came from towns in northern Israel to
worship in Jerusalem probably indicates that some people in
the former northern kingdom had accepted and remained
faithful to Josiah's reformation of 622 B.C., based upon the
demands of Deuteronomy, one of the chief characteristics of
which is the centralization of worship to one sanctuary, that
is, Jerusalem (cp. Deut. 12; 2 Kings 23). *They had shaved off
their beards, their clothes were rent and their bodies gashed:* these

were signs of mourning and penitence. The offerings they were bringing with them to Jerusalem indicate that notwithstanding the destruction of the temple itself, its site remained sacred (as indeed one would expect) and that cultic worship, even if in considerably reduced form, continued there, at least for some time, after 587 B.C.

6-7. It is difficult to see what reason Ishmael had, other than wanton brutality, for killing these pilgrims.

8. *we have a secret hoard in the country, wheat and barley, oil and honey:* at a time such as is presupposed by this narrative, such a hoard of provisions would have been highly desirable. Since Ishmael apparently did not intend to remain in Judah (cp. verse 10), he no doubt wanted such provisions for the journey to Ammon. But we are not told that he acquired the hoard at this time and it is possible that he planned to use these provisions on some future occasion when he would return to Judah with his raiding-party.

9. *the pit which King Asa had made:* cp. 1 Kings 15: 22.

10. *the king's daughters:* we learn that Zedekiah's daughters had escaped the dreadful fate of their father and brothers.

12. *the great pool in Gibeon:* it was by this same pool that the blood-thirsty incident recorded in 2 Sam. 2: 12-16 took place. The huge hewn-out pit, which is 82 feet (nearly 25 m) deep, has been discovered by archaeologists at Gibeon, the modern el-Jib, about 6 miles (approximately 9½ km) northwest of Jerusalem. It was originally a cistern for collecting and storing water and there were steps hewn out down the side of it, from top to bottom, down which the people went to fetch water.

15. *with eight men:* Ishmael's band of desperadoes was small, perhaps consisting of no more than the eight men here mentioned. Having succeeded in his plot to kill Gedaliah, Ishmael made his way back to his co-conspirator, Baalis of Ammon. We know nothing more of either of them.

16-18. The immediate result of Ishmael's treachery is the decision of the leaders of the community to go to Egypt in flight from the Babylonians whom they expected (not without good reason!) to take vengeance for the murder of their appointed governor as well as some of their own people, perhaps troops, at Mizpah.

17. *Kimham's holding near Bethlehem:* as indicated in this verse, the community had already started out for Egypt and had already arrived at the region of Bethlehem, about 6 miles south-south-west of Jerusalem. At this point they break their journey to consult Jeremiah (cp. 42: 1). This can only mean that the prophet had moved to Bethlehem some time before this. *Kimham's holding:* Kimham was a son of Barzillai. The latter had given generous help to David during the rebellion of Absalom. He escorted David across the Jordan on the latter's triumphant return to Jerusalem, but because of his advanced years was unable to accept the king's invitation to become a member of the royal household in the capital and instead suggested that his son should receive the honour (cp. 2 Sam. 19: 31–40). This was agreed and Kimham, as well as becoming a member of the royal household, received a grant of land near Bethlehem which was known henceforth as 'the holding of Kimham'. But its location is unknown. *

JEREMIAH IS CONSULTED

All the captains of the armed bands, including Johanan **42** son of Kareah and Azariah[a] son of Hoshaiah, together with the people, high and low, came to the prophet Jeremiah and said to him, 'May our petition be acceptable 2 to you: Pray to the LORD your God on our behalf and on behalf of this remnant; for, as you see for yourself, only a few of us remain out of many. Pray that the LORD your 3 God may tell us which way we ought to go and what we ought to do.' Then the prophet Jeremiah said to them, 4

[a] So Sept., cp. 43: 2; Heb. Jezaniah.

'I have heard your request and will pray to the LORD your God as you desire, and whatever answer the LORD gives 5 I will tell you; I will keep nothing back.' They said to Jeremiah, 'May the LORD be a true and faithful witness against us if we do not keep our oath! We swear that we will do whatever the LORD your God sends you to tell 6 us. Whether we like it or not, we will obey the LORD our God to whom we send you, in order that it may be well with us; we will obey the LORD our God.'

✻ Jeremiah is not mentioned in the narrative in 40: 7 – 41: 18 concerning Gedaliah's governorship at Mizpah and his assassination by Ishmael. But the prophet now appears again on the scene to be consulted as God's spokesman by the community who, in the new crisis brought about by Ishmael's treachery, seek to know God's will for them and what they should now do. At the same time, this introduces the final phase of Jeremiah's prophetic activity, for the chain of events now set in motion was to lead to his exile to Egypt where his ministry came to an end and where, we must suppose, he died, probably not long after arriving.

1. *Azariah son of Hoshaiah:* the reading 'Jezaniah' in the Hebrew text possibly arose because a copyist thought the names of the officers here should correspond as closely as possible with those mentioned in 40: 8. The mention of Azariah son of Hoshaiah in 43: 2 confirms the reading adopted by the N.E.B. which is also, as noted in the footnote, supported by the Septuagint.

4–6. The narrator's report of Jeremiah's response to the people's request and the people's solemn undertaking to obey God's command whatever it may be already alerts the reader to expect the subsequent conflict between the community and the prophet and their rejection of the word of God. The emphatic manner in which the people pledge themselves to obey (verses 5–6) serves to heighten their subsequent disobedience. ✻

GOD'S PROMISE AND WARNING
TO THE COMMUNITY

Within ten days the word of the LORD came to Jere- 7
miah; so he summoned Johanan son of Kareah, all the 8
captains of the armed bands with him, and all the people,
both high and low. He said to them, These are the words 9
of the LORD the God of Israel, to whom you sent me to
present your petition: If you will stay in this land, then 10
I will build you up and not pull you down, I will plant
you and not uproot you; I grieve for the disaster which
I have brought upon you. Do not be afraid of the king 11
of Babylon whom you now fear. Do not be afraid of him,
says the LORD; for I am with you, to save you and deliver
you from his power. I will show you compassion, and 12
he too will have compassion on you; he will let you stay
on your own soil. But it may be that you will disobey 13
the LORD your God and say, 'We will not stay in this
land. No, we will go to Egypt, where we shall see no 14
sign of war, never hear the sound of the trumpet, and
not starve for want of bread; and there we will live.'
Then hear the word of the LORD, you remnant of Judah. 15
These are the words of the LORD of Hosts the God of
Israel: If you are bent on going to Egypt, if you do settle
there, then the sword you fear will overtake you in 16
Egypt, and the famine you dread will still be with you,
even in Egypt, and there you will die. All the men who 17
are bent on going to Egypt and settling there will die by
sword, by famine, or by pestilence; not one shall escape
or survive the calamity which I will bring upon them.
These are the words of the LORD of Hosts the God of 18

Israel: As my anger and my wrath were poured out upon the inhabitants of Jerusalem, so will my wrath be poured out upon you when you go to Egypt; you will become an object of execration and horror, of ridicule and
19 reproach; you will never see this place again. To you, then, remnant of Judah, the LORD says, Do not go to Egypt. Make no mistake, I can bear witness against you
20 this day. You deceived yourselves when you sent me to the LORD your God and said, 'Pray for us to the LORD our God; tell us all that the LORD our God says and we will
21 do it.' I have told you everything today; but you have not obeyed the LORD your God in what he sent me to tell
22 you. So now be sure of this: you will die by sword, by famine, and by pestilence in the place where you desire to go and make your home.

☆ After some days Jeremiah brings God's response to the community. He announces God's will and plans for them: they are bidden to remain in Judah and are promised that if they do so they will suffer no harm from the Babylonians and will gain God's blessing for their future as his people. At the same time the terrible consequences of going to Egypt in defiance of God's command are declared.

This passage, like the entire section 40: 7 – 44: 30, is composed in the characteristic prose style of the book and, like other similar narratives and speeches, derives from the Deuteronomic editors of the book. Once again, however, this does not mean that the historicity of the events described need be questioned. But it is a further example of the way in which Deuteronomic authors, active in the period of the exile, recorded and adapted an incident and saying of Jeremiah in order to reveal the continued relevance and importance of the prophet's message for the people in exile and for their future beyond the judgement which had befallen them.

7. *Within ten days:* the Hebrew reads literally 'at the end of ten days'. The time it took for Jeremiah to ascertain God's will for the people gives us an insight into the nature of prophecy. Possibly the prophet had already formed his own opinion as to what course of action the community should adopt. But his own conclusions were not necessarily what God would demand of the community. We may be sure, therefore, that the days were spent in prayer and meditation and that when he was finally prepared to announce God's will to the people he was sure that it was God's word for them and not just his own counsel. Only by such prayer and meditation, by 'waiting upon God' as we may put it, was Jeremiah able to distinguish between the word of God and the promptings of his own heart.

10. *I will build you up and not pull you down, I will plant you and not uproot you:* we have already come across this terminology, which is peculiar to the prose material in the book, several times (cp. for example 31: 28) and we have seen that it centres on one of the main themes of the book as a whole, the theme of judgement and restoration after judgement. The use of this terminology to describe God's will for the remnant in Judah after 587 B.C. is accordingly of great significance. For it means that this remnant was not merely being promised protection from further attack by the Babylonians, but was graciously being given the promise of renewal and restoration as the people of God: through them the whole nation would be restored. Had they committed themselves to God and stood by his command to them at this time, this promise would have been realized. But by their further rebellion against him they cut themselves off from his grace and so forfeited his promise for the future. As we have already seen, the main purpose of the author of 40: 7 – 44: 30 was to describe the possibility the remnant left in Judah had for the future and the circumstances and events which culminated in the annulment of that possibility. In other words, the author of these chapters sought to show in a negative way what has been announced positively

elsewhere in the book (cp. especially chs. 24 and 29) that the future of Israel as God's people lay with the exiles in Babylon: neither in the homeland nor amongst those who fled to Egypt would the promised new beginning for the people of God materialize. *I grieve for the disaster which I have brought upon you:* this further emphasizes that the judgement is now past and that God's will for his people is blessing and renewal. The word here translated *I grieve* is rendered in some other English translations as 'I repent'. But this is obviously misleading. The primary meaning of the Hebrew verb in question is 'to take a (deep) breath' and in the present context it clearly means 'to sigh sorrowfully' or the like. The N.E.B. translation is most suitable.

11. Not unnaturally, the community feared that Nebuchadrezzar would exact vengeance for the treachery of Ishmael. They would also have had good reason to fear that in doing so the Babylonian king would not concern himself unduly with discriminating between the guilty and the innocent!

12. *he will let you stay on your own soil:* the Hebrew text reads 'he will cause you to return to your own land'. The N.E.B. reading is achieved by a very slight alteration in the vowel points in the Hebrew text.

15. *If you are bent on going to Egypt:* like the introduction in verses 4-6, where the manner in which the narrator has emphasized the people's pledge to obey raises our suspicions that in the event they will not do so, this statement also prompts the reader to anticipate their decision to disobey and to go to Egypt.

17f. *by sword, by famine, or by pestilence* (cp. also verse 22): this is one of the prose author's favourite descriptions of the terrible judgement inflicted upon Israel for its disobedience and apostasy. The same is true also of the expression *you will become an object of execration and horror, of ridicule and reproach*.

19-22. Here we are left in no doubt of the decision of the people to go to Egypt in defiance of God's command. So much is their decision to go presupposed as a *fait accompli* in these verses, that a number of commentators have suggested that these verses should be transferred to follow 43: 1–3. On the other hand, whilst this suggestion has obvious plausibility, we have seen that the author has throughout the chapter led us to anticipate the community's disobedience. From this point of view verses 19–22 do not come unexpectedly. The artistry and intention of a good author are not always best served by strict logic. ✻

THE COMMUNITY GOES TO EGYPT

When Jeremiah had finished reciting to the people all **43** that the LORD their God had sent him to say, Azariah son 2 of Hoshaiah and Johanan son of Kareah and their party had the effrontery to say to*ᵃ* Jeremiah, 'You are lying; the LORD our God has not sent you to forbid us to go and make our home in Egypt. Baruch son of Neriah has 3 incited you against us in order to put us in the power of the Chaldaeans, so that they may kill us or deport us to Babylon.' Johanan son of Kareah and the captains of the 4 armed bands and all the people refused to obey the LORD and stay in Judah. So Johanan son of Kareah and the 5 captains collected the remnant of Judah, all who had returned from the countries among which they had been scattered to make their home in Judah – men, women 6 and children, including the king's daughters, all the people whom Nebuzaradan captain of the guard had left with Gedaliah son of Ahikam, son of Shaphan, as well as the prophet Jeremiah and Baruch son of Neriah; these 7 all went to Egypt and came to Tahpanhes, disobeying the LORD.

[a] to say to: *or* to say: It is being said to.

✻ Notwithstanding either the promise of blessing or the threat of disaster, the community reject Jeremiah's word and go to Egypt, bringing both Jeremiah and Baruch with them. In this way the hope of renewal and revival amongst those left in the land by the Babylonians is finally lost.

3. *Baruch son of Neriah has incited you against us:* this verse provides an interesting though at the same time somewhat frustrating snippet of information about Baruch. It is interesting because it indicates that he was more than a mere secretary to Jeremiah. The accusation here levelled against him – its authenticity need not be questioned – indicates that he was known to have a mind of his own, so to speak, on vital national issues and that he was believed to have exercised some degree of influence upon Jeremiah. It is frustrating precisely because it is only a meagre amount of information about someone of whom we would like to have more knowledge but unfortunately probably never will (cp. the commentary on ch. 45).

5–6. It is doubtful whether the community which fled to Egypt was as numerous and extensive as is here suggested. Some commentators believe that those mentioned in verse 6 alone constituted the group which fled. That is, those who went to Egypt consisted primarily of the leaders mentioned in 42: 1, 8 and 43: 2 together with those who had lived at Mizpah and had escaped Ishmael's murderous attack. The intention of the author in stating that nothing less than *the remnant of Judah* went to Egypt was to indicate that there could no longer be any hope of future renewal in Judah itself; the community which had been left there by the Babylonians had rebelled further against God's will and had left the homeland; they were now written off without hope for the future. To all intents and purposes they no longer existed.

6. *as well as the prophet Jeremiah and Baruch son of Neriah:* it is not stated whether Jeremiah and Baruch voluntarily went with the refugees to Egypt or were forced to accompany them. It is unlikely, however, that the prophet would willingly have

gone with those who chose to go to Egypt in defiance of God's command announced to them by him. It seems probable, therefore, that the leaders forced him to go with them, though one wonders why they should have done so.

7. *Tahpanhes:* cp. the note on 2: 16. *

A SYMBOL OF JUDGEMENT IN EGYPT

The word of the LORD came to Jeremiah at Tahpanhes: 8 Take some large stones and set them in cement in the 9 pavement at the entrance to Pharaoh's palace in Tahpan-hes. Let the Judaeans see you do it and say to them, These 10 are the words of the LORD of Hosts the God of Israel: I will send for my servant Nebuchadrezzar king of Babylon, and he[a] will place his throne on these stones that I have set there, and spread his canopy over them. He will then proceed to strike Egypt down, killing those 11 doomed to death, taking captive those who are for captivity, and putting to the sword those who are for the sword. He[a] will set fire to the temples of the Egyptian 12 gods, burning the buildings and carrying the gods into captivity. He will scour the land of Egypt as a shepherd scours his clothes to rid them of lice. He will leave Egypt with his purpose achieved. He will smash the sacred pillars 13 of Beth-shemesh[b] in Egypt and burn down the temples of the Egyptian gods.

* This report of a declaration of judgement upon the community which was now resident at Tahpanhes is already antici-pated in 42: 15 ff. where the people's belief that they would be safe in Egypt from further Babylonian attack and punish-ment is refuted. At Tahpanhes Jeremiah by means of a symbolic act and a prophecy announces that the strong, conquering

[a] *So Sept.; Heb.* I.
[b] Heliopolis *in Sept.*

arm of the Babylonians would overrun Egypt. Those who had fled and settled there would gain no respite. Some commentators have suggested that this passage is fictional and thus historically worthless and that it was probably composed by an author who wished to place on the lips of the prophet a condemnation of the idolatrous cults and sanctuaries of Egypt. Since the passage is composed in the characteristic prose style of the book we can expect it to reflect, like other prose speeches and narratives in the book, something with which those responsible for it were concerned. But this does not mean that these editors had no historical or authentic basis for this passage. It is important to note that it is only the second half of the passage (verses 12–13) which concerns the destruction of the Egyptian cults and sanctuaries. Since this cannot be said to have been a direct threat to the Judaean refugees themselves it is possible that it was solely the product of the authors of the prose and had no basis in anything Jeremiah said. But the first half of the passage where the judgement declared against Egypt is obviously at the same time judgement upon the Judaeans there is surely based on a historical incident and there are no serious grounds for doubting that it is based on a reliable tradition of an announcement of judgement by Jeremiah on the occasion described. Furthermore, there is undoubtedly a very authentic ring about the symbolic act here described, an act so original and striking that we cannot seriously doubt that it was performed by Jeremiah. For these reasons, therefore, it seems very probable that the passage provides another instance of a saying of Jeremiah which has subsequently been worked over and developed by an editor.

The question arises whether this prophecy, which envisages an invasion of Egypt by the Babylonians, was fulfilled. Our knowledge of the history of the Babylonian empire at this time is very sketchy. We know, however, that Nebuchadrezzar invaded Egypt in his thirty-seventh year (568/567 B.C.) and fought a battle with Pharaoh Amasis (570–526 B.C.). But the text recording this (it is contained in J. B. Pritchard, *Ancient Near Eastern Texts Relating to the Old Testament* (3rd edition, Princeton 1969), p. 308) is very fragmentary and we do not know the result of this battle or the extent of Nebuchadrezzar's invasion at that time. It is clear, however, that the country remained independent and it is very doubtful whether Egypt suffered much destruction. The very fact that this prophecy was not literally fulfilled is probably an indication that it is based on a genuine oracle of Jeremiah.

9. *Take some large stones and set them in cement in the pavement at the entrance to Pharaoh's palace in Tahpanhes:* the nature of this symbolic act is clear. The large stones were intended as a sort of pedestal on which, according to Jeremiah's prophecy, Nebuchadrezzar would erect his throne as a sign of his conquest of Egypt. The building in question, though referred to as Pharaoh's palace, cannot have been so, since the capital of Egypt was not Tahpanhes. Probably it was simply a government building in this frontier town and may have been used by the Pharaoh on visits to Tahpanhes.

10. *and he will place:* as noted in the footnote, the N.E.B. here and in verse 12 adopts the Septuagint reading 'he' instead of the first person singular in the Hebrew text. But the latter is surely all right and there is no need to emend it. *his canopy:* the Hebrew word here occurs only once in the Old Testament and is obscure. It could also mean a carpet but the translation here adopted suits the context better.

12. *He will scour the land of Egypt as a shepherd scours his clothes to rid them of lice:* this translation is supported by the Septuagint which uses a word meaning literally 'to delouse'.

13. *Beth-shemesh:* 'House of the Sun' (the Septuagint translates it 'Heliopolis'). The text adds 'in Egypt' no doubt to distinguish it from the town of the same name in Palestine. It is located about 5 miles (approximately 8 km) north-east of Cairo. As its name indicates, it was renowned in ancient times as a centre of the cult of the Sun-god, known to the Egyptians as Re. ✳

APOSTASY IN EGYPT

✳ Ch. 44 takes the form of a long prose discourse, abounding in Deuteronomic words and expressions, which describes the apostasy of several communities of Judaeans (cp. the note on verse 1) living in Egypt. In spite of all that had happened and the catastrophic punishment which God had inflicted in judgement upon Judah and Jerusalem, idolatry persisted (verses 1–10). Not only did it persist; it was now openly defended by those in Egypt who engaged in it (verses 15–19). Because of this all who had fled to Egypt and there committed such idolatry were condemned, and condemned in language which is amongst the most bitter and vehement in the whole book (verses 11 ff., 24 ff.): 'not one of them shall survive, not one escape' (verse 14).

As already noted, the passage as a whole is markedly Deuteronomic in style and phraseology. In addition, familiar Deuteronomic themes and motifs are well in evidence in the chapter (see the notes below). It has been suggested by some commentators that the condemnation of the cult of the queen of heaven contained in this chapter derives from Jeremiah. Against this, however, we note that the only other reference to this cult is in 7: 18, which is another prose passage and shows all the signs of having been composed by a Deuteronomic editor. Probably, therefore, this long prose discourse was freely composed by a Deuteronomic editor who, still further developing the declaration of judgement in ch. 43: 8–13, has sought to emphasize even more forcefully the apostasy of those who fled to Egypt and the terrible judgement they thus incurred. In this way the author of the history of the Judaean 'remnant' contained in 40: 7 – 44: 30 brings his account to its climax: the hopes which arose for that 'remnant' after the catastrophe of 587 B.C. were but short-lived; by its wanton disobedience and apostasy the community left in the land forfeited God's promises for renewal and revival. ✳

NO REMORSE, NO REVERENCE

The word that came to Jeremiah for all the Judaeans **44** who were living in Egypt, in Migdol, Tahpanhes, Noph, and the district of Pathros: These are the words of the 2 LORD of Hosts the God of Israel: You have seen the calamity that I brought upon Jerusalem and all the cities of Judah: today they are laid waste and left uninhabited, all because of the wickedness of those who provoked me 3 to anger by going after other gods, gods unknown to them, by burning sacrifices to them.[a] It was you and your fathers who did this. I took pains to send all my 4 servants the prophets to you with this warning: 'Do not do this abominable thing which I hate.' But your fathers 5 would not listen; they paid no heed. They did not give up their wickedness or cease to burn sacrifices to other gods; so my anger and wrath raged like a fire through 6 the cities of Judah and the streets of Jerusalem, and they became the desolate ruin that they are today.

Now these are the words of the LORD the God of Hosts, 7 the God of Israel: Why bring so great a disaster upon yourselves? Why bring destruction upon Judaeans, men and women, children and babes, and leave yourselves without a survivor? This is what comes of your provoking 8 me by all your idolatry in burning sacrifices to other gods in Egypt where you have made your home. You will destroy yourselves and become an object of ridicule and reproach to all the nations of the earth. Have you for- 9 gotten all the wickedness committed by your forefathers, by the kings of Judah and their wives, by yourselves and

[a] *So Sept.; Heb. adds* to worship.

your wives in the land of Judah and in the streets of

10 Jerusalem? To this day you*a* have shown no remorse, no reverence; you have not conformed to the law and the statutes which I set before you and your forefathers.

11 These, therefore, are the words of the LORD of Hosts the God of Israel: I have made up my mind to bring calamity

12 upon you and exterminate the people of Judah. I will deal with the remnant of Judah who were bent on going to make their home in Egypt; in Egypt they shall all meet their end. Some shall fall by the sword, others will meet their end by famine. High and low alike will die by sword or by famine and will be an object of execration

13 and horror, of ridicule and reproach. I will punish those who live in Egypt as I punished those in Jerusalem, by

14 sword, famine, and pestilence. Those who had remained in Judah came to make their home in Egypt, confident that they would return and live once more in Judah. But they shall not return;*b* not one of them shall survive, not one escape.

✷ 1-10. Judah's past sins and the judgement these brought upon the land and people are briefly stated. Yet the obvious lesson to be drawn from all this had been ignored, with the result that still further and even more terrible judgement was being incurred.

1. *all the Judaeans who were living in Egypt:* in addition to the community which had settled at Tahpanhes, other groups of Judaean refugees are now mentioned and placed under judgement. Though not referred to here, a Jewish community is known to have lived at Elephantine, an island on the Nile in southern Egypt, during the fifth century B.C. From a number of papyri documents discovered at Elephantine, it is clear that this community had been there well before the Persian

[a] *Lit.* they.   [b] *Prob. rdg.; Heb. adds* except fugitives.

conquest of Egypt in 525 B.C. Unfortunately we do not know precisely when they emigrated, but it is not improbable that they did so in the late seventh century or early in the sixth century B.C. *Migdol:* a town or city bearing this name is also mentioned in connection with the route of the exodus from Egypt (Exod. 14: 2; Num. 33: 7) and again in Ezek. 29: 10 and 30: 6 where it is located in northern Egypt. We do not know whether these texts all refer to one and the same town, but probably they do. The name Migdol means a 'tower' (probably used for defensive purposes). It is a Semitic word borrowed by the Egyptians. For *Noph* and *Tahpanhes* see the note on 2: 16. *Pathros:* this was the name for Upper Egypt. It means literally 'land of the south'.

4. *I took pains to send all my servants the prophets to you:* we have already come across this expression several times in the prose in Jeremiah (cp. 7: 25; 25: 4; 26: 5; 29: 19; 35: 15) and we have seen that it expresses a theme which is characteristic of the Deuteronomic theology (cp. especially 2 Kings 17: 13).

10. *you have not conformed to the law and the statutes which I set before you:* as we have seen, Israel's disobedience to the law (the Torah) of God is a central theme in the prose in Jeremiah and forms the basis of several passages (cp. the commentary on 7; 11; 17: 19–27; 34: 8-22). As we have also seen, this is a dominant theme of the Deuteronomic theology and further evidence of the Deuteronomic authorship of this chapter.

11–14. The judgement upon the Judaeans in Egypt is to be complete and final. Note the intensity of the judgement here declared against them: *calamity* will befall them, God will *exterminate* them; *High and low alike* will perish; *sword, famine, and pestilence* will overtake them; they will be *an object of execration and horror, of ridicule and reproach; not one of them shall survive, not one escape.*

12. Note that the various groups of Judaeans mentioned in verse 1 are all here described as *the remnant of Judah.* This conforms to the main theme of chs. 40: 7 – 44: 30 which,

as we have seen, is to describe the history and fate of the 'remnant' left in the land after 587 B.C. and to show that because of their disobedience and apostasy and their eventual flight to Egypt they cut themselves off from God's promises for the future of his people. There could now be no hope for revival and renewal either in Judah or amongst the community in Egypt. The future restoration was to be effected through the exiles in Babylon (cp. the commentary on chs. 24 and 29).

14. *But they shall not return:* as noted in the footnote in the N.E.B., the Hebrew text adds 'except fugitives'. In view of the judgement of total extermination so harrowingly emphasized in verses 11–14, 26–8, this comment together with the similar statement in the Hebrew text of verse 27 (see again the N.E.B. footnote) could be an editorial gloss. On the other hand, it may be nothing more than a means of further emphasizing the extent of the judgement upon the community in Egypt and as such need not necessarily be a gloss. ✽

IN DEFENCE OF IDOLATRY

15 Then all the men who knew that their wives were burning sacrifices to other gods and the crowds of women
16 standing by*a* answered Jeremiah, 'We will not listen to
17 what you tell us in the name of the LORD. We intend to fulfil all the promises by which we have bound ourselves: we will burn sacrifices to the queen of heaven and pour drink-offerings to her as we used to do, we and our fathers, our kings and our princes, in the cities of Judah and in the streets of Jerusalem. We then had food in
18 plenty and were content; no calamity touched us. But from the time we left off burning sacrifices to the queen of heaven and pouring drink-offerings to her, we have been in great want, and in the end we have fallen victims

[a] *Prob. rdg.; Heb. adds* and all the people who lived in Egypt, in Pathros.

to sword and famine.' And the women said,[a] 'When we 19
burnt sacrifices to the queen of heaven and poured drink-
offerings to her, our husbands knew full well that we
were making crescent-cakes marked with her image and
pouring drink-offerings to her.'

* An argument such as is recorded here may well have been
advanced by not a few people in the wake of 587 B.C. After all,
in spite of Josiah's reformation in 621 B.C. and the campaign
against idolatry and apostasy in Judah at that time, within a
relatively short period a series of disasters had befallen Judah,
beginning with the tragic and untimely death of Josiah himself (609 B.C.) and continuing through one crisis after another
until the final destruction of Judah and Jerusalem in 587 B.C.
Many may well have interpreted all this in the manner here
described in 44: 15–19. Similarly, the counter-argument here
placed on the lips of Jeremiah (verses 20–3) must have been
employed or accepted by many others who understood the
catastrophe of 587 B.C. as God's just and necessary judgement
upon Judah: notwithstanding the reformation and such good
as came from it, they would have claimed, the nation's sin was
so deep-seated and pervasive that nothing short of a radical
break with the past and a completely new beginning was now
possible.

18. *But from the time we left off burning sacrifices to the queen of
heaven:* as already implied above, this must be understood as
a reference to Josiah's reformation which sought to abolish
all foreign and idolatrous cults from Judah and Jerusalem.
Although such long-established and deeply rooted cultic practices, such as the cult of the queen of heaven, would have been
impossible to wipe out completely, we need not doubt that
the reformation, at least initially, was carried out vigorously
and that at the same time many in the land would willingly
and enthusiastically have supported its principles, especially

[a] And the women said. So Luc. Sept., Heb. om.

157

since the reformation was also linked with a movement for national independence and renewal. The bitter disappointment of Josiah's death at Megiddo in 609 B.C. and subsequent calamities must have brought with them widespread disillusion. *the queen of heaven:* probably the Canaanite goddess of fertility (cp. the commentary on 7: 16–20).

19. *crescent-cakes marked with her image:* cp. the comment on 7: 18. ✳

A FINAL CONDEMNATION

20 When Jeremiah received this answer from these men
21 and women and all the people, he said, 'The LORD did not forget those sacrifices which you and your fathers, your kings and princes and the people of the land burnt in the cities of Judah and in the streets of Jerusalem, and
22 they mounted up in his mind until he could no longer tolerate them, so wicked were your deeds and so abominable the things you did. Your land became a desolate waste, an object of horror and ridicule, with no inhabi-
23 tants, as it still is. This calamity has come upon you because you burnt these sacrifices and sinned against the LORD and did not obey the LORD or conform to his laws, statutes, and teachings.'[a]

24 Jeremiah further said to all the people and to the women, Listen to the word of the LORD, all you from
25 Judah who live in Egypt. These are the words of the LORD of Hosts the God of Israel: You women[b] have made your actions match your words. 'We will carry out our vows', you said, 'to burn sacrifices to the queen of heaven and to pour drink-offerings to her.' Well then,

[a] *So Sept.; Heb. adds* as at this day.
[b] You women: *so Sept.; Heb.* You and your wives.

fulfil your vows by all means, and make your words good. But listen to the word of the LORD, all you from Judah 26 who live in Egypt. I have sworn by my great name, says the LORD, that my name shall never again be on the lips of the men of Judah; they shall no longer swear in Egypt, 'By the life of the Lord GOD.' I am on the watch to 27 bring you evil and not good, and all the men of Judah who are in Egypt shall meet their end by sword and by famine until not one is left.*a* It is then that all the survivors 28 of Judah who have made their home in Egypt shall know whose word prevails, theirs or mine.

This is the sign I give you, says the LORD, that I intend 29 to punish you in this place, so that you may learn that my words against you will prevail to bring evil upon you: These are the words of the LORD: I will hand over 30 Pharaoh Hophra king of Egypt to his enemies and to those who seek his life, just as I handed over Zedekiah king of Judah to his enemy Nebuchadrezzar king of Babylon who was seeking to take his life.

* The third and final section of the chapter comprises (a) verses 20-3, a refutation of the people's argument described in verses 15-19; and (b) verses 24-30, a further declaration of judgement upon the Judaeans now resident in Egypt.

(a) This refutation of the people's argument is a summary of the Deuteronomic interpretation of the catastrophe of 587 B.C. and the ensuing exile: that catastrophe was God's judgement upon the nation's long and deeply imbedded cultic apostasy and its failure to obey God's 'laws, statutes, and teachings' (cp. the note on verse 23).

(b) The judgement which is to overtake those in Egypt is

[a] *Prob. rdg.; Heb. adds* Few will escape the sword in Egypt to return to Judah.

159

to be final and complete. No ray of hope is here held out, no thought of a fresh beginning after that judgement: that judgement will pursue an unrelenting and terrible path 'until not one is left'.

21. *the people of the land:* this expression, which occurs in quite a number of texts throughout the Old Testament, is widely regarded as a technical term designating a specific class or group within Judah's population (for example, the landed gentry). Here, however, it is clearly best understood as designating the people in general.

23. *his laws:* the Hebrew has the singular, 'his law', and is to be preferred here. The expression as a whole is a favourite one in the Deuteronomic literature in Deuteronomy–2 Kings where it designates 'the Book of the Law', that is, in Deuteronomy.

25. *You women:* since what follows is addressed specifically to the women, it seems best to adopt, with the N.E.B., the reading of the Septuagint in which the words are addressed to the women only.

27. *until not one is left:* cp. the note on verse 14.

30. *Pharaoh Hophra:* this Pharaoh ruled from 589 to 570 B.C. He was the Pharaoh who pledged his support for Zedekiah in the revolt against Nebuchadrezzar in 588 B.C. and sent an army against the Babylonians at that time (cp. 37: 5). Towards the end of his reign there was a rising against him among some sections of the army who proclaimed Amasis king. Hophra and Amasis reigned as co-regents but after only three years a further struggle took place between them as a result of which Hophra was executed. The knowledge of how Hophra met his end as well as the fact that this section, like the chapter as a whole, is composed in the Deuteronomic style, must be taken as indicating that the 'sign' here given is a 'prophecy after the event'. ✳

A PROMISE TO BARUCH

The word which the prophet Jeremiah spoke to Baruch **45**
son of Neriah when he wrote these words in a book at
Jeremiah's dictation in the fourth year of Jehoiakim son
of Josiah, king of Judah: These are the words of the LORD 2
the God of Israel concerning you, Baruch: You said, 3
'Woe is me, for the LORD has added grief to all my trials.
I have worn myself out with my labours and have had
no respite.' This is what you shall say to Baruch, These are 4
the words of the LORD: What I have built, I demolish;
what I have planted, I uproot. So it will be with the
whole earth. You seek great things for yourself. Leave off 5
seeking them; for I will bring disaster upon all mankind,
says the LORD, and I will let you live wherever you go,
but you shall save your life and nothing more.[a]

* As far as we know, Baruch was Jeremiah's sole disciple,
at least in the active sense of the word, during the turbulent
years of the prophet's ministry. It was Baruch who was
employed by Jeremiah to write down his oracles for the scroll
compiled in 605/604 B.C. (cp. ch. 36) and there is no reason
to doubt that he continued to record the prophet's sayings and
oracles of later years. But he was not merely a secretary
passively committing to writing what his master uttered.
He appears to have been much more involved in Jeremiah's
ministry than this and to have identified himself closely with
the prophet's preaching against Judah. In some instances this
placed Baruch in the same perilous situation as Jeremiah and
incurred for him the same hatred with which the prophet was
opposed (cp. 36: 19, 26; 43: 3). Many scholars believe that
Baruch not only wrote down and preserved his master's words

[a] *See note on 21: 9.*

but also wrote a 'biography' of Jeremiah, all or part of which they identify with the many narratives in the book recording incidents and events in Jeremiah's ministry. But we have seen that these narratives very probably were composed by Deuteronomic authors and that it is in any case a misunderstanding of them to classify them as 'biographical'. Nevertheless, Baruch surely played a key part in the origin of the book and clearly much of its contents must have been derived from the records he made of Jeremiah's oracles and sayings. Furthermore, even though the narratives in the book were not actually composed by him, those who did compose them must have acquired much of the information about Jeremiah contained in these narratives from Baruch. We shall probably never know whether this information came directly from him or from written records he made or from others to whom he had related episodes in his master's life, or indeed in all three ways. Thus, whatever his own ambitions or aspirations may have been, whatever 'great things' he sought for himself (verse 5), his loyalty to his master has gained for him a place of honour beyond anything he could ever have desired.

3. *Woe is me, for the LORD has added grief to all my trials:* this is reminiscent of Jeremiah's own cries of lament in his 'confessions' earlier in the book. As indicated in 43:6 Baruch was taken to Egypt with Jeremiah after the murder of Gedaliah. We know nothing more of him after this. However, since the editors of the book of Jeremiah were able to record what happened in Egypt when the community settled there, it is not impossible that Baruch eventually escaped and returned to Judah or even journeyed to Babylon to join the exiles there and was able to tell what took place in Egypt. But we shall probably never know for certain what became of him.

4. *What I have built, I demolish; what I have planted, I uproot:* for the terminology see the note on 31:28.

5. *but you shall save your life and nothing more:* see the comment on 21:9. ✳

Prophecies against the nations

⌐HIS CAME TO THE PROPHET JEREMIAH as the word **46**
⌐of the LORD concerning the nations.

✻ Chs. 46–51 comprise a series of oracles announcing judgement upon foreign nations. The Septuagint places these
chapters after 25: 13a (omitting verse 14) and concludes them
with 25: 15–38. This was probably their original position and
we note in support of this that in the other two major prophetic books in the Old Testament, Isaiah and Ezekiel, similar
collections of oracles against foreign nations are found in the
middle rather than at the end of each book (Isa. 13–23; Ezek.
25–32).

  In addition to the collections of oracles against foreign
nations in Isaiah, Jeremiah and Ezekiel, there is a collection of
similar oracles in Amos 1–2, whilst the oracles of Nahum
against Nineveh and those of Obadiah concerning Edom
clearly belong to the same category. All of this can only mean
that there was in ancient Israel a particular kind of prophecy
which concerned itself with foreign nations and that the
prophets mentioned above adopted this type of prophecy in
their preaching. Scholars are not agreed on the original
sphere in which this type of prophecy had its home. Some
believe that it originated in the sphere of war when the nation's
enemy or enemies were solemnly cursed by prophets who
accompanied the Israelite army to battle. Others believe that
the form had its original setting in the cult where, it is main-
tained, the forces of chaos ranged against Yahweh the creator
of the world were symbolized by the nations; the enemies of
God were identified with the enemies of his people. A background in a cultic festival celebrating God's victory over his
enemies would certainly explain the marked monotheism of

such oracles. Still others suggest that the cursing of enemies may have taken place in the royal court.

Each of these three views has some evidence to support it. That preparations for war may have been the setting for such a type of oracle is obviously a plausible theory. The same is true of the royal court, where foreign nations would clearly have been the concern of the king and his counsellors. As to the view that the form originated in the cult, such psalms as Pss. 2, 46 and 47 portray the theme of the nations acting together against Yahweh and his people and being subdued by his power; it has been suggested that this theme was the subject of a ritual 'conflict' carried out periodically in the Jerusalem temple.

This is a problem with which Old Testament scholars will continue to concern themselves and perhaps new evidence will emerge to settle the question. What may be said here is that this type of oracle may have been influenced by various spheres in Israel's life, both military and political as well as cultic, without having been exclusively limited to any one of them. As to their presence in the prophetic literature, they indicate on the one hand that there emerged in Israel the belief that Yahweh was not just the national God of Israel but was Lord over all the nations of the world and, on the other hand, that prophets such as Isaiah, Jeremiah and Ezekiel believed themselves to have been entrusted with a message not only for their own people but for the nations of the world whose destiny was in the hands of God. For this reason these oracles against the nations, though perhaps the least read of all the contents of the prophetic books, are of great importance for our understanding of the development of Israel's religion and the theology of the Old Testament. *

CONCERNING EGYPT

* With the exception of verses 27–8, which announce the future restoration of Israel, ch. 46 comprises two poems

announcing the destruction of Egypt by the Babylonians under Nebuchadrezzar (verses 2-12 and 13–24), followed by a short saying further announcing the conquest of Egypt by Nebuchadrezzar but ending with a promise of the future restoration of Egypt (verses 25-6). Of these, the poem in verses 2–12, which is amongst the most vivid and striking in the entire book, concerns the rout of the Egyptians at Carchemish on the Euphrates by Nebuchadrezzar in 605 B.C. That it was composed by Jeremiah himself either just before or after the event described is agreed by most commentators. It has been much disputed whether Jeremiah composed the second poem, verses 13–24. This passage appears to presuppose the invasion of Egypt by the Babylonians. But the victory of Nebuchadrezzar over Pharaoh Necho at Carchemish in 605 B.C. was not followed up by an invasion of Egypt itself. It was not until 568 B.C., by which time Jeremiah was very probably dead, that Nebuchadrezzar invaded Egypt, though the report of the Jewish historian Josephus (first century A.D.) that five years after the fall of Jerusalem, that is, in 582 B.C., the Babylonians subjugated the Ammonites and the Moabites and followed this up by an invasion of Egypt may be trustworthy. If this report of Josephus is reliable, it is possible that the composition of verses 13–24 is to be connected with Jeremiah's prophecy in 43: 8–13. Alternatively, it has been suggested that the advance of Nebuchadrezzar's forces into the Philistine plain after his victory at Carchemish may have been the occasion when this poem was composed, since the occupation of the coastal plain would have been an obvious base from which to move down against Egyptian territory. Or again, it is not impossible that the victory and apparent invincibility of the Babylonians in 587 B.C. prompted the poem. But whatever the occasion, there are no sound grounds for questioning that this poem comes from Jeremiah. *

THE EGYPTIAN ARMY ROUTED AT CARCHEMISH

2 Of Egypt: concerning the army of Pharaoh Necho king of Egypt at Carchemish on the river Euphrates, which Nebuchadrezzar king of Babylon defeated in the fourth year of Jehoiakim son of Josiah, king of Judah.

3   Hold shield and buckler ready
      and advance to battle;
4   harness the horses, let the riders mount;
    form up, your helmets on, your lances burnished;
      on with your coats of mail!
5   But now, what sight is this?
  They are broken and routed,
    their warriors beaten down;
  they have turned to flight and do not look behind
      them.
    Terror let loose!
    This is the very word of the LORD.

6   Can the swift escape, can the warrior save himself?
    In the north, by the river Euphrates,
      they stumble and fall.
7   Who is this rising like the Nile,
  like its streams turbulent in flood?
8   Egypt is rising like the Nile,
  like its streams turbulent in flood.

He[a] says:
    I will rise and cover the earth,
    I will destroy both city and people.

[a] *Or* It.

Charge, horsemen! On, you flashing chariots, on!   9
    Forward, the warriors,
  Cushites and men of Put carrying shields,
  Lydians grasping their bent bows!
This is the day of the Lord, the GOD of Hosts,   10
  a day of vengeance, vengeance on his enemies;
  the sword shall devour and be sated,
    drunk with their blood.
For the GOD of Hosts, the Lord, holds sacrifice
    in a northern land, by the river Euphrates.
Go up into Gilead and fetch balm,   11
    O virgin people of Egypt.
  You have tried many remedies, all in vain;
    no skin shall grow over your wounds.
The nations have heard your cry,[a]   12
and the earth echoes with your screams;
    warrior stumbles against warrior
    and both fall together.

✻ The poem presents a vivid picture of the march forward to battle of the Egyptian army, equipped and confident for the engagement, only to be miserably defeated and set in total disarray.

2. *Of Egypt:* the title of the first section of the oracles against foreign nations (cp. e.g. 48: 1). For most of the second millennium B.C. the Egyptians held sway over the territory of Syria–Palestine. But towards the end of this millennium Egypt's power declined and the Egyptians never regained control of the empire they once ruled over. There were but moments of power during the first millennium, as when the Pharaoh Shishak invaded Palestine during the reign of Rehoboam (cp. 1 Kings 14: 25–6), and the Egyptians

[a] your cry: *so Sept.; Heb.* your shame.

intrigued and at times launched attacks, rarely with success and never for long, against the Assyrians, Babylonians and Persians, who successively ruled over the territory of Syria–Palestine.

3. *Hold shield and buckler ready:* the *shield* (Hebrew *ṣinnah*) was heavier and larger than the buckler (Hebrew *magen*) (cp. 1 Kings 10: 16–17).

4. *coats of mail:* made of leather or perhaps some thick woven material coated with metal scales.

5. *they have turned to flight and do not look behind:* this together with verse 12, 'warrior stumbles against warrior and both fall together', gives a graphic picture of the soldiers fleeing in disarray and confusion from the battle-field. *Terror let loose!* this expression is used in 6: 25 concerning the 'foe from the north' who is to invade Israel, in 20: 3 of Jeremiah's opponent and persecutor Pashhur son of Immer and in 20: 10 (cp. N.E.B. footnote) of those who plot against him and here in 46: 5 of the Babylonians before whom the Egyptian armies flee in terror. It is also found in Ps. 31: 13 (there translated 'threats from every side') where it is used of the psalmist's enemies. The application of this phrase in these different contexts suggests that it was a 'proverbial' curse formula.

8. *Egypt is rising like the Nile, like its streams turbulent in flood:* the annual flooding of the Nile valley was of paramount importance in Egypt. Its waters spread out over the surrounding land, parched by the sun, and thus brought new life and vegetation to the barren soil. During the summer the river begins to swell, at first slowly but gradually gathering momentum until eventually it can become a rushing torrent, bursting its banks and spreading out over the adjoining land. So also, boast the Egyptians, will they *rise and cover the earth*. A similar metaphor is used by Isaiah to describe the invasion of Judah by the Assyrians (cp. Isa. 8: 7–8).

9. *Cushites* were Ethiopians. The location of *Put* is disputed, some placing it along the east coast of Africa, others believing that it refers to some part of Libya. The *Lydians* here

mentioned are unlikely to have been from Lydia in Asia Minor. More likely they were people who lived in north Africa and near Egypt (cp. Gen. 10: 13). Alternatively, it has been suggested that the Hebrew word here, *Ludim*, should be slightly emended to read *Lubim* = Libyans. This suggestion finds some support in Nahum 3: 9 where 'Put and the Libyans' are said to have helped Egypt. Probably the various groups mentioned were mercenary soldiers in the service of the Pharaoh.

10. *a day of vengeance, vengeance on his enemies:* perhaps the vengeance here mentioned had in mind the untimely death of Josiah at the hands of Pharaoh Necho at Megiddo in 609 B.C. But the mention of *the day of the Lord* probably indicates that the vengeance in question is to be understood more generally as in many other statements about 'the day of the LORD' in the Old Testament. *For the GOD of Hosts, the Lord, holds sacrifice:* a graphic description of the defeat of the Egyptians at Carchemish.

11. *Go up into Gilead and fetch balm:* see the note on 8: 22. ✶

DISASTER UPON EGYPT

The word which the LORD spoke to the prophet Jere- 13
miah when Nebuchadrezzar king of Babylon was
coming to harry the land of Egypt:

Announce it in Egypt, proclaim it in Migdol,   14
    proclaim it in Noph and Tahpanhes.
Say, Stand to! Be ready!
for a sword devours all around you.
Why does Apis flee, why does your bull-god   5
    not*a* stand fast?
    The LORD has thrust him out.

[a] Why does Apis. . .not: *or* Why is your bull-god routed, why does
he not . . .

16   The rabble of Egypt stumbles and falls,
          man against man;
      each says, 'Quick, back to our people,
      to the land of our birth, far from the cruel sword!'
17   Give Pharaoh of Egypt the title King Bombast,
          the man who missed his moment.
18   By my life, says the King
      whose name is the LORD of Hosts,
      one shall come mighty as Tabor among the hills,
          as Carmel by the sea.
19   Make ready your baggage for exile,
          you native people of Egypt;
      for Noph shall become a waste,
          ruined and unpeopled.

20   Egypt was a lovely heifer,
      but a gadfly from the north descended on her.[a]
21   The mercenaries in her land were like stall-fed calves;
      but they too turned and fled,
          not one of them stood his ground.
      The hour of their downfall has come upon them,
          their day of reckoning.
22   Hark, she is hissing[b] like a snake,
          for the enemy has come in all his force.
      They fall upon her with axes
          like woodcutters at their work.
23   They cut down her forest, says the LORD,
          and it flaunts itself no more;
      for they are many as locusts and past counting.

[a] on her: *so many MSS.; others obscure in context.*
[b] Hark. . .hissing: *so Sept.; Heb. obscure.*

170

The Egyptians are put to shame, enslaved to a   24
    northern race.

* Egypt is summoned to prepare for imminent disaster. Once
again the vividness of this poem is striking, its phraseology and
staccato expressions heightening the description of the
destruction to befall Egypt.

14. On *Migdol, Noph* and *Tahpanhes*, see the note on 2: 16
and 44: 1.

15. *Why does Apis flee, why does your bull-god not stand fast?*
Apis was the sacred bull worshipped in Memphis (Noph) from
very ancient times. The representation of fertility deities in
the form of a bull was widely practised in the ancient Near
East and was apparently not unknown in Israel (cp. Hos. 8:
5–6). Apis, though originally believed to be the incarnation
of the god Ptah, became more and more associated with the
god Osiris, the god of vegetation and regeneration. The reference in this verse is probably to an image of Apis, perhaps
carried into battle as the context suggests, though it is known
that the priests in charge of the cult of Apis kept and honoured
a specially selected live bull as the representative of the god.

17. *Give Pharaoh of Egypt the title King Bombast:* literally the
Hebrew means 'the loud noise that lets the appointed time
pass by'. The N.E.B. translation understands the phrase to
mean that the Pharaoh was full of talk about what he would do
but quite ineffective in carrying out his boastful plans. The
suggestion has been made that one of the Hebrew words in
the phrase 'the loud noise that lets the time pass by' is a pun
upon the name of Apries (Hophra) who was Pharaoh during
the period 588–569 B.C. But the word-play is not close.

18. *mighty as Tabor among the hills:* Tabor is a mountain in
the plain of Jezreel in northern Israel. It is little over 1800 feet
(nearly 549 m) high, but the fact that it stands isolated from
any other mountains and has steep sides gives the impression
of great height and makes it a striking land-mark, visible for
miles around. *Carmel by the sea:* the prominent mountain on

the coast of northern Israel, known especially as the place of the 'contest' between Elijah and the prophets of Baal (see 1 Kings 18: 19–40). At its highest point it is just over 1700 feet (about 518 m). Thus as Tabor towers high over the hills and as Carmel rises loftily above the sea, so the foe who comes against Egypt will be mightier than other conquerors.

20. *but a gadfly from the north descended on her:* the Hebrew word is literally 'the nipper'. These flies approach with a loud hum and inflict a particularly painful wound on cattle. The image is therefore of a healthy heifer with a good hide being attacked by gadflies who create wounds and sores all over it. *from the north:* the dreaded 'foe from the north', so characteristic a feature of Jeremiah's preaching.

21. *The mercenaries in her land were like stall-fed calves:* mercenary soldiers (the Hebrew word means literally 'hired ones') were common to armies in the ancient Near East. *stall-fed calves:* calves specially fed and fattened to supply veal for feasts. The meaning appears to be that Egypt's mercenaries were particularly well treated by their masters and well equipped and trained for war but that even they fled before the victorious enemy.

22. *Hark, she is hissing like a snake:* Egypt is likened to a snake driven away from its lair by the approach of woodcutters and impotent to do anything more than hiss at them. The metaphor is perhaps all the more apt since the snake was of such importance in Egyptian religion and in Egyptian royal insignia. ✻

A FINAL ORACLE CONCERNING EGYPT

25   The LORD of Hosts the God of Israel has spoken:
        I will punish Amon god of No,[a]
      Egypt with her gods and her princes,
      Pharaoh and all who trust in him.

[a] *Prob. rdg.; Heb. adds* and Pharaoh.

I will deliver them to those bent on their destruction, 26
to Nebuchadrezzar king of Babylon and his troops;
yet in after time the land shall be peopled as of old.
    This is the very word of the LORD.

✻ 25. *I will punish Amon god of No: No* was the Egyptian
name for Thebes, the capital of Upper Egypt. *Amon* was the
chief god worshipped at Thebes. Eventually at Thebes Amon
was 'merged' with Re to become Amon-Re, king of the gods
and the imperial god.

    26. This verse is not found in the Septuagint and may be a
later addition to verse 25. The statement *yet in after time the
land shall be peopled as of old* may have been based on the
knowledge that although the Babylonians invaded Egypt in
568 B.C. they apparently did not succeed in making the
Egyptians subject to them for long. ✻

A PROMISE TO ISRAEL

But you, Jacob my servant, have no fear,   27
    despair not, O Israel;
for I will bring you back safe from afar
    and your offspring from the land where they are
           captives;
and Jacob shall be at rest once more,
    prosperous and unafraid.
O Jacob my servant, have no fear,   28
says the LORD; for I am with you.
    I will make an end of all the nations
        amongst whom I have banished you;
    but I will not make an end of you;
        though I punish you as you deserve,
        I will not sweep you clean away.

* These verses are found, with only minor differences in the text, in 30: 10–11 (see the commentary on ch. 30). Their proper context is ch. 30. They have been placed at the end of ch. 46 either because an editor wished to follow the promise concerning Egypt's future in verse 26 with one concerning the restoration of Israel from exile, or perhaps because (if verse 26 was originally absent from this chapter) he wished to contrast the fate of Egypt with the promise of blessing upon Israel. *

CONCERNING THE PHILISTINES

47 This came to the prophet Jeremiah as the word of the LORD concerning the Philistines before Pharaoh's harry-
2 ing of Gaza: The LORD has spoken:

> See how waters are rising from the north
> and swelling to a torrent in spate,
> flooding the land and all that is in it,
>> cities and all who live in them.
>> Men shall shriek in alarm
> and all who live in the land shall howl.

3   Hark, the pounding of his chargers' hooves,
> the rattle of his chariots and their rumbling wheels!
> Fathers spare no thought for their children;
>> their hands hang powerless,

4   because the day is upon them when Philistia will be
>> despoiled,
> and Tyre and Sidon destroyed to the last defender;
> for the LORD will despoil the Philistines,
>> that remnant of the isle of Caphtor.

5   Gaza is shorn bare, Ashkelon ruined.
> Poor remnant of their strength,
> how long will you gash yourselves[a] and cry:

> [a] gash yourselves: *or, with Scroll*, roll about.

Ah, sword in the hand of the LORD, 6
    how long will it be before you rest?
Sheathe yourself, rest and be quiet.
How can it*a* rest? for the LORD has given it work to do 7
    against Ashkelon and the plain by the sea;
    there he has assigned the sword its task.

* There are no substantial grounds for questioning that the poem contained in this chapter comes from Jeremiah. It shares the same vivid style as the material in ch. 46. But the poem is by no means without problems. Verse 1 appears to connect it with an attack on Gaza by the Egyptians. From verse 2 onwards, however, it is clearly not the Egyptians but the Babylonians from the north who are the enemy about to destroy the Philistines. The Greek historian Herodotus (fifth century B.C.) records that after Pharaoh Necho had defeated Josiah at Megiddo in 609 B.C., he attacked and conquered the city Kadytis, which is widely agreed to be Gaza. In view of this, some commentators suggest that the occasion when the poem was composed was therefore 609 B.C. though its contents concern not Pharaoh's attack upon Gaza but a later destruction of the Philistines here being prophesied by Jeremiah. In other words, the prophecy was made in 609 B.C. concerning events which took place in 604 B.C. when Nebuchadrezzar, after his victory against the Egyptians at Carchemish in 605 B.C., swept down into the coastal plain in Palestine to the territory of the Philistines. (We know from Babylonian records that the Philistine city Ashkelon was captured by them in 604 B.C.) But there is another possibility. The Septuagint version of 47: 1 omits any reference to the Egyptians, and has simply 'Concerning the Philistines', a title like 'Of Moab' at 48: 1, though not in quite the same form (cp. the title at 50: 1). It is possible therefore, that the verse as found in the Hebrew text is due to a later editor, who

[a] *So Sept.; Heb.* you.

erroneously related the poem, perhaps because of the reference to the destruction of Gaza in verse 5, to Necho's attack on this city in 609 B.C. If the reference to Pharaoh in verse 1 is a later and erroneous expansion of the text, the poem could be dated during the period after the Babylonian victory at Carchemish when Jeremiah's message that the Babylonians would be masters of both Judah and the surrounding nations gathered momentum (cp. the commentary on ch. 36). Of these two possibilities, the second is perhaps preferable, especially in view of the evidence of the Septuagint which, as we have had occasion to observe, preserves what appears to be an earlier form of the book of Jeremiah in a number of places.

2. *See how waters are rising from the north:* for a similar metaphor see Isa. 8: 7–8.

4. *and Tyre and Sidon destroyed to the last defender:* Tyre and Sidon were Phoenician cities and the mention of them here is surprising. But perhaps, as many commentators suggest, there was an alliance between these cities and the Philistines. *that remnant of the isle of Caphtor:* Caphtor, according to biblical tradition (cp. Amos 9: 7), was the original home of the Philistines. It is usually identified with Crete but was perhaps originally used more generally for the Aegean area from which not only the Philistines but also other similar groups (referred to in Egyptian texts as 'the sea peoples') came and settled along the coast of Phoenicia and Palestine in the twelfth and eleventh centuries B.C.

5. *Ashkelon:* one of the five cities of the Philistines, comprising this city and Gaza, Ashdod, Gath, and Ekron. *Poor remnant of their strength:* until recently the Hebrew here was somewhat obscure. The Authorized Version, for example, translated it 'the remnant of their valley', whilst the Revised Standard Version, adopting the reading of the Septuagint, has 'O remnant of the Anakim'. But the Hebrew word which has been the source of the difficulty (*'emeq*), though it can mean 'valley', is here best understood as parallel to a similar word in Ugaritic meaning 'strength'. (Ugaritic is a language

belonging to the same family as Hebrew and was once spoken in ancient Syria. Tablets with Ugaritic inscribed on them were first discovered in 1928 and quickly deciphered. They have proved invaluable in illuminating many features not only of the Hebrew language but also of Israelite religion and culture.) *how long will you gash yourselves:* see the note on 41: 5. *

CONCERNING MOAB

* Ch. 48 comprises a number of sayings, mostly in poetry but with a few short passages in prose, announcing disaster upon Moab, its cities and inhabitants. It is surprising that Moab should receive such lengthy treatment compared with the other small nations surrounding Israel (the Philistines in ch. 47 and the nations dealt with in ch. 49). We know of no reason why this should be so, for Moab does not appear to have been a more hated enemy of Israel than, for example, the Ammonites or the Edomites who are dealt with much more briefly in ch. 49.

That Jeremiah himself uttered oracles against Moab need not be questioned (cp. ch. 27). But the chapter of oracles against Moab as we have it shows clear signs of the work of authors other than the prophet. This is particularly evident from the fact that not a little of the chapter displays heavy dependence upon Isa. 15–16. (It is inherently very unlikely that someone with the creative impulse and genius of Jeremiah would have felt it necessary to borrow so much from an earlier source.) So complex is the chapter, however, that there is little point in attempting to isolate from it such parts of it as may have been composed by Jeremiah.

From ch. 27 it was ascertained that Moab was party to a rebellion planned by various small states against Babylon in 594 B.C. Nothing came of the plans for revolt in that year and thereafter Moab appears to have remained loyal to Babylon for some years. But the Jewish historian Josephus (first century A.D.) records that the Babylonians invaded Moab and Ammon in 582 B.C. (It may have been at this time also that the third deportation of Judaeans mentioned in 52: 30 took place. Cp. the commentary on 41: 1.) It is known that after 582 B.C. Moab was invaded, not for the first time (see below), by Arab tribes from the east and Moab ceased to exist as a nation. Accordingly, whilst the present chapter may have been somewhat 'touched up' or rearranged at a later time, most, if not all, of it was completed during the first quarter of the sixth century. As already noted, this chapter in places shows dependence upon Isa. 15–16. There are good reasons for believing that the material in these chapters comes from the middle of the seventh century B.C. when Moab was invaded by Arab tribes from the east. It would appear, therefore, that an editor, working during the first quarter of the sixth century B.C., has taken up some of the material in Isa. 15–16 together with other sayings, some probably from Jeremiah himself, and has arranged and supplemented them to form the present chapter.

For the rest, it remains to be noted that the most striking feature of this chapter is the great number of place-names it contains (cp. also Isa. 15–16). But many of the places mentioned have thus far not been identified. ✷

DISASTER UPON MOAB

48 Of Moab. The LORD of Hosts the God of Israel has spoken:

> Alas for Nebo! it is laid waste;
> Kiriathaim is put to shame and captured,
> Misgab reduced to shame and dismay;
2   Moab is renowned no longer.
> In Heshbon they plot evil against her:
>   Come, destroy her, and leave her no longer a
>   nation.

And you who live in Madmen shall be struck down,
your people pursued by the sword.
    Hark to the cries of anguish from Horonaim: 3
great havoc and disaster!
    Moab is broken.   4
Their cries are heard as far as Zoar.
    On the ascent of Luhith   5
    men go up weeping bitterly;
    on the descent of Horonaim
cries of 'Disaster!' are heard.
Flee, flee for your lives   6
like a sand-grouse in the wilderness.
Because you have trusted in your defences and your   7
    arsenals,
    you too will be captured,
and Kemosh will go into exile,
his priests and his captains with him;
and a spoiler shall descend on every city.   8
    No city shall escape,
valley and tableland will be laid waste and plundered;
    the LORD has spoken.

Let a warning flash to Moab,[a]   9
for she shall be laid in ruins[b]
and her cities shall become waste places
    with no inhabitant.
A curse on him who is slack in doing the LORD's   10
    work!
A curse on him who withholds his sword from
    bloodshed!

[a] Let. . .Moab: *or* Doom Moab to become saltings.
[b] laid in ruins: *prob. rdg.; Heb. obscure.*

✻ Moab and its cities are overthrown. Their inhabitants can do nothing but flee for their lives. Both gods and those who worship them will be taken into exile.

1. *Of Moab:* the title, cp. on 46: 2. The territory of Moab is east of the Dead Sea. Its southern boundary was marked by the gorge of the Zared and its northern boundary by the river Arnon, though in some periods it was further north than this. The land is a plateau rich in cultivable terrain. *Nebo:* mentioned as one of the cities of the tribe Reuben in Transjordan (Num. 32: 3, 38) and on the Moabite Stone (a ninth-century inscription by Mesha, king of Moab) as a city of Moab. Its location is unknown, though from its name it may have been near Mount Nebo, about 12 miles (approximately 19 km) east of the northern tip of the Dead Sea. *Kiriathaim:* like Nebo, Kiriathaim also is mentioned as a city of the tribe Reuben in Transjordan (Josh. 13: 19) and on the Moabite Stone as a Moabite city. It is possibly to be identified with the modern el-Qereiyat just over 5 miles (about 8 km) north-west of Dibon. *Misgab:* nothing is known of this place. (Some translations understand the word to be a noun meaning 'fortress'.)

2. *In Heshbon they plot:* Heshbon was the capital of the Amorite king Sihon (cp. Num. 21: 25–30). It is listed in Josh. 13: 26 as a city of the tribe of Gad but in Josh. 13: 17 as a city of the Reubenites. It later became a Moabite city and is identified with the modern Hesban (about 50 miles (80 km) due east of Jerusalem). The Hebrew translated 'they plot' is a play upon the word Heshbon. The location of *Madmen* is unknown. The Hebrew word translated *shall be struck down* is a play upon the word Madmen.

3. *Horonaim:* Horonaim is also mentioned on the Moabite Stone, but its location is unknown.

.4. *Zoar:* Zoar was one of the 'cities of the Plain' mentioned in Gen.13 : 10 ff. which also included Sodom and Gomorrah. From early times the territory of Zoar and the other 'cities of the Plain' has been located in the shallow southern end of the Dead Sea, though some scholars locate them north of the Dead Sea.

5. This verse is almost identical with the second half of Isa. 15: 5. The location of *Luhith* is unknown.

6. *like a sand-grouse in the wilderness:* the translation *sand-grouse* is based upon an Arabic word not recognized until recently to be cognate with the Hebrew word here. This discovery removes the difficulty which translators have hitherto had with the verse.

7. *and Kemosh will go into exile:* Kemosh was the god of the Moabites. On the Moabite Stone this god is referred to as Ashtar-Kemosh and since Ashtar was the Canaanite god of the morning star it suggests that Kemosh was worshipped as an astral deity. According to 1 Kings 11: 7 Solomon 'built a hill-shrine for Kemosh, the loathsome god of Moab', no doubt for the use of the Moabite women in his harem.

10. This verse has all the appearance of being an editorial insertion in the text at this point. *

MOAB'S EASE COMES TO AN END

All his life long, Moab has laid undisturbed   11
   like wine settled on its lees,
     not emptied from vessel to vessel;
      he has not gone into exile.
Therefore the taste of him is unaltered,
    and the flavour stays unchanged.
Therefore the days are coming, says the LORD,   12
   when I will send men to tilt the jars; they shall tilt them
   and empty his vessels and smash his jars;
    and Moab shall be betrayed by Kemosh,   13
    as Israel was betrayed by Bethel,
     a god in whom he trusted.

11. *All his life long, Moab has lain undisturbed:* for long periods of its history Moab had been subject to Israel. But defeat and humiliation in battle and even subjection to another power

are surpassed by exile. *like wine settled on its lees, not emptied from vessel to vessel:* Moab is compared to wine not strained of its dregs and sediment (*lees*) by being carefully poured from one vessel to another. The metaphor conveys the complacency of Moab; the oracle announces that it is a complacency soon to be violently terminated.

12. The metaphor is continued. As men might throw out wine from jars and smash the jars in pieces, so would Moab be destroyed and thrown into exile.

13. *and Moab shall be betrayed by Kemosh:* on the Moabite Stone Kemosh, the god of Moab is portrayed, as we might expect, as the deliverer of his people from their enemies; the author of the inscription, King Mesha, could say of Kemosh 'he saved me from all the kings and let me see my desire upon my adversaries'. But in the disaster now to befall Moab, Kemosh would be of no avail, an empty illusion. *as Israel was betrayed by Bethel:* Bethel is here not the name of the town and sanctuary in Israel bearing this name but of a god. This god is known to have been worshipped in Syria and elsewhere in the ancient Near East. That he was worshipped in Israel is shown by documents deriving from a Jewish colony at Elephantine in Egypt in the fifth century B.C. which mention this god. It is probable that this community had brought the worship of this god with them from Palestine. It is possible, however, that though Israel's worship of Bethel is condemned in this verse, he was in Israel identified with Yahweh just as other Canaanite gods such as, for example, El Elyon ('God most high') were gradually taken over by Israel and identified with the national God Yahweh. ✳

JUDGEMENT HAS COME UPON MOAB

14   How can you say, 'We are warriors
      and men valiant in battle'?
15   The spoiler of Moab and her cities has come up,

and the flower of her army goes down to the
    slaughter.

This is the very word of the King whose name is the
LORD of Hosts.

    The downfall of Moab is near at hand,   16
    disaster rushes swiftly upon him.
    Grieve for him, all you his neighbours   17
      and all who acknowledge him,
    and say, 'Alas! The commander's staff is broken,
      broken is the baton of honour.'
    Come down from your place of honour,   18
sit on the thirsty ground, you natives of Dibon;
for the spoiler of Moab has come upon you
    and destroyed your citadels.
You that live in Aroer, stand on the roadside and   19
    watch,
    ask the fugitives, the man running, the woman
      escaping,
    ask them, 'What has happened?'

    Moab is reduced to shame and dismay: 20
    howl and shriek,
proclaim by the Arnon that Moab is despoiled,
and that judgement has come to the tableland, to Holon 21
and Jahazah, Mephaath and Dibon, Nebo and Bethdib- 22
lathaim and Kiriathaim, Beth-gamul, Beth-meon, Kirioth 23, 24
and Bozrah, and to all the cities of Moab far and near.

* This passage comprises several short sayings announcing
the imminent destruction of Moab.
  14–15. Moab's proud warriors, *the flower of her army*, are
wiped out.

16–17. The nations around Moab are summoned to grieve its downfall.

17. *The commander's staff is broken, broken is the baton of honour:* characteristic of the royal insignia of ancient Near Eastern kings was an official staff or baton, better known as the sceptre. It was emblematic of the king's power. The Hebrew text here is literally 'broken is the staff of strength, the baton of honour' and may therefore be a reference directly to the king's sceptre. The N.E.B. translation refers it to the commander. This also could be taken to refer to the king (the 'commander-in-chief' as we might designate him). But it is known that a royal official could carry such a staff as a sign of his authority under the king. In this case the commander would have been the leader of the army on the battle-field.

18. *Dibon:* it was at Dibon (modern Diban) that the Moabite Stone was discovered. This town is mentioned in it.

19–24. Verses 20–4 are probably to be taken as the reply to the question in verse 19.

19. *Aroer:* several cities bearing this name (it means 'junipers') are mentioned in the Old Testament. The city in question here is the Aroer just north of the river Arnon and a few miles south-west of Dibon.

21–4. Of the towns mentioned in these verses, *Jahazah* (= Jahaz in verse 34), *Beth-diblathaim, Beth-meon,* and *Kirioth* are mentioned in the Moabite Stone, as also is *Bozrah* which may be the same as Bezer located about 8 miles (nearly 13 km) north-east of Medeba. The location of *Holon* and Kirioth are unknown, and that of Jahazah uncertain. *Mephaath* is probably to be identified with Tell Jawah about 6 miles (approximately $9\frac{1}{2}$ km) south of Amman in Jordan. Beth-diblathaim appears to have been located near Medeba as also were Beth-meon and *Beth-gamul.* ✳

MOAB IS REVILED

Moab's horn is hacked off   25
   and his strong arm is broken,
   says the LORD.

Make Moab drunk – he has defied the LORD –   26
until he overflows with his vomit
and even he becomes a butt for derision.
But was Israel ever your butt?   27
   Was he ever in company with thieves,
that whenever you spoke of him you should shake
     your head?
Leave your cities, you inhabitants of Moab,   28
   and find a home among the crags;
become like a dove which nests
   in the rock-face at the mouth of a cavern.

✵ 25. This is an isolated saying describing the destruction of
Moab's might. The word *horn* is often used as a description or
emblem of strength in the Old Testament.
26–8. The imagery of drunkenness recalls 25: 15–29. Moab
is depicted in a situation at once disgusting and ridiculous, a
sheer laughing-stock.
27. *But was Israel ever your butt?* Moab had treated Israel as a
laughing-stock, a people to be treated as contemptuously as a
thief. But now Moab itself has become an object of ridicule
and derision. ✵

A LAMENT OVER MOAB

We have heard of Moab's pride, and proud indeed   29
     he is,
proud, presumptuous, overbearing, insolent.
I know his arrogance, says the LORD;   30

his boasting is false, false are his deeds.

31   Therefore I will howl over Moab
        and cry in anguish at the fate of every soul in
           Moab;
     I[a] will moan over the men of Kir-heres.

32   I will weep for you more than I wept for Jazer,
        O vine of Sibmah
     whose branches spread out to the sea
        and stretch as far as Jazer.[b]
     The despoiler has fallen on your fruit and on your
        vintage,

33   gladness and joy are taken away
        from the meadows of Moab,
     and I have stopped the flow of wine from the vats;
     nor shall shout follow shout from the harvesters – not
        one shout.

34 Heshbon and[c] Elealeh utter cries of anguish which are
heard in Jahaz; the sound carries from Zoar to Horonaim
and[d] Eglath-shelishiyah; for the waters of Nimrim have
35 become a desolate waste. In Moab I will stop their sacri-
ficing at hill-shrines and burning of offerings to their gods,
36 says the LORD. Therefore my heart wails for Moab like a
reed-pipe, wails like a pipe for the men of Kir-heres.
37 Their hard-earned wealth has vanished. Every man's head
is shorn in mourning, every beard shaved, every hand
38 gashed, and every waist girded with sackcloth. On
Moab's roofs and in her broad streets nothing is heard but

[a] *So one MS.; others* he.
[b] as far as Jazer: *so some MSS., cp. Isa. 16: 8; others* the sea of Jazer.
[c] and: *prob. rdg., cp. Isa. 15: 4; Heb.* as far as.
[d] and: *so Sept.; Heb. om.*

lamentation; for I have broken Moab like a useless thing.[a]
Moab in her dismay[b] has shamefully turned to flight. 39
Moab has become a butt of derision and a cause of dismay to all her neighbours.

* This entire section is heavily dependent upon Isa. 15 and 16.
The many similarities between the passages are so obvious
that there is no need to cite them here.

31. *I will moan over the men of Kir-heres:* also known as
Kir-hareseth (cp. 2 Kings 3: 25; Isa. 16: 7), it has been identified with el-Kerak, about 17 miles (approximately 27 km)
south of the river Arnon and about 11 miles (nearly 18 km)
east of the Dead Sea. It is possible that its proper name was
Kir-hadesheth, 'the new city', and that this was corrupted in
Hebrew to Kir-hareseth 'wall of the potsherds'.

32. *Jazer:* this was in the territory of the Ammonites, but
like many other towns in this area it was apparently conquered by Mesha even though it is not mentioned in the
Moabite Stone. The location of *Sibmah* is uncertain.

34. *Elealeh* is modern el-'Al north of Heshbon. The name
Eglath-shelishiyah ('the third Eglath') may have been used to
distinguish this town, whose location is unknown, from two
other towns in the same region or locality also having Eglath
as their names or as part of their names. The location of *the
waters of Nimrim* is uncertain. Some commentators identify it
with a small stream known as the Wadi en-Numeirah which
flows into the Dead Sea from the east a few miles north of its
southern tip. Others would identify it with the Wadi Nimrim
which flows into the Jordan from the east about 8 miles
(nearly 13 km) north of the Dead Sea.

36. *Therefore my heart wails for Moab like a reed-pipe:* the
instrument here mentioned (some argue that it is really a
primitive clarinet) was also known elsewhere in the ancient

[a] *Prob. rdg.; Heb. adds* says the LORD.
[b] *So Sept.; Heb. adds* they howl.

Near East and could be used for expressing great joy or deep lament.

37. All these were expressions of grief and mourning in the ancient Near East (cp. the comment on 41: 5). ✳

THE ENEMY SWOOPS UPON MOAB

40   For the LORD has spoken:

> A vulture shall swoop down
> and spread out his wings over Moab.

41   The towns are captured, the strongholds taken;
> on that day the spirit of Moab's warriors shall fail
> like the spirit of a woman in childbirth.

42   Then Moab shall be destroyed, no more to be
>   a nation;
>   for he defied the LORD.

43   The hunter's scare, the pit, and the trap
>   threaten all who dwell in Moab,
>   says the LORD.

44   If a man runs from the scare
>   he will fall into the pit;
> if he climbs out of the pit
>   he will be caught in the trap.

> All this will I bring on Moab in the year of their
>   reckoning.
>   This is the very word of the LORD.

45   In the shadow of Heshbon the fugitives stand helpless;
>   for fire has blazed out from Heshbon,
>   flames have shot out from the palace of[a] Sihon;
>   they devour the homeland of Moab

[a] from the palace of: *so some MSS.; others* from between.

and the country[a] of the sons of tumult.

Alas for you, Moab! the people of Kemosh have   46
    vanished,
  for your sons are taken into captivity
  and your daughters led away captive.
Yet in days to come I will restore Moab's fortunes.   47
    This is the very word of the LORD.

Here ends the sentence on Moab.

* 40–1. Of these two verses the Septuagint has only 'Kirioth
is captured, the strongholds taken' (the parallelism is best
suited by taking the Hebrew word *kirioth* here to refer to
'cities', as in the N.E.B., rather than to Kirioth). This was
possibly all there was originally of these two verses, the
remainder of which may have been inserted, with the
necessary alteration of the proper names, from 49: 22.

44. With the imagery employed here we may compare
Amos 5: 19.

45–7. These verses are not found in the Septuagint which,
after verse 44, has the vision of the 'cup of fiery wine' (25:
15–29). Verses 45–6 are for the most part taken from Num.
21: 28–9. *

CONCERNING AMMON

Of the people of Ammon. Thus says the LORD: **49**

Has Israel no sons? Has he no heir?
Why has Milcom inherited the land of Gad,
  and why do his people live in the cities of Gad?
Look, therefore, a time is coming,   2
    says the LORD,
when I will make Rabbath Ammon hear the
    battle-cry,

[a] *So some MSS.; others* crown (of head).

189

when it will become a desolate mound of ruins
and its villages will be burnt to ashes,
and Israel shall disinherit those who disinherited
him,
says the LORD.

3 Howl, Heshbon, for Ai is despoiled.
Cry aloud, you villages round Rabbath Ammon,
put on sackcloth and beat your breast,
and score your bodies with gashes.[a]
For Milcom will go into exile,
and with him his priests and officers.

4 Why do you boast of your resources,
you whose resources are melting away,
you wayward people who trust in your arsenals,
and say, 'Who will dare attack me?'

5 Beware, I am bringing fear upon you from every
side,[b]
and every one of you shall be driven headlong
with no man to round up the stragglers.

6 Yet after this I will restore the fortunes of Ammon.
This is the very word of the LORD.

☆ The Ammonites, like the Moabites, were involved in the plot to rebel against Nebuchadrezzar in 594 B.C. recorded in ch. 27. Ezek. 21: 18ff. indicates that Ammon, like Judah, rebelled against the Babylonians in 589 B.C. But evidently the Ammonites escaped the avenging wrath of Nebuchadrezzar, for after the fall of Jerusalem in 587 B.C. Baalis king of Ammon was Ishmael's co-conspirator in the assassination of Gedaliah (cp. 40: 13f.). It was probably as a result of Ammon's involvement in this that Nebuchadrezzar invaded it in 582 B.C. (see

[a] *Prob. rdg., cp. Targ.; Heb.* fences.
[b] *Prob. rdg.; Heb. adds* says the Lord GOD of Hosts.

above, p. 165). Subsequently, Ammon, like Moab, was overrun
by Arab invasions and by the middle of the sixth century B.C.
had ceased to exist as a nation.

1. *Of the people of Ammon:* the title, cp. on 46: 2. The
Ammonites were a people who lived on the borders of the
Syrian desert in central Transjordan from about 1300–580
B.C. They were thus, like the Moabites, close neighbours of
Israel and the Old Testament records frequent hostilities and
wars between the two peoples. *Why has Milcom inherited the
land of Gad:* the territory of the tribe of Gad lay east of the
river Jordan and north of the Dead Sea. In 734 B.C. the
Assyrian king Tiglath-pileser invaded this territory and exiled
its people. The Ammonites took advantage of this and invaded
this region. It is to this occupation of Israelite territory that
verse 1 refers. *Milcom* was the national god of Ammon. The
name means 'the king'. From 1 Kings 11: 7 it is clear that
Milcom and Molech were the same god (cp. the commentary
on 2: 23 and 7: 30 – 8: 3).

2. *I will make Rabbath Ammon hear the battle-cry:* Rabbath
Ammon was the capital of Ammon. It is identified with modern
Amman, the capital of Jordan. *a desolate mound of ruins:* see the
note on 30: 18.

3. *Howl, Heshbon, for Ai is despoiled:* from this it appears
that there was a Moabite town called Ai (literally 'ruin') in
addition to the Israelite town bearing the same name. But we
do not know the location of this Moabite city. The text
implies that at this time Ammon was in control of some
Moabite territory. *and score your bodies with gashes:* see the
note on 41: 5.

4. *Why do you boast of your resources:* the word here translated *resources* is the same as that translated 'strength' in 47: 5
(see the note on this verse). The discovery of such a meaning
for the Hebrew word here solves an old problem in understanding this verse. ✻

CONCERNING EDOM

7   Of Edom. The LORD of Hosts has said:

Is wisdom no longer to be found in Teman?
Have her sages no skill in counsel?
    Has their wisdom decayed?
8   The people of Dedan have turned and fled
    and taken refuge in remote places;
for I will bring Esau's calamity upon him
    when his day of reckoning comes.
9[a] When the vintagers come to you
    they will surely leave gleanings;
and if thieves raid your early crop in the night,
    they will take only as much as they want.
10   But I have ransacked Esau's treasure,
    I have uncovered his hiding-places,
    and he has nowhere to conceal himself;
his children, his kinsfolk and his neighbours are
        despoiled;
    there is no one to help him.
11   What! am I to save alive your fatherless children?
    Are your widows to trust in me?

12   For the LORD has spoken: Those who were not doomed
to drink the cup shall drink it none the less. Are you alone
to go unpunished? You shall not go unpunished; you
13 shall drink it. For by my life, says the LORD, Bozrah shall
become a horror and reproach, a byword and a thing of
ridicule; and all her towns shall be a byword for ever.

[a] *Verses 9 and 10: cp. Obad. 5, 6.*

When a herald was sent among the nations, crying, 14[a]
'Gather together and march against her,
   rouse yourselves for battle',
I heard this message from the LORD:
Look, I make you the least of all nations,   15
   an object of all men's contempt.
Your overbearing arrogance and your insolent heart 16
   have led you astray,
you who haunt the crannies among the rocks
and keep your hold on the heights of the hills.
Though you build your nest high as a vulture,
   thence I will bring you down.
   This is the very word of the LORD.
Edom shall become a scene of horror,   17
all who pass that way shall be horror-struck
and shall jeer in derision at the blows she has borne,
overthrown like Sodom and Gomorrah and their 18
   neighbours,[b]
   says the LORD.
No man shall live there,
no mortal make a home in her.
Look, like a lion coming up   19
from Jordan's dense thickets to the perennial
   pastures,
in a moment I will chase every one away
and round up the choicest of[c] her rams.
For who is like me? Who is my equal?
What shepherd can stand his ground before me?
Therefore listen to the LORD's whole purpose against 20

[a] *Verses 14–16: cp. Obad. 1–4.*
[b] *Or inhabitants.*
[c] the choicest of: *prob. rdg.; Heb.* who is chosen?

Edom and all his plans against the people of Teman:

The young ones of the flock shall be carried off,
and their pasture shall be horrified at their fate.

21   At the sound of their fall the land quakes;
it cries out, and the cry is heard at the Red Sea.[a]

22   A vulture shall soar and swoop down
and spread out his wings over Bozrah,
and on that day the spirit of Edom's warriors shall
fail
like the spirit of a woman in labour.

✻ Gen. 36 designates the Edomites as descendants of Esau,
Jacob's brother, and Edom is referred to in the present passage
as Esau. But of all Israel's neighbours, Edom is singled out as
an object of particular hatred by the Jews after 587 B.C. From
ch. 27 it appears that Edom was confederate with Judah in the
abortive plans to rebel against Babylon. But when Zedekiah
rebelled against Nebuchadrezzar in 589 B.C. the Edomites
came out on the Babylonian side (cp. especially Ps. 137: 7).
Like the Moabites and Ammonites, however, Edom was later
overrun by Arab tribes. The Edomites at this time moved into
southern Judah and occupied it. This explains why this area
came to be known at a later time as Idumea.

This passage contains some material found elsewhere in the
Old Testament. Verses 9–10 are closely parallel to Obad.
verses 5–6, whilst verses 14–16 are closely akin to Obad.
verses 1–4. In addition, some verses or parts of verses are found
elsewhere in the book of Jeremiah itself. The passage has therefore all the appearance of being editorial, though it may contain a kernel of material from Jeremiah. The passage as it now
stands was probably composed in the period immediately
following 587 B.C. but it is possible that the material it has in
common with Obadiah (also composed after 587 B.C.) derives
from an earlier source.

[a] *Or* the Sea of Reeds.

7. *Of Edom:* the title, cp. on 46: 2. The territory of Edom lay south of the Dead Sea with its southern border north of the Gulf of Aqabah. *Is wisdom no longer to be found in Teman?:* the association here drawn between wisdom and Edom has been taken, together with some other texts in the Old Testament, as an indication that Edom was famous for its wisdom. But there is little evidence for this and certainly the present text need not be taken as implying it. *Teman* was a region of Edom but its location is disputed. As this text implies, the name could be used of Edom as a whole.

8. *The people of Dedan:* in north-west Arabia, possibly a district or boundary of Edom.

9-10. (Cp. Obad. verses 5-6.) The meaning appears to be that whereas men picking grapes do not glean the vines completely and that whereas thieves who raid a crop in the night take only what they need, God would utterly destroy Edom.

12. This verse is clearly an allusion to 25: 15 ff. (cp. especially 25: 28, 29).

13. *Bozrah:* not to be confused with the Moabite town of the same name mentioned in 48: 24, this Edomite town, Bozrah, is possibly to be identified with the modern Buseira, about 25 miles (approximately 40 km) south-east of the Dead Sea.

14-16. As already noted, these verses are, with minor differences, the same as Obad. verses 1-4.

18. *overthrown like Sodom and Gomorrah:* the fate to befall Edom is likened to that of these two infamous cities which God overthrew and completely destroyed. *and their neighbours:* unless this refers to the inhabitants of these cities (cp. the N.E.B. footnote), it probably means Admah and Zeboyim (cp. Deut. 29: 23). Verse 18 is also found in 50: 40.

19-21. These verses are also found in 50: 44-6, where they apply to Babylon.

19. *Look, like a lion coming up from Jordan's dense thickets:* see the note on 5: 6.

22. This verse was probably used in the composition of 48: 40-1 (see the note on these verses). ✻

OF DAMASCUS

23   Of Damascus.

Hamath and Arpad are in confusion,
    for they have heard news of disaster;
they are tossed up and down in anxiety
    like the unresting sea.

24   Damascus has lost heart and turns to flight;
        trembling has seized her,
the pangs of childbirth have gripped her.

25   How forlorn is the town of joyful song,
        the city of gladness[a]!

26   Therefore her young men shall fall in her streets
    and all her warriors lie still in death that day.
        This is the very word of the LORD of Hosts.

27   Then will I kindle a fire against the wall of Damascus
    and it shall consume the palaces of Ben-hadad.

* Damascus, Hamath and Arpad were the capital cities of
three Syrian states in the ancient Near East. All three, but
especially Damascus, played a part in the history of Syria–
Palestine during much of the monarchical period in Israel's
history. But all three were invaded by the Assyrians in
the middle of the eighth century B.C. and were of little or no
importance thereafter. We read in 2 Kings 24: 2 of Aramaean
troops together with other marauding bands attacking Judah.
But apart from this the Aramaeans were of no consequence in
the history of Judah during Jeremiah's lifetime. For this reason
it is possible that this passage is based upon an earlier saying
concerning the peoples mentioned and has been placed here
so as to include the Aramaeans among the other states border-
ing or close to Israel dealt with in the present chapter.

[a] *So Pesh.; Heb.* of my gladness.

23. *Of Damascus:* the title, cp. on 46: 2. Ancient Damascus was situated at the foot of Mount Hermon on the Syro–Arabian desert. *Hamath* was situated on the River Orontes in Syria, whilst *Arpad* is probably to be identified with the modern Tell Erfad about 25 miles (approximately 40 km) north of Aleppo.

26. This verse is also found in 50: 30 where it is probably original, since *Therefore* at the beginning of the verse shows it to be the proper sequel to the words of 50: 29; it is not appropriate here.

27. This verse is very similar to Amos 1: 4 on which it may have been based. *Ben-hadad* ('son of (the god) Hadad') was the name of at least two kings of Damascus. Hadad was the storm-god worshipped by the Aramaeans. He is the same as the Canaanite god Baal much more frequently mentioned in the Old Testament. ✳

CONCERNING KEDAR AND HAZER

Of Kedar and the royal princes[a] of Hazer which 28 Nebuchadrezzar king of Babylon subdued. The LORD has said:

> Come, attack Kedar,
>> despoil the Arabs of the east.
>
> Carry off their tents and their flocks,   29
>> their tent-hangings and all their vessels,
>> drive off their camels too,
>
> and a cry shall go up: 'Terror let loose!'
> Flee, flee; make haste,   30
>> take refuge in remote places, O people of Hazer,
>> for the king of Babylon[b] has laid his plans
>> and formed a design against you,
>>> says the LORD.

[a] royal princes: *or* kingdom.
[b] *So Sept.; Heb. adds* Nebuchadrezzar.

31   Come, let us attack a nation living at peace,
             in fancied security,[a]
          with neither gates nor bars,
          sufficient to themselves.
32   Their camels shall be carried off as booty,
             their vast herds of cattle as plunder;
          I will scatter them before the wind to roam the
             fringes of the desert,[b]
          and bring ruin upon them from every side.
33   Hazer shall become a haunt of wolves,
             for ever desolate;
          no man shall live there,
          no mortal make a home in her.
          This is the very word of the LORD.

✻ Kedar was an important Arab tribe frequently mentioned in the Old Testament. It lived in the Syro–Arabian desert east of present-day Jordan. *Hazer* (not Hazor, as the word is vocalized in the Hebrew text) was also the name of an Arab tribe in the eastern desert. We noted earlier (see the commentary on ch. 48 and 49: 1–6) that in the middle of the seventh century B.C. and again in the sixth century B.C. Arab tribes from the east overran the territory of Moab and Ammon in Transjordan. Babylonian records indicate that Nebuchadrezzar attacked these Arab tribes early in the sixth century B.C. Possibly this passage was composed at that time.

29. The mention of *tents* and *camels* here indicates that the people in question were nomads rather than settled tribes. *Terror let loose:* cp. the note on 46: 5.

32. *the fringes of the desert:* see the note on 9: 26. ✻

[a] So Sept.; *Heb. adds* says the LORD.
[b] them. . .desert: *or* to the wind those who clip the hair on their temples.

CONCERNING ELAM

This came to the prophet Jeremiah as the word of the 34
LORD concerning Elam, at the beginning of the reign of
Zedekiah king of Judah: Thus says the LORD of Hosts: 35

> Listen, I will break the bow of Elam,
>> the chief weapon of their might;
> I will bring four winds against Elam   36
>> from the four quarters of heaven;
> I will scatter them before these four winds,
>> and there shall be no nation
> to which the exiles from Elam shall not come.
> I will break Elam before their foes,   37
>> before those who are bent on their destruction;
> I will vent my anger upon them in disaster;[a]
> I will harry them with the sword
>> until I make an end of them.
> Then I will set my throne in Elam,   38
> and there I will destroy the king and his officers.
>> This is the very word of the LORD.
> Yet in days to come I will restore the fortunes of   39
>> Elam.
>> This is the very word of the LORD.

* Elam is the name of the country to the east of Babylon in
modern Persia. It was conquered by the Assyrians under
Ashurbanipal about 640 B.C. but probably regained independence in the years after about 630 B.C. But our knowledge of
the history of Elam in the years after this is very meagre and
there is no sure information about any events involving the

[a] *So Sept.; Heb. adds* says the LORD.

Elamites during the reign of Zedekiah which may have prompted the present oracle. Perhaps future discoveries will shed light on this.

35. *the chief weapon of their might:* this together with the reference to Elam in Isa. 22: 6 suggests that Elam was famous for its archers.

38. *Then I will set my throne in Elam:* the throne of a conquering king is set up in the land which he has invaded and which he can then proceed to subjugate and bring under his control (cp. 1: 15; 43: 8–13). ✳

CONCERNING BABYLON

✳ The remaining two chapters of the oracles against the nations are concerned exclusively with Babylon. In length these two chapters are not far short of the material in chs. 46–9 concerning the other nations dealt with in this section of the book. That Jeremiah himself uttered oracles of such a nature concerning the eventual downfall of Babylon is all to be expected. But once again there is evidence that these two chapters owe their present form to editors who have embodied in them sayings from Jeremiah himself which they have supplemented with material of their own composition or from other authors.

That such a large proportion of the oracles against the foreign nations should concern Babylon can occasion no surprise. For Israel the destruction of Jerusalem by the Babylonians and the ensuing exile marked the greatest tragedy which had hitherto befallen the nation, even including the devastation wrought by the Assyrians on northern Israel in 722 B.C. and the exile which took place at that time. It is against the Babylonians that what is probably the most gruesome and horrifying curse in the Old Testament is levelled (Ps. 137: 9). The present chapters are characterized by an intensely vengeful announcement of the coming destruction of Babylon. Their contents may be summarized as a proclamation of Babylon's destruction and the deliverance of God's people from captivity.

After the death of Nebuchadrezzar in 562 B.C. the neo-Babylonian power began a steady decline. His son and successor, Amel Marduk (Evil-merodach, as he is named in the Old Testament), was assassinated in 560 B.C. by his brother-in-law Neriglissar (560–556 B.C.). Neriglissar's heir and successor, Labashi-Marduk, reigned for only a very brief period before being supplanted by Nabonidus (556–539 B.C.), the last king of the neo-Babylonian Empire. Meanwhile the Persians to the east under Cyrus (550–530 B.C.) were emerging as future conquerors of the Near East and in 539 B.C. entered the city of Babylon 'without battle', as a Babylonian record states. Under Cyrus the Jews in exile were permitted to return to their homeland. The fact that these two chapters speak of devastation being wrought upon Babylon by its conquering enemy and appear to be unaware of what turned out to be a battle-free occupation of Babylon by Cyrus points to the period before these events for the composition of these chapters.

Not all of the sayings and oracles in these chapters can be isolated from each other, since in many places they have been fused together by the editors. Some individual sections can be separated out, but in other places sections have been marked off for convenience. ✳

BABYLON'S DOWNFALL AND ISRAEL'S RESTORATION

The word which the LORD spoke concerning Babylon, **50** concerning the land of the Chaldaeans, through the prophet Jeremiah:

> Declare and proclaim among the nations,[a]   2
> keep nothing back, spread the news:
>> Babylon is taken,

[a] *So Sept.; Heb. adds* and raise a standard, proclaim.

Bel is put to shame, Marduk is in despair;
   the idols of Babylon are put to shame,
   her false gods are in despair.

3   For a nation out of the north has fallen upon her;
   they will make her land a desolate waste
   where neither man nor beast shall live.[a]

4   In those days, at that time, says the LORD, the people of Israel and the people of Judah shall come together and 5 go in tears to seek the LORD their God; they shall ask after Zion, turning their faces towards her, and they shall come and join[b] themselves to the LORD in an everlasting covenant which shall not be forgotten.

6   My people were lost sheep, whose shepherds let them stray and run wild on the mountains; they went from 7 mountain to hill and forgot their fold. Whoever found them devoured them, and their enemies said, 'We incur no guilt, because they have sinned against the LORD, the LORD who is the true goal and the hope of all their fathers.'

✳ This passage comprises two obviously separate sections, the first (verses 1–3) in poetry and the second (verses 4–7) in prose. But both are appropriate here at the beginning of these two chapters for they introduce the two major themes which characterize these chapters, the downfall of Babylon upon whom vengeance is to be taken for what they did to God's people (introduced by the first section) and the restoration of Israel from exile (introduced by the second section).

2. *Bel is put to shame, Marduk is in despair:* Bel is another name for the god Marduk, the state-god of Babylon. He was

[a] So Sept.; Heb. *adds* they have fled, they have gone.
[b] and they shall come and join: *so one MS.; others* come, and they shall join.

worshipped above all as the creator-god who championed over the chaos-waters to be acclaimed as king of the gods.

4. *the people of Israel and the people of Judah shall come together:* as in the 'book of consolation' the future restoration of God's people includes the people of both former kingdoms, northern Israel and Judah.

5. *they shall ask after Zion:* see the comment on 31: 6. *an everlasting covenant which shall not be forgotten:* a clear allusion to the new covenant passages in 31: 31 ff. and 32: 40.

6. *whose shepherds let them stray:* a reference to the nation's kings but possibly also, in this context, to priests and prophets who had fostered and encouraged apostasy. ✳

VENGEANCE UPON BABLYON

Flee from Babylon, from the land of the   8
    Chaldaeans;
go forth, and be like he-goats leading the flock.
For I will stir up a host of mighty nations   9
    and bring them against Babylon,
    marshalled against her from a northern land;
    and from the north she shall be captured.
Their arrows shall be like a practised warrior
    who never comes back empty-handed;
    the Chaldaeans shall be plundered,   10
and all who plunder them shall take their fill.
    This is the very word of the LORD.
You ravaged my patrimony; but though you   11
    rejoice and exult,
    though you run free like a heifer after threshing,
    though you neigh like a stallion,
your mother shall be cruelly disgraced,   12
    she who bore you shall be put to shame.

Look at her, the mere rump of the nations,
a wilderness, parched and desert,

13   unpeopled through the wrath of the LORD,
nothing but a desolate waste;
all who pass by Babylon shall be horror-struck
and jeer in derision at the sight of her wounds.

14   Marshal your forces against Babylon, on every side,
you whose bows are ready strung;
shoot at her, spare no arrows.[a]

15   Shout in triumph over her,[b] she has thrown up
her hands,
her bastions are down, her walls demolished;
this is the vengeance of the LORD.
Take vengeance on her;
as she has done, so do to her.

16   Destroy every sower in Babylon,
every reaper with his sickle at harvest-time.
Before the cruel sword every man will go back to his
people,
every man flee to his own land.

✻ As Babylon ravaged Israel so also she would be ravaged.
9. *marshalled against her from a northern land:* as Babylon, 'the foe from the north', had invaded and destroyed Israel, so now an enemy from the north would invade and destroy Babylon.

11. *You ravaged my patrimony:* in ancient Israel one's *patrimony* was the land inherited from one's ancestors (cp. the note on 37: 12). So the land of Israel is figuratively described as God's 'patrimony'.

[a] *So Sept.; Heb. adds* for she has sinned against the LORD.
[b] *So Sept.; Heb. adds* around her.

12. *your mother:* that is, the city of Babylon, personified here as the *mother* of the inhabitants.

15. *Take vengeance on her:* the note of vengeance runs through both chapters. ✳

FURTHER SAYINGS CONCERNING BABYLON
AND ISRAEL

Israel is a scattered flock　　　　　　　　　　　　　　17
　　harried and chased by lions:
as the king of Assyria was the first to feed on him,
so the king of Babylon*ᵃ* was the last to gnaw his
　　　bones.

Therefore the LORD of Hosts the God of Israel says this: 18

I will punish the king of Babylon and his country
as I have punished the king of Assyria.
I will bring Israel back to his pasture,　　　　　　　19
and he shall graze on Carmel and Bashan;
in the hills of Ephraim and Gilead he shall eat his fill.

In those days, says the LORD, when that time comes, 20
search shall be made for the iniquity of Israel but there
shall be none, and for the sin of Judah but it shall not be
found; for those whom I leave as a remnant I will forgive.

Attack the land of Merathaim;　　　　　　　　　　21
attack it and the inhabitants of Pekod;
put all to the sword and destroy them,*ᵇ*
and do whatever I bid you.
　　This is the very word of the LORD.

[a] *So Sept.; Heb. adds* Nebuchadrezzar.
[b] them: *prob. rdg., cp. Pesh.; Heb.* after them.

22   Hark, the sound of war in the land
          and great destruction!

23   See how the hammer of all the earth
          is hacked and broken in pieces,
      how Babylon has become
          a horror among the nations.

24   O Babylon, you have laid a snare to be your own
              undoing;
      you have been trapped, all unawares;
      there you are, you are caught,
          because you have challenged the LORD.

25   The LORD has opened his arsenal
          and brought out the weapons of his wrath;
      for this is work for the Lord the GOD of Hosts
          in the land of the Chaldaeans.

26   Her harvest-time has come:*a*
      throw open her granaries,*b* pile her in heaps;*c*
      destroy her, let no survivor be left.

27   Put all her warriors*d* to the sword;
          let them be led to the slaughter.
      Woe upon them! for their time has come,
          their day of reckoning.

28   I hear the fugitives escaping from the land of
              Babylon
      to proclaim in Zion the vengeance of the LORD our
              God.*e*

[*a*] Her...come: *prob. rdg., cp. Sept.; Heb.* Enter her from every
side.
[*b*] *Or* cattle-pens.
[*c*] in heaps: *or, with Targ.,* like men piling up corn.
[*d*] *Lit.* her bulls.
[*e*] *So Sept.; Heb. adds* vengeance for his temple.

Let your arrows be heard whistling against   29
   Babylon,
  all you whose bows are ready strung.
Pitch your tents all around her
  so that no one escapes.
Pay her back for all her misdeeds;
  as she has done, so do to her,
for she has insulted the LORD the Holy One of Israel.
Therefore her young men shall fall in her streets,   30
and all her warriors shall lie still in death that day.
  This is the very word of the LORD.

I am against you, insolent city;   31
for your time has come, your day of reckoning.
  This is the very word of the Lord GOD of Hosts.
Insolence shall stumble and fall   32
  and no one shall lift her up,
and I will kindle fire in the heath*a* around her
  and it shall consume everything round about.

The LORD of Hosts has said this: 33
The peoples of Israel and Judah together are oppressed;
  their captors hold them firmly and refuse to release
    them.
  But they have a powerful advocate,   34
  whose name is the LORD of Hosts;
  he himself will plead their cause,
bringing distress on Babylon and turmoil on its people.

A sword hangs over the Chaldaeans,   35
over the people of Babylon, her officers and her wise
    men,
  says the LORD.

[*a*] heath: so *Sept.*; *Heb.* cities

36   A sword over the false prophets, and they are made
            fools,
        a sword over her warriors, and they despair,

37   a sword over her horses and her chariots
            and over all the rabble within her,
            and they shall become like women;
        a sword over her treasures, and they shall be
            plundered,

38   a sword over her waters, and they shall dry up;
            for it is a land of idols
            that glories in its dreaded gods.[a]

39 Therefore marmots and jackals shall skulk in it, desert-
    owls shall haunt it, nevermore shall it be inhabited by
    men and no one shall dwell in it through all the ages.

40 As when God overthrew Sodom and Gomorrah and their
    neighbours,[b] says the LORD, no man shall live there, no
    mortal make a home in her.

    ✻ Verses 17–20 comprise two separate sayings which are,
    however, closely related in content. The first announces
    judgement upon Babylon and the restoration of Israel (verses
    17-19), the second, which is in prose, announces Israel's future
    faithfulness to God. Once again the note of vengeance is struck.
    In verses 21–32 the theme of vengeance upon Babylon recurs
    and her foes are incited to attack her. In verses 33–4 Israel's
    deliverance from her oppressor is again announced, whilst in
    verses 35–40 there is a graphic description of the total devasta-
    tion to be inflicted upon Babylon, its people and their leaders
    and sages, their prophets, their army, their treasures. Their
    copious supplies of water will be dried up, bringing devasta-
    tion and want to the land and making it a barren territory
    inhabited only by wild animals.

    [a] dreaded gods: *or* dire portents.   [b] *Or* inhabitants.

17. *as the king of Assyria was the first to feed on him:* a reference to the invasion and destruction of northern Israel by the Assyrians in 722 B.C. and the exile of many from northern Israel at that time.

18. *as I have punished the king of Assyria:* after the death of the Assyrian king Assurbanipal about 630 B.C., Assyria fell from power and was defeated by the Babylonians in 612 B.C.

19. God's 'flock', Israel, will return to its land and prosper.

20. This verse echoes the promise announced in the new covenant passage in 31: 31–4 that Israel's future would be one of perfect harmony with God, when never again would rebellion and sin separate her from him.

21. *Attack the land of Merathaim:* this was the name of a region in southern Babylon. But the name is also a play upon the Hebrew word 'to rebel' and is in grammatical form a 'dual'. Thus Babylon's name is 'twofold rebel', a 'rebel of rebels'. *the inhabitants of Pekod:* this is the name of a Babylonian tribe. But again the word is a play upon the Hebrew word 'to punish'.

23. *the hammer of all the earth:* a graphic description of the Babylonians who had beaten the nations of the Near East into subjection to her, devastating their lands in the process.

28. *to proclaim in Zion the vengeance of the LORD our God:* the fugitives are probably to be thought of as Jewish fugitives making their way back to Jerusalem to announce the overthrow of the nation's hated oppressor.

29. *Pay her back for all her misdeeds:* once more the note of revenge is struck. *for she has insulted the LORD:* the basic meaning of the word here translated *insulted* is 'to act presumptuously *or* rebelliously' against someone. The Babylonians had arrogantly discounted Israel's God as being of no importance and powerless.

34. *But they have a powerful advocate:* the word here translated *advocate* is the same as the word rendered 'redeemed' in 31: 11 (see the comment on this verse). *he himself will plead their cause:* the imagery is of a strong and successful counsel for

the defence in a court case. We recall that in ch. 2 God 'brought a charge' against his own people, acting as both plaintiff and counsel for the prosecution, so to speak, against them. Here he is their own advocate against those who have wronged them and upon whom he will execute judgement.

39. *marmots* are stout, burrowing rodents. *desert-owls:* this is preferable to the translation 'ostrich' found in some other English translations.

40. *Sodom and Gomorrah and their neighbours:* see the note on 49: 18. *

THE AGONY OF BABYLON

41 See, a people is coming from the north, a great nation,
    mighty*a* kings rouse themselves from earth's farthest
        corners;
42 armed with bow and sabre, they are cruel and
        pitiless;
    bestriding horses, they sound like the thunder
        of the sea;
    they are like men arrayed for battle against
        you, Babylon.
43 The king of Babylon has heard news of them
      and his hands hang limp;
    agony grips him, anguish as of a woman in labour.
44 Look, like a lion coming up
    from Jordan's dense thickets to the perennial
        pastures,
      in a moment I will chase every one away
      and round up the choicest of*b* the rams.
    For who is like me? Who is my equal?
    What shepherd can stand his ground before me?

[a] *Or* many.
[b] the choicest of: *prob. rdg.; Heb.* who is chosen?

Therefore listen to the LORD's whole purpose against 45
Babylon and all his plans against the land of the Chaldaeans:

> The young ones of the flock shall be carried off
> and their pasture shall be horrified at their fate.
> At the sound of the capture of Babylon   46
> the land quakes and her cry is heard among the
>   nations.

* This final passage in ch. 50 provides an interesting example
of the way in which a prophetic saying can be applied to a
situation other than that for which it was first composed. We
have come across many examples throughout the book of
original sayings of Jeremiah being applied to conditions of a
later period than that in which he lived and ministered. In
particular, there are not a few prose passages in the book from
Deuteronomic authors which have been based on an oracle or
saying by Jeremiah and which bring out the continued relevance of the prophet's message for a later time (an excellent
example is provided by ch. 24). In the case of the present
passage a saying originally referring to the defeat of Judah at
the hands of an enemy from the north (6: 22–4) has been
adapted (whether by Jeremiah himself or by a later editor need
not concern us) to the fate of Babylon. Accordingly, the
message of this passage is that just as Babylon had been the
terrible enemy from the north which invaded and destroyed
Israel, so now Babylon itself was to suffer a similar fate from
an equally terrible foe from the north (cp. verse 43 with 6: 24).

44. This verse, here applied to Babylon, is repeated from
49: 19, where it applies to Edom. *What shepherd can stand his
ground before me?* that is, what earthly ruler, however powerful, can match the power of God or resist his will?

45–6. These verses have been adapted from 49: 20-1. *

ISRAEL AND JUDAH NOT FORSAKEN BY GOD

51 For thus says the LORD:

I will raise a destroying wind
   against Babylon and those who live in Kambul,[a]
2 and I will send winnowers to Babylon,
   who shall winnow her and empty her land;
for they shall assail her on all sides on the day of
     disaster.
3 How shall the archer then string his bow
   or put on his coat of mail?

Spare none of her young men, destroy all her host,
4 and let them fall dead in the land of the Chaldaeans,
   pierced through in her streets.
5 Israel and Judah are not left widowed
   by their God, by the LORD of Hosts;
but the land of the Chaldaeans is full of guilt,
   condemned by the Holy One of Israel.

6 Flee out of Babylon, every man for himself,
   or you will be struck down for her sin;
for this is the LORD's day of vengeance,
   and he is paying her full recompense.
7 Babylon has been a gold cup in the LORD's hand
   to make all the earth drunk;
the nations have drunk of her wine,
   and that has made them mad.
8 Babylon falls suddenly and is broken.
   Howl over her,
fetch balm for her wound;

[a] Kambul: *prob. rdg.*; *Heb.* the heart of my opponents.

perhaps she will be healed.

We would have healed Babylon, but she would not   9
    be*ᵃ* healed.

Leave her and let us be off, each to his own country;
    for her doom reaches to heaven
    and mounts up to the skies.

The LORD has made our innocence plain to see;   10
come, let us proclaim in Zion
    what the LORD our God has done.

✻ As in other passages in these two chapters the announcement of Babylon's downfall is coupled with an announcement of Israel's restoration.

  1. *Kambul:* this reading is achieved by changing one of the
letters of the two Hebrew words which it translates and then
rearranging the letters. As it stands the Hebrew words mean
'the heart of my opponents'. Most commentators believe
that these two words are an example of the device of 'Atbash'
and that they are a cipher for Kasdim = Chaldaeans. ('Atbash'
is a device whereby a consonant in the Hebrew alphabet is
replaced by the corresponding consonant numbered from the
opposite end of the alphabet. Cp. the note on 25: 26.) This
suggestion has the support of the Septuagint which reads
'Chaldaeans'. Whilst such an understanding of these two
words remains possible, it is nevertheless difficult to see why
a cipher should be used here when Babylon has already been
referred to directly in this verse. Accordingly, the N.E.B.
suggestion that we should read *Kambul*, thus understanding
the text to have referred originally to a place, would appear
to make better sense. But the exact location of *Kambul* is
unknown (it may have been a district in southern Babylon) so
that the N.E.B. reading itself remains only a possibility.

  5. *Israel and Judah are not left widowed:* one of a number of

[a] would not be: *or* was not.

promises in these two chapters concerning the restoration of Israel and Judah. We note once again that all Israel, both northerners and Judaeans, is the subject of this promise. The use of the word *widowed* recalls the description of Israel as God's 'bride' in ch. 2.

6. *Flee out of Babylon, every man for himself:* those to whom this is addressed are not named. But verse 10 (cp. also verse 45) suggests that the Jews in exile in Babylon are intended (cp. Zech. 2: 6–7). *for this is the LORD's day of vengeance:* once more the note of vengeance which permeates these two chapters is sounded.

7. *Babylon has been a gold cup in the LORD's hand:* the imagery is similar to that in 25: 15ff. But here Babylon itself is portrayed as the cup of fury in God's hand, whilst in 25: 15–29 Babylon itself is to drink the 'cup' of God's fury. Here the imagery is rather of Babylon, once the 'cup' of God's wrath, being smashed (verse 8).

10. *come, let us proclaim in Zion what the LORD our God has done:* see the comment on 50: 28. ✳

BABYLON'S END HAS COME

11   Sharpen the arrows, fill the quivers.
      The LORD has roused the spirit of the king[a] of the
          Medes;
          for the LORD's purpose against Babylon is to destroy
              it,
          and his vengeance is the avenging of his temple.
12   Raise the standard against Babylon's walls,
      mount a strong guard, post a watch, set an ambush;
      for the LORD has both planned and carried out
      what he threatened to do to the people of Babylon.
13   O opulent city, standing beside great waters,

[a] So Sept.; Heb. kings.

your end has come, your destiny[a] is certain.
The LORD of Hosts has sworn by himself, saying,   14
Once I filled you with men, countless as locusts,
    yet a song of triumph shall be chanted over you.

God made the earth by his power,   15[b]
fixed the world in place by his wisdom,
unfurled the skies by his understanding.
At the thunder of his voice the waters in heaven are   16
        amazed;[c]
he brings up the mist from the ends of the earth,
he opens rifts[d] for the rain
and brings the wind out of his storehouses.
All men are brutish and ignorant,   17
every goldsmith is discredited by his idol;
for the figures he casts are a sham,
there is no breath in them.
They are worth nothing, mere mockeries,   18
which perish when their day of reckoning comes.
God, Jacob's creator, is not like these;   19
    for he is the maker of all.
    Israel[e] is the people he claims as his own;
    the LORD of Hosts is his name.

You are my battle-axe, my weapon of war;   20
with you I will break nations in pieces,
and with you I will destroy kingdoms.
With you I will break horse and rider,   21

[a] destiny: *lit.* cutting off (the thread of life).
[b] *Verses 15–19: cp. 10: 12–16.*
[c] At the thunder...amazed: *prob. rdg.; Heb.* At the sound of his giving tumult of waters in heaven.
[d] rifts: *prob. rdg.; Heb.* lightnings.
[e] *So many MSS.; others om.*

with you I will break chariot and rider,
22   with you I will break man and woman,
with you I will break young and old,
with you I will break young man and maiden,
23   with you I will break shepherd and flock,
with you I will break ploughman and team,
with you I will break viceroys and governors.
24   So will I repay Babylon and the people of Chaldaea
for all the wrong which they did in Zion in your
        sight.
        This is the very word of the LORD.

✷ This passage comprises three sections, verses 11–14, 15–19, 20–4. Of these, verses 15–19 are, with minor differences, inserted here from 10: 12–16. They may have been placed here after 11–14 to announce and emphasize, by asserting his omnipotence, God's power to accomplish his plans against Babylon (cp. verse 12 and for comments on verses 15–19 see the notes on 10: 12–16). It is difficult to determine who is being addressed in verses 20–4. Some commentators, taking verses 15–19 to be a secondary insertion into the text, link verses 20–4 with 11–14 and understand verses 20–4 to refer to the Babylonians and cite in support of this the reference in 50: 23 to Babylon as 'the hammer of all the earth' as well as 51: 25 where Babylon is described as a 'destroying mountain' which destroys 'the whole earth'. But as the N.E.B. translation of the passage as referring not to present or past action but to future action ('with you I will destroy kingdoms') suggests, the reference may be to Cyrus (cp. verse 11 and Isa. 41: 2–4). In view of the contents of verse 24, the latter understanding of the passage is preferable.

11. *Sharpen the arrows, fill the quivers:* once again the enemy is vehemently incited against Babylon. *The LORD has roused the spirit of the king of the Medes:* the Medes inhabited an

area in north-west Iran. Their capital was Ecbatana. They were invaded and subjugated by Cyrus in 550 B.C. As noted in the N.E.B. footnote, the Hebrew is 'kings of the Medes'. But the Medes never invaded Babylon. Cyrus's mother was a Mede and the Medes and Persians are linked together in several texts in the Old Testament (e.g. Dan. 5: 28; 6: 8, 12, 15). This, together with the fact that the Septuagint reads the singular 'king', suggests that we should understand the reference here to be to Cyrus. On the other hand, there is some evidence that an invasion of Babylon by the Medes was expected, even though it never materialized, about 561–560 B.C. so that it remains possible that these verses come from this time. *and his vengeance is the avenging of his temple* (cp. also the N.E.B. footnote on 50: 28): a specific reference to the Babylonian destruction and pillaging of the temple (cp. 52: 12f., 17–23).

13. *standing beside great waters* (cp. Ps. 137: 1): the River Euphrates with its numerous canals, near which the city of Babylon was situated, gave the city a perennial supply of water. In addition, we know that the copious amount of water in the vicinity was channelled into artificially-made ditches and lakes to strengthen the security of the city against attack by an enemy.

20–3. Like 49: 35–8, these verses present a picture of total annihilation.

24. *for all the wrong which they did in Zion:* once again the note of vengeance is struck. ✳

BABYLON IS DEFEATED

I am against you, O destroying mountain,[a][b]   25
    you who destroy the whole earth,
and I will stretch out my hand against you

[a] *Or* O Mount of the Destroyer.
[b] *So Sept.; Heb. adds* says the LORD.

and send you tumbling from your terraces
and make you a burnt-out mountain.

26 No stone of yours shall be used as a corner-stone,
no stone for a foundation;
but you shall be desolate, for ever waste.
This is the very word of the LORD.

27 Raise a standard in the land,[a]
blow the trumpet among the nations,
hallow the nations for war against her,
summon the kingdoms of Ararat, Minni, and
Ashkenaz,
appoint a commander-in-chief against her,
bring up the horses like a dark swarm of locusts;[b]

28 hallow the nations for war against her,
the king[c] of the Medes, his viceroys and governors,
and all the lands of his realm.

29 The earth quakes and writhes;
for the LORD's designs against Babylon are fulfilled,
to make the land of Babylon desolate and unpeopled.

30 Babylon's warriors have given up the fight,
they skulk in the forts;
their courage has failed, they have become like women.
Her buildings are set on fire, the bars of her gates
broken.

31 Runner speeds to meet runner,
messenger to meet messenger,
bringing news to the king of Babylon
that every quarter of his city is taken,

32 the river-crossings are seized,

[a] Or earth.   [b] Or hoppers.
[c] So Sept. (cp. verse 11); Heb. kings.

the guard-towers set on fire
and the garrison stricken with panic.

For the LORD of Hosts the God of Israel has spoken: 33

Babylon is like a threshing-floor when it is trodden;
soon, very soon, harvest-time will come.

'Nebuchadrezzar king of Babylon has devoured me   34
and sucked me dry,
he has set me aside like an empty jar.
Like a dragon he has gulped me down;
he has filled his maw with my delicate flesh
and spewed me up.
On Babylon be the violence done to me,   35
the vengeance taken upon me!',
Zion's people shall say.
'My blood be upon the Chaldaeans!',
Jerusalem shall say.

Therefore the LORD says: 36

I will plead your cause, I will avenge you;
I will dry up her sea[a] and make her waters fail;
and Babylon shall become a heap of ruins, a haunt of 37
wolves,
a scene of horror and derision, with no inhabitant.

⁎ This passage comprises three separate sayings. The first
(verses 25–6) is a short saying announcing the destruction of
the city of Babylon, the second (verses 27–32) returns to the
description of Babylon's rout before its enemies. The third
(verses 33–7) continues this theme and emphasizes the note of
vengeance upon Babylon which is characteristic of these
chapters.

[a] *Possibly the Euphrates.*

25. *and make you a burnt-out mountain:* as noted above (p. 201) Cyrus occupied the city of Babylon without resistance and the city was left intact. Almost certainly, therefore, the description of the devastation of the city here, as elsewhere in these two chapters, comes from the period before the fall of the Babylonians to Cyrus.

27. *Raise a standard in the land, blow the trumpet among the nations:* once again a summons to Babylon's enemies to muster their troops for attack. *hallow the nations for war against her:* it was a characteristic of the preparation of armies for war in the ancient Near East, including Israel, that religious rites were performed. The troops were ritually prepared for battle under the leadership of the nation's god(s). *Ararat, Minni, and Ashkenaz:* the first of these is roughly the territory of Armenia, the second is probably a region called Manna in Assyrian texts and was also probably located in Armenia, whilst the third was also probably in Armenia.

28. *the king of the Medes:* see the note on 51: 11.

29. *The earth quakes and writhes:* language such as this is associated elsewhere in the Old Testament, as here, with the coming of Israel's God Yahweh in war against his (and his people's) enemies (cp. for example Judg. 5: 4).

31. *Runner speeds to meet runner:* in the conduct of warfare in the ancient Near East, specially trained men were *runners* responsible for bringing news from the scene of the battle to the king or his commanders at headquarters (cp. 2 Sam. 18: 19ff.). The picture here is of these runners or couriers meeting each other as they come from all directions in panic to bring news to the king of the defeat of his army in the field. This verse and the next gives a graphic description of the invasion and destruction of the city.

33. *Babylon is like a threshing-floor when it is trodden:* as a threshing-floor is pounded down and levelled out in readiness for threshing the ingathered corn, so Babylon is to be levelled to the ground. *soon, very soon, harvest-time will come:* another metaphor taken from the same sphere as that immediately

preceding it and referring to the coming destruction of Babylon (cp. 50: 26).

34–5. The exiles cry out for vengeance upon their captors.

36–7. God responds to this plea for vengeance: he will avenge his people. *her sea* (see the note on 51: 13): this probably refers, as the N.E.B. footnote states, to the Euphrates, the source of Babylon's copious water-supply.

37. Much the same description is applied to Judah and Jerusalem in 9: 11. *

AGAIN THE DESTRUCTION OF BABYLON

Together they roar like young lions,   38
they growl like the whelps of a lioness.
I will cause their drinking bouts to end in fever   39
and make them so drunk that they will writhe and toss,
then sink into unending sleep, never to wake.
   This is the very word of the LORD.
I will bring them like lambs to the slaughter,   40
   rams and he-goats together.
Sheshak[a] is captured,   41
   the pride of the whole earth taken;
Babylon has become a horror amongst the nations!
The sea has surged over Babylon,   42
   she is covered by its roaring waves.
Her cities have become waste places,   43
   a land dried up and desert,
a land in whose cities no man lives
and through which no mortal travels.
I will punish Bel in Babylon   44
and make him bring up what he has swallowed;
nations shall never again come streaming to him.

[a] *A name for Babylon.*

The wall of Babylon has fallen;
45   come out of her, O my people,
        and let every man save himself
            from the anger of the LORD.
46   Then beware of losing heart,
        fear no rumours spread abroad in the land,
            as rumour follows rumour,
            each year a new one:
        violence on earth and ruler against ruler.
47   Therefore a time is coming
            when I will punish Babylon's idols,
            and all her land shall be put to shame,
            and all her slain shall lie fallen in her midst.
48   Heaven and earth and all that is in them
            shall sing in triumph over Babylon;
        for marauders from the north shall overrun her.
        This is the very word of the LORD.

✳ This passage comprises a number of short sayings describing in different ways the coming destruction of Babylon.

38. *Together they roar like young lions:* like lions and their whelps growling with satisfaction over their prey, so do the Babylonians gloat with satisfaction over the nations upon whom they have preyed.

39. *I will cause their drinking bouts to end in fever:* but their drunken celebrations will end in disaster. They will sink into a lethal stupor, never to regain consciousness.

41. In the note on 25: 26 in vol. 1 of this commentary, it was suggested that the word *Sheshak* was a way of referring to Babylon by means of the device known as 'Atbash'. Taken as an example of 'Atbash', *Sheshak* was a cipher for Babel. Since the completion of vol. 1, however, my attention has been drawn to some evidence that Sheshak was a genuine

name for Babylon and need not therefore be understood as a cipher. In addition, in view of the numerous oracles and sayings in chs. 50–1 explicitly referring to Babylon and announcing its downfall and destruction, it is pertinent to ask why a cipher such as Sheshak is alleged to be would have been necessary (see the note on 51: 1). This consideration would support the understanding of *Sheshak* as a genuine name. But in the absence of firmer evidence for the occurrence of this name in Babylonian texts, it seems wisest to leave both possibilities open. Future discoveries may decide the matter.

42. *The sea has surged over Babylon:* according to the Babylonian myth of creation the god Marduk fought against and destroyed the chaos-waters (Tiamat). The present verse may well be an allusion to this myth (it can scarcely refer to the Euphrates) and would therefore mean that Babylon would be overcome by chaos.

44. *I will punish Bel in Babylon:* on the god Bel, see the comment on 50: 1.

45. *come out of her, O my people:* the exiles are summoned to leave Babylon which is soon to perish.

46. *Then beware of losing heart:* the exiles are beckoned to take courage. The confusion of the day, the rumours of victory and defeat, the uncertainty of such news as came through to them of the ongoings of the struggle between nations for power and control must have evoked a feeling of hopelessness among those in exile.

47–8. But Babylon's downfall is certain – this was *the very word of the LORD.* ✷

BABYLON IS REPAID IN FULL

49 Babylon must fall for the sake of[a] Israel's slain,
as the slain of all the world fell for the sake of Babylon.

50 You who have escaped from her sword, off with you,
        do not linger.
    Remember the LORD from afar
    and call Jerusalem to mind.

51 We are put to shame by the reproaches we have heard,
    and our faces are covered with confusion:
strangers have entered the sacred courts of the
        LORD's house.

52 A time is coming therefore, says the LORD,
        when I will punish her idols,
        and all through the land there shall be the groaning
            of the wounded.

53 Though Babylon should reach to the skies
    and make her high towers inaccessible,
I will send marauders to overrun her.
        This is the very word of the LORD.

54 Hark, cries of agony from Babylon!
    Sounds of destruction from the land of the
        Chaldaeans!

55 For the LORD is despoiling Babylon
and will silence the hum of the city,
before the advancing wave that booms and roars
        like mighty waters.

56 For marauders march on Babylon herself,
    her warriors are captured and their bows are broken;
    for the LORD, a God of retribution, will repay in full.

[a] for the sake of: *prob. rdg.; Heb. om.*

I will make her princes and her wise men drunk,   57
her viceroys and governors and warriors,
and they shall sink into unending sleep,
    never to wake.
  This is the very word of the King,
  whose name is the LORD of Hosts.

The LORD of Hosts says: 58

The walls of broad Babylon shall be razed to the
    ground,
her lofty gates shall be set on fire.
Worthless now is the thing for which the nations
    toiled;
the peoples wore themselves out for a mere
    nothing.

☆ 49. Yet again the note of vengeance upon Babylon for her deeds against Israel is sounded.

50. The exiles who escaped death at the hands of the Babylonians are bidden to go forth from her doomed land. They are summoned to *Remember the LORD from afar*, that is, to put their trust in him and to have faith again in the future of the holy city.

51–2. Verse 51 is the reply of the exiles to the exhortation of verse 50. The implication of the reply is that the gods whose nations invaded the very temple of Yahweh in Jerusalem are supreme. But the gods of the Babylonians are mere idols soon to be overthrown by Yahweh.

53. *and make her high towers inaccessible:* under Nebuchadrezzar an extensive programme of building was implemented and carried out in the city of Babylon. The reference here is to the lofty buildings of the city.

56. *for the LORD, a God of retribution, will repay in full:* yet

another example of the note of vengeance which permeates chs. 50–1.

57. This verse repeats the thought and imagery of verse 39.

58. See the comment on 51: 25. *

A SYMBOLIC ACT AGAINST BABYLON

59 The instructions given by the prophet Jeremiah to the quartermaster Seraiah son of Neriah and grandson of Mahseiah, when he went to Babylon with Zedekiah king of Judah in the fourth year of his reign.

60 Jeremiah, having written down in a[a] book[b] a full description of the disaster which would come upon

61 Babylon, said to Seraiah, 'When you come to Babylon,

62 look at this, read it all and then say, "Thou, O LORD, hast declared thy purpose to destroy this place and leave it with no one living in it, man or beast; it shall be

63 desolate, for ever waste." When you have finished reading the book, tie a stone to it and throw it into the

64 Euphrates, and then say, "So shall Babylon sink, never to rise again after the disaster which I shall bring upon her."'

Thus far are the collected sayings of Jeremiah.

* This final section of ch. 51 provides another good example of a symbolic act (see the note on 28: 2). The oracles announcing Babylon's downfall are written in a 'book' or scroll and are taken to Babylon and cast into the river Euphrates. This symbolic act is accompanied with the saying 'So shall Baby-

[a] *Or* one.
[b] *Prob. rdg.; Heb. adds* all these things which are written concerning Babylon.

lon sink, never to rise again after the disaster which I shall bring upon her.'

59. *when he went to Babylon with Zedekiah king of Judah in the fourth year of his reign:* this was the year 594/593 B.C. If this narrative is reliable, it is probably to be understood in connection with the events recorded in ch. 27. It is possible that the plot to rebel against Babylon which is narrated in that chapter and in which Zedekiah evidently played a leading part became known to Nebuchadrezzar and that Zedekiah, after the plot had proved to be abortive, was summoned by Nebuchadrezzar or perhaps went of his own accord to Babylon to repledge his loyalty to his overlord. Some commentators would associate the letter sent by Jeremiah to the exiles (ch. 29) with what is recorded here. But the royal official to whom the prophet entrusted the scroll of oracles against Babylon is not mentioned in ch. 29, where two different envoys are mentioned. Jeremiah's letter was probably sent on an earlier occasion than that described here in 51: 59–64. It is possible that the messengers from Zedekiah to Nebuchadrezzar on the occasion alluded to in 29: 3 were sent to assure the Babylonians that the authorities in Judah had not been in any way behind the disturbances which, as 29: 21–3 appears to imply, some of the exiles of 597 B.C. had created in Babylon.

64. *Thus far are the collected sayings of Jeremiah:* this is obviously an editorial note. The final chapter of the book is a historical appendix and is for the most part parallel to 2 Kings 24: 18 – 25: 30. ✳

Historical note about the fall of Jerusalem

✳ The final chapter of the book of Jeremiah is for the most part parallel to the narrative in 2 Kings 24: 18–25: 30. The two major differences between them are: the brief account of the appointment of Gedaliah as governor of Judah after 587 B.C. and his subsequent assassination by Ishmael in 2 Kings 25: 22–6 is not found in Jer. 52, probably because it has been more extensively dealt with earlier in the book (chs. 40–1), whilst the record of the number of people deported by the Babylonians from Judah in Jer. 52: 28–30 is not found in 2 Kings 25. Other differences between the two narratives are minor variations in the text. The section 52: 4–16 is a somewhat more expansive account of the narrative also found in 39: 1–10 (see the notes below). ✳

THE FALL OF JERUSALEM

52 1[a] ZEDEKIAH WAS TWENTY-ONE YEARS OLD when he came to the throne, and he reigned in Jerusalem for eleven years; his mother was Hamutal daughter of 2 Jeremiah of Libnah. He did what was wrong in the eyes 3 of the LORD, as Jehoiakim had done. Jerusalem and Judah so angered the LORD that in the end he banished them from his sight; and Zedekiah rebelled against the king of Babylon.

4   In the ninth year of his reign, in the tenth month, on the tenth day of the month, Nebuchadrezzar king of Babylon advanced with all his army against Jerusalem,

[a] *Verses 1–27: cp. 39: 1–10 and 2 Kgs. 24: 18–25: 21.*

invested it and erected watch-towers against it on every
side; the siege lasted till the eleventh year of King Zede- 5
kiah. In the fourth month of that year, on the ninth day 6
of the month, when famine was severe in the city and
there was no food for the common people, the city was
thrown open. When Zedekiah king of Judah saw this, 7
he and[a] all his armed escort left the city and fled by night
through the gate called Between the Two Walls, near
the king's garden. They escaped towards the Arabah,
although the Chaldaeans were surrounding the city.
But the Chaldaean army pursued the king and overtook 8
him in the lowlands of Jericho; and all his company was
dispersed. The king was seized and brought before the 9
king of Babylon at Riblah in the land of Hamath, where
he pleaded his case before him. The king of Babylon slew 10
Zedekiah's sons before his eyes; he also put to death all
the princes of Judah in Riblah. Then the king of Babylon 11
put Zedekiah's eyes out, bound him with fetters of
bronze, brought him to Babylon and committed him
to prison till the day of his death.

In the fifth month, on the tenth day of the month, in 12
the nineteenth year of Nebuchadrezzar king of Babylon,
Nebuzaradan, captain of the king's bodyguard,[b] came to
Jerusalem and set fire to the house of the LORD and the 13
royal palace; all the houses in the city, including the
mansion of Gedaliah,[c] were burnt down. The Chaldaean 14
forces with the captain of the guard pulled down the

[a] When Zedekiah. . .and: *prob. rdg., cp. 39: 4; Heb. om.*
[b] captain . . . bodyguard: *prob. rdg., cp. 2 Kgs. 25: 8; Heb.* captain of
the bodyguard stood before the king of Babylon.
[c] Gedaliah: *prob. rdg.; Heb.* the great man.

15 walls all round Jerusalem. ^aNebuzaradan captain of the
guard deported the rest of the people left in the city,
those who had deserted to the king of Babylon and any
16 remaining artisans. The captain of the guard left only the
weakest class of people to be vine-dressers and labourers.

✷ 1. *Zedekiah was twenty-one years old when he came to the
throne:* Zedekiah was his throne-name. His name before this
was Mattaniah (cp. 2 Kings 24: 17). For a brief description of
his reign see pp. 7ff. (cp. the notes on 38: 5, 25–6).

4. *on the tenth day of the month:* this detail is not supplied in
39: 1–10. *invested it and erected watch-towers against it on every
side:* 39: 1 reads simply 'they laid siege to it'.

6. *In the fourth month of that year:* see the note on 39: 2.
*when famine was severe in the city and there was no food for the
common people:* a further detail of information not found in
39: 1–10.

7. *When Zedekiah king of Judah saw this, he and:* as noted in
the N.E.B. footnote, this has been supplied from 39: 4 (see
the note on this verse). Cp. also 2 Kings 25: 4. *They escaped
towards the Arabah:* see the note on 39: 4. *although the Chaldaeans were surrounding the city:* Zedekiah and his entourage
somehow managed to get through the tight cordon which no
doubt the Babylonians had thrown around the city. This
note also is absent in 39: 1–10.

8. The capture of the king here recorded may be what is
alluded to in Lam. 4: 19–20. *and all his company was dispersed:*
a further detail of information not found in the parallel
passage in 39: 1–10.

9. *Riblah in the land of Hamath:* see the note on 39: 5.

10–11. See the note on 39: 6-7.

11. *and committed him to prison:* this is not mentioned in
39: 7. In view of the brutal punishment inflicted upon him by

[a] *Prob. rdg., cp. 39: 9 and 2 Kgs. 25: 11; Heb. prefixes* The weakest class
of the people (*cp. verse 16*).

the Babylonians at Riblah, Zedekiah cannot have survived long.

12. This verse is not found in 39: 1–10.

13. *Gedaliah:* this reading is achieved by a slight emendation of the Hebrew text which reads 'and all the house of the great man' and makes little sense.

16. *The captain of the guard left only the weakest class of people:* since a community of some importance was left in the land under Gedaliah, this note may refer only to Jerusalem. But see the note on verse 27. ✳

THE SACKING OF THE TEMPLE

The Chaldaeans broke up the pillars of bronze in the 17 house of the LORD, the trolleys, and the sea of bronze, and took the metal to Babylon. They took also the pots, 18 shovels, snuffers, tossing-bowls, saucers, and all the vessels of bronze used in the service of the temple. The captain 19 of the guard took away the precious metal, whether gold or silver, of which the cups, firepans, tossing-bowls, pots, lamp-stands, saucers, and flagons were made. The bronze 20 of the two pillars, of the one sea and of the twelve oxen supporting it,[a] which King Solomon had made for the house of the LORD, was beyond weighing. The one pillar 21 was eighteen cubits high and twelve cubits in circumference; it was hollow and the metal was four fingers thick. It had a capital of bronze, five cubits high, and a 22 decoration of network and pomegranates ran all round it, wholly of bronze. The other pillar, with its pomegranates, was exactly like it. Ninety-six pomegranates were 23

[a] supporting it: *so Sept.; Heb.* which were under the trolleys (*or,* with *some change of text,* which supported it, and the ten trolleys).

exposed to view[a] and there were a hundred in all on the network all round.

24   The captain of the guard took Seraiah the chief priest and Zephaniah the deputy chief priest and the three on
25 duty at the entrance; he took also from the city a eunuch who was in charge of the fighting men, seven of those with right of access to the king who were still in the city, the adjutant-general[b] whose duty was to muster the people for war, and sixty men of the people who were
26 still there. These Nebuzaradan captain of the guard brought
27 to the king of Babylon at Riblah. There, in the land of Hamath, the king of Babylon had them flogged and put to death. So Judah went into exile from their own land.

☆ Before destroying the temple, the Babylonians looted it, taking away with them all the objects of bronze, silver and gold they found there. After their capture of the city in 597 B.C. they had also seized various objects (cp. 27: 16). Seen within the context of the book of Jeremiah, this passage records the fulfilment of Jeremiah's prophecy recorded in 27: 19-22. The narrative in 2 Kings 25: 13–17 is much briefer than Jer. 52: 17–23.

17. *the pillars of bronze in the house of the LORD, the trolleys, and the sea of bronze:* see the note on 27: 19.

18. *the pots, shovels, snuffers, tossing-bowls, saucers:* the *pots* were probably used for removing fat and ashes from the altar. The *shovels* were no doubt used for removing ashes from the altar and placing them in the pots. The *snuffers* were used for trimming the wicks of the lamps. The *tossing-bowls* were probably used to throw the blood of sacrifices against the sides of the altar. The *saucers* may have been used for burning incense.

[a] exposed to view: *mng. of Heb. word uncertain.*
[b] *Prob. rdg.; Heb. adds* commander-in-chief.

19. *the cups, firepans, tossing-bowls, pots, lamp-stands, saucers, and flagons:* of the objects here not already mentioned in verse 18, the *cups* were used for containing the blood of sacrifices (cp. Exod. 12: 22, 23) and perhaps also for pouring out libations; the *firepans* were used for carrying live coals to and from the altar and could also be used as censers; the *lamp-stands* were used for elevating lamps so as to light up as wide an area as possible; the *flagons* were used for pouring out libations (cp. Exod. 25: 29).

20. *which King Solomon had made for the house of the LORD:* the building of the temple and its elaborate decoration and furnishing are described in 1 Kings 6–7 (see the commentary on these two chapters in the volume on 1 Kings in this series).

27. *So Judah went into exile from their own land:* we have already seen (cp. the commentary on chs. 24; 29: 16–20; 40–4) that for Jeremiah and those who transmitted and developed his message the future of God's people lay with the community in exile in Babylon. The same belief is shared by both Deutero-Isaiah and Ezekiel. The people in the homeland are not considered heirs of God's promises for the nation's future. We have seen that the book of Jeremiah writes off those in Judah and those who fled to the land of Egypt as without hope for the future. So the editors of the book of Jeremiah can state that *Judah went into exile from their own land*; those left in the land were only 'the weakest class of people' (verse 16). ✳

THE NUMBERS DEPORTED TO BABYLON

These were the people deported by Nebuchadrezzar 28 in the seventeenth[a] year: three thousand and twenty-three Judaeans. In his eighteenth year, eight hundred and 29 thirty-two people from Jerusalem; in his twenty-third 30 year, seven hundred and forty-five Judaeans were deported by Nebuzaradan the captain of the bodyguard: all together four thousand six hundred people.

[a] *Prob. rdg.; Heb.* seventh.

✽ These verses are not contained in the Septuagint text of this chapter and are not found in 2 Kings 25.

28. *the seventeenth year:* as indicated in the N.E.B. footnote, the Hebrew text reads 'seventh'. Nebuchadrezzar succeeded his father Nabopolassar in 605 B.C. so that the seventh year would have been 598 B.C. There was a deportation in 597 B.C., Nebuchadrezzar's eighth year (cp. 2 Kings 24: 12), but not, as far as we know, in 598 B.C. It seems best, therefore, to emend, with the N.E.B., the text to read *seventeenth*. This would have been the year 588 B.C. when Judah but not Jerusalem itself had fallen to the Babylonians. In this year there was a deportation of people from Judah excluding Jerusalem, as the text indicates by reading *Judaeans*. In the eighteenth year (587 B.C.) citizens of Jerusalem, now captured by the Babylonians, were deported (verse 29). The third deportation, which is dated in Nebuchadrezzar's twenty-third year, would have been 582 B.C. and may have been the result of the assassination of Gedaliah (cp. the note on 41: 1).

29–30. The numbers of the exiles from Judah and Jerusalem mentioned in these verses and in verse 28 show all the signs of being authentic. These numbers probably refer to adult male citizens only. When their families are added the number of people altogether deported would have been much greater. (The number exiled in 597 B.C., according to 2 Kings 24: 14–16, was 18,000. This may be an exaggeration, though it is possible that it represents the total number, deported in that year, that is, male adults and their families, in round figures.) The fact that the editors of the book of Jeremiah included such details concerning the numbers of Judaeans carried into exile is probably yet another indication that they believed the future of God's people to be with the exiles whose numbers they have so carefully recorded. We have seen that such an attitude towards the exiles in Babylon is characteristic of the book's message for the nation's future (cp. the commentary on 29: 16–20, and on 40–4; cp. also ch. 24 in vol. i).

THE RELEASE OF JEHOIACHIN FROM PRISON

In the thirty-seventh year of the exile of Jehoaichin 31[a]
king of Judah, on the twenty-fifth day of the twelfth
month, Evil-merodach king of Babylon in the year of his
accession showed favour to Jehoiachin king of Judah.
He brought him out of prison, treated him kindly and 32
gave him a seat at table above the kings with him in
Babylon. So Jehoiachin discarded his prison clothes and 33
lived as a pensioner of the king for the rest of his life. For 34
his maintenance a regular daily allowance was given him
by the king of Babylon as long as he lived, to the day of
his death.

* Jehoiachin was taken into exile in 597 B.C. and evidently
remained in prison in Babylon until his release in 562 B.C.
(cp. the commentary on 22: 24–30). His survival in exile,
where he appears to have been regarded by the exiles as king
of Judah (see pp. 7f.), and his release and treatment by the
Babylonians may well have given rise to new hopes among the
exiles that God had remained faithful to his promises to the
line of David.

31. *In the thirty-seventh year of the exile:* taking it from the
year 597 B.C. this gives us the year 561/560 B.C. as the year of
Jehoiachin's release. Amel-Marduk's (Evil-merodach) first
year as king was 562/561 B.C. It is probable that Jehoiachin's
release actually took place on the occasion of the accession of
Amel-marduk as king of Babylon, as the text states. The
accession of a new monarch necessitated or provided the
opportunity for a re-affirmation of the oath of vassaldom on
the part of Babylon's vassal kings. Jehoiachin's release may
well have been connected with this.

[a] *Verses 31–4: cp. 2 Kgs. 25: 27–30.*

32. *treated him kindly:* there is some evidence that this may refer not merely to kindness on the part of the Babylonian king to his prisoner, but refers specifically to the re-establishment of the desirable amity between overlord and vassal. In other words, it is possible that Amel-Marduk was here re-establishing a treaty between himself and Jehoiachin king of Judah. But the fact that Jehoiachin was not allowed to return home places a question mark against such an understanding of the phrase.

34. *For his maintenance a regular daily allowance was given him:* Babylonian texts from the reign of Nebuchadrezzar have been discovered and mention the allowances provided by the Babylonians for Jehoiachin and his sons with him in exile. ✳

A NOTE ON FURTHER READING

Other recent commentaries on the book of Jeremiah are J. Bright, *Jeremiah* (The Anchor Bible, Doubleday, 1965), which contains an extensive introduction to the book and the life and times of Jeremiah, and J. P. Hyatt, 'Jeremiah – Text, Exegesis, and Exposition', *The Interpreter's Bible*, vol. 5 (Abingdon, 1956). A shorter but useful commentary is that by H. Cunliffe-Jones, *Jeremiah: God in History* (S.C.M. Torch Bible, 2nd ed., 1966). Older but still very useful are A. S. Peake, *Jeremiah*, vols. 1 and 2 (The Century Bible, Edinburgh, 1910–11) and A. W. Streane, *The Book of the Prophet Jeremiah together with The Lamentations* (Cambridge, 1913). J. Skinner, *Prophecy and Religion: Studies in the Life of Jeremiah* (Cambridge, 1922, paperback ed. 1961) remains a classic. The chapter on 'The Age of Jeremiah' in G. von Rad, *Old Testament Theology*, vol. 2, translated by D. M. Stalker (Oliver and Boyd, 1965), pp. 188–219 reprinted in his *The Message of the Prophets* (London, 1968), pp. 161–88, is characteristically perceptive and stimulating. On the problem of the prose sections in Jeremiah see the detailed discussion in E. W. Nicholson, *Preaching to the Exiles: A Study of the Prose Tradition in the Book of Jeremiah* (Basil Blackwell, 1970). For a more detailed description of the historical background to the life and times of Jeremiah, J. Bright, *A History of Israel* (2nd ed., S.C.M., 1972) and M. Noth, *The History of Israel* (2nd ed. with a revised translation by P. R. Ackroyd, A. and C. Black, 1960) may be consulted.

INDEX

239

Jeremiah (*cont.*)

i. 90, 92, 111–12, 114, 169; out-cries for vengeance i. 159; ultimate despair i. 170–1; visions i. 154–5, 202–4, 206; *see also* symbolic acts
Jeremiah, book of: content and themes i. 10–15, 26–7; ii. 10–15; date i. 3, 11; ii. 3, 11; origin and growth ii. 104, 105, 112; religious ideas i. 16–19; ii. 16–19; role of Deuteronomic authors i. 10–14; ii. 10–14; textual differences i. 15–16; ii. 15–16; *see also* Deutero-nomic authors and editors; Hebrew text of Old Testament; prose passages; Septuagint; sermons
Jeroboam I, king of Israel ii. 61
Jerusalem i. 51, 175, 183, 187; assaults on, and sieges i. 7, 8, 104, 125, 173; ii. 7, 8, 74, 76, 94, 95, 114–15; belief in inviolability i. 6, 77, 78; centralization of worship in i. 3; ii. 3, 38–40; fall and destruction i. 9–10, 15, 66–7, 108, 137, 199; ii. 9–10, 15, 56, 126, 200; judgement i. 127, 155; sinfulness i. 82, 92–3; throne of the LORD i. 45
Jesus: and new covenant ii. 70; say-ings of i. 39, 77–8
Jezebel, wife of Ahab ii. 101
Job i. 171, 214
Johanan, son of Kareah ii. 137
Jonadab, son of Rechab ii. 101, 102, 103
Jonathan the scribe ii. 117, 118
Joseph, son of Jacob ii. 66
Josephus, Jewish historian i. 119; ii. 165, 177
Josiah, king of Judah i. 1, 2, 3, 4; ii. 1, 2, 3, 4, 20, 27, 28, 106; contrast with Jehoiakim i. 6, 186; ii. 6, 110–11; defeat and death i. 35, 184; ii. 157, 158, 169, 175; reformation i. 2, 37, 115, 194; ii. 2, 25, 66, 139, 157; renewal of covenant ii. 96
Jotham, king of Judah i. 167; ii. 25

Judah: i. 98, 105, 127; comparison with Israel i. 28, 43–4; inevitable subjection by Babylon i. 139–40; invasions of i. 50–6, 73, 119, 135, 136–7; sinfulness i. 128, 155; union with Israel i. 47, 165
judgement: theme i. 12–13, 14, 69, 76, 119, 121, 144–5, 209; ii. 12–13, 14, 21; Jeremiah's message of i. 173, 176–7, 197–8, 204–6; ii. 49; and renewal after judgement i. 26, 122, 155, 174, 176–7, 191, 204–6; ii. 35, 55, 49–50, 69; set in motion by symbolic acts i. 165–6, 167; *see also* restoration of Israel and Judah
just, fate of the i. 116–17, 148

Kambul (location unknown) ii. 213
Kedar i. 33; oracle concerning ii. 197–8
Kemosh, god of Moab ii. 181, 182
Kenites ii. 101
Kidron valley ii. 28, 73
Kimham's holding (location un-known) ii. 141
king: personification of nation ii. 26; responsibilities i. 13, 179, 181–2; ii. 13, 26
Kings, books of i. 15, 76, 108, 181; ii. 15, 228, 234
kingship in Israel ii. 178, 181; ii. 88–9
Kir-heres (el Kerak) ii. 187
Kiriathim (possibly el-Qereiyat) ii. 180
Kiriath-jearim ('town of the forest thickets', Tell el-Azhar) ii. 27
Kirioth (location unknown) ii. 184, 189
Kittim (Cyprus) i. 33

Labashi-Marduk, king of Babylon i. 175; ii. 201
Lachish (Tell ed-Duweir) ii. 92
Lachish letters ii. 92, 120
lament i. 112–13, 128–9, 131–2, 135; of God over his people i. 118–19; of Jeremiah over Israel i. 89–90, 94,

INDEX

lament (*cont.*)
95–6; by Jerusalem i. 104; on Jerusalem i. 135–7; in time of defeat and famine i. 133–5; in time of drought i. 129–30
Lamentations, book of i. 199
law, God's: importance i. 13; ii. 13; Israels' refusal and incapacity to obey i. 71; ii. 21, 70–1, 79, 159; prophetic proclamation i. 13, 76, 107; ii. 13; scribes and 87–8
Lebanon i. 183, 187, 188
Leviathan i. 63
Luhith (location unknown) ii. 181
Lydians ii. 168–9

Maaseiah, son of Shallum ii. 102
Madmen (location unknown) ii. 180
mager-missabib ('terror let loose') i. 73, 167
Maher-shalal-hash-baz, son of Isaiah i. 165
Malchiah the king's son ii. 118
Malchiah, son of Rechab ii. 103–4
Manasseh, king of Judah i. 1, 2, 4, 135, 182; ii. 1, 2, 4
Marduk, state of god of Babylon ii. 202–3, 223
Mattaniah *see* Zedekiah
Medes i. 214; ii. 216–17
Megiddo, battle of i. 2, 5, 184; ii. 2, 5, 158, 169, 175
Memphis *see* Noph
Mephaath (probably Tell Jawah) ii. 184
Merathaim ii. 209
mercenary soldiers ii. 169, 172
Mesha, king of Maob ii. 180, 182, 187
Messiah ('anointed one') i. 178, 179
messianism i. 192
Micah i. 97; ii. 24–5, 26
Micaiah, son of Gemariah ii. 107
Migdol ('tower') ii. 155, 171
Milcom, god of Ammon ii. 191; *see also* Molech
Minni ii. 220
Misgab (location unknown) ii. 180

Mizpah (probably Tell en-Nasbeh) i. 10; ii. 10, 126, 129, 130, 131–2, 134, 138, 139
Moab i. 8, 214; ii. 8, 29, 180; invasions ii. 177–8, 198; oracles concerning ii. 177–89
Moabite Stone ii. 180, 182, 184, 187
Moabites i. 7, 119; ii. 7, 101, 165, 194
Molech, Ammonite god i. 6, 37, 83; ii. 6, 81
monarchy, judgement upon 171, 174, 191; *see also* king, kingship
monotheism i. 16, 101; ii. 16, 86; in oracles against nations ii. 163–4
Moresheth-gath ii. 25
Moses i. 12, 71, 187; ii. 12, 63; his call i. 23, 25; first of the prophets i. 13, 26, 76, 107, 109; ii. 13
mourning rites i. 96, 143; ii. 139–40, 188

Nabonidus, king of Babylon ii. 201
Nabopolassar, king of Babylon i. 175; ii. 234
Naboth ii. 77
Nahum ii. 163
Nazarites i. 81–2; ii. 101
Nebo (location unknown) ii. 180
Nebo, Mount i. 187; ii. 180
Nebuchadrezzar, king of Babylon i. 1, 7, 125, 175, 187; ii. 1, 7, 29, 40, 45, 126, 146, 198, 201, 225, 227, 234; as God's servant i. 210–11; ii. 32; invasions and subjection of Judah i. 7, 9, 10, 119, 189; ii. 1, 7, 10; treatment of enemies i. 9, 176; ii. 34, 91, 127; victory at Carchemish i. 7; ii. 7, 165, 175
Nebuzaradan, captain of Nebuchadrezzar's bodyguard i. 9; ii. 9, 126, 131
Necho, Pharaoh i. 5, 184; ii. 5, 20, 165, 169, 175, 176
Negeb i. 126, 154
Nehemiah i. 19
Nehushta, mother of Jehoiachin i. 125; ii. 27

244